THE MIRACLE MAN

I0456253

RoyalKye Aurelius Fünk

THE MIRACLE MAN

Published by
Miracle Maker Publishing™
United States of America

ISBN
Paperback: 979-8-9904433-4-1

Format Notice
This publication is available in print, digital, and audio formats.

Disclaimer
This book is not intended to be a substitute for professional medical, psychological, legal, or financial advice. The author is not a licensed medical doctor, therapist, or counselor. The content reflects the author's personal experiences, insights, and perspectives and is provided for educational and inspirational purposes only.

Trademark Notice
"Miracle Maker™," "Miracle Maker Publishing™," and associated logos are used as common-law trademarks and are the intellectual property of the publisher.

Edition
First Edition
Printed in the United States of America

Dedication

This book stands as a tribute to the boundless mercy, miracles, and grace of God, forever illuminating the path of healing, redemption, and empowerment beyond all human understanding. To the almighty Alpha and Omega, Lord of the Skies, be all the praise and honor.

To Lolu, whose hidden broken heart led to the cracking open of my very soul amidst the burning ashes, guiding me to discover God and Jesus within all my being. Our experience ignited a journey I will forever cherish. May you find solace and peace on your own path, for this book would never have come about without you. I promised you this dedication, and I intend to honor that promise.

To my future family, beautiful wife, and God-willing legacy, anything is possible with the belief in such and the divine guiding the way. Stand tall, stand proud, and stand true to the virtues that reside in your soul.

To my Mom and Dad, thanks for all your sacrifice, love, and support over the years and for never giving up on me.

With deepest gratitude,

Royal Kye Aurelius Funk

THE MIRACLE MAN

Page Left Blank Intentionally

Acknowledgment

First and foremost, I must thank my Creator for keeping me alive through all of my turmoil, madness, and debauchery as a young man suffering and ignorant of better. I am astounded by your mercy and grace and left perplexed by the wonders you have performed in my life and the lives of those you have touched with your goodness.

I would like to express my deepest appreciation and gratitude to all the individuals who have played both a significant and minimal role in shaping my life and contributing to the foundation of this book, "The Miracle Man." Whether the impact was positive or negative, each person has helped me learn important lessons and grow into the man I am today - full of life, love, and miracles.

Secondly, I would like to acknowledge my experiences as a Federal Fire Fighter. The challenges and triumphs I faced in that role have instilled a sense of resilience, courage, leadership, and dedication that have greatly influenced my life, experiences, and writing.

I am also grateful for my involvement in various sales, marketing, and international business endeavors. These experiences have broadened my perspective, exposed me to diverse cultures, and enriched my understanding of human interactions, which have undoubtedly influenced the themes explored in this book.

To my ex-wife, who loved me dearly, I want to express my heartfelt appreciation and gratitude for you. Although I was unable to fully receive your love due to the trauma I faced as a child and the negative coping mechanisms I was in, your unwavering support and affection have left a permanent mark on my journey of healing and self-discovery. Mahalo, for your love and your support and for helping me become the man I am today. I wouldn't be here without you, chamaquita, and I wish you and your family the best.

I would also like to acknowledge the women who broke my heart and shattered me into a million pieces along the way, and I theirs. I've been able to find profound and enduring serenity as a result of our interactions as they helped me find forgiveness for others and myself, rising from the ashes like a phoenix reborn and rediscovering the God inside. Their presence in my life has taught me valuable lessons about true love, resiliency, the power of boundaries, and honoring oneself.

In addition, I would like to thank my family for not only their love and support but the difficult situations and challenges that I faced in our family unit. Without that very resistance and the difficult childhood growing up, my soul wouldn't have been able to experience the greatness within and rise to the challenge of becoming the best version of myself.

Lastly, I want to extend my sincere apologies to anyone I may have unintentionally hurt along my path. As I reflect on my journey, I recognize that I have made decisions and caused pain to others unknowingly. I am deeply sorry for any hurt I may have caused and hope that this book serves as a testament to my growth and commitment to becoming a better person.

In conclusion, I am immensely grateful for the individuals who have shaped my life and contributed to the creation of "The Miracle Man" - my teachers, my coaches, my mentors, my leaders, my family and friends, my lovers, my haters, and the strangers. Your influence, whether positive or negative, has been instrumental in my personal and literary development. Thank you all for being a part of my journey.

Sincerely,

RoyalKye Aurelius Fünk - Aka RK "The Lightning Lion "

THE MIRACLE MAN

Table of Contents

Chapter 1: A Message To The Men… 32

Chapter 2: The Early Years… 59

Chapter 3: Battling The Blaze… 85

Chapter 4: Returning From Death's Doorstep…..... 109

Chapter 5: Mistakes or Learning Lessons… 140

Chapter 6: Hustle Game - Sales/Business. 170

Chapter 7: Surrendering to the Flow..................... 203

Chapter 8: Ancestral Connections… 228

Chapter 9: Body/Mind Medicine. 264

Chapter 10: Boundaries & Self Value… 303

Chapter 11: Miracle Flow… 338

Chapter 12: Godpower or Willpower..................... 371

Chapter 13: Belief Systems… 393

Chapter 14: Your Magic… 408

Chapter 15: Healing the Hurt. 428

About the Author

RoyalKye Aurelius Fünk is a renowned specialist in the fields of self-mastery, personal transformation, and spirituality. With a deep passion for his own personal growth and transformation, he has dedicated his life to helping individuals unlock their full potential and find deep and lasting inner peace.

Born in Salt Lake City, UT, and having been raised in the Wild West of the mountain country in Wyoming, RoyalKye developed a keen interest in exploring the realms of the mind, body, and spirit from an early age with a spiritual connection he was innately tapped into. It progressed with a greater understanding of the body/mind connection through the foundation of an intense dedication to sports, Federal Fire Operations, and healing rapidly from a near-fatal motorcycle accident - NDE (Near Death Experience), baffling doctors at his rapid and miraculous rate of recovery.

From hopping out of helicopters into raging forest fires, cage fighting for fun, surfing motorcycles down canyon corridors, or free diving far below the ocean's surface in one breath, he has always been interested in pushing the limits of what he thought possible and blazing his own path.

Traumatic childhood experiences and PTSD from Federal Fire Operations propelled him into years of chaos and destruction, culminating in his profound realization and embodiment of resiliency, empowerment, and miracles. Since then, he has emerged as a sought-after speaker, coach, and author, captivating audiences and clients worldwide with his illuminating insights and guiding them toward self-discovery and profound empowerment.

Throughout his journey, he has touched the lives of countless individuals, providing them with practical tools and profound insights to navigate the complexities of life and achieve personal growth, connecting to God within.

With a unique blend of wisdom, compassion, and practicality, RoyalKye has earned a reputation for delivering transformative teachings that resonate with individuals from all walks of life. His writing style is characterized by a deep understanding of human psychology, spirituality, and the power of self-reflection and taking massive action.

In addition to his writing, he speaks globally, conducts workshops, seminars, and retreats worldwide, guiding participants on a transformative journey of self-discovery and liberation.

When RoyalKye is not writing, speaking, or teaching, he enjoys traveling the world and spending time in nature, specifically the ocean, whether it be surfing, scuba diving, snorkeling, or free diving.

Through his latest book, *The Miracle Man*, RoyalKye invites readers to embark on a transformative journey of self-mastery, a deeper embodiment of their personal spirituality, and the deconstruction of archaic self and world paradigms. It offers practical tools, insightful guidance, and profound wisdom to help individuals awaken their true potential and live a life of purpose and ultimate fulfillment.

RoyalKye is committed to empowering individuals to embrace their authentic selves, cultivate inner peace, and create positive change in their lives and the world around them. Together, he believes that we can alter the course of human history and mankind on the planet for the highest good of all, with God leading the way and working together toward a common goal of self-mastery, empowerment, and realizing the God within us all.

THE MIRACLE MAN

Page left blank intentionally

ENTER THE MIRACLE MAKER EXPERIENCE

Scanning this code brings you into the complete Miracle Maker ecosystem — including the audiobook, workbook, and guided integration resources.

This book is not meant to be consumed. It is meant to be entered.

If you are holding The Miracle Man, you are standing at a threshold — where the old story no longer fits and alignment begins.

Scanning this code brings you into the Miracle Maker Digital Bundle, including the full audiobook, and companion chapter-by-chapter workbook designed for embodiment, clarity, and action.

This is not bonus material. It is the next layer of the work.

For those ready to move beyond insight into direction, you may also request a private 15-minute Clarity Call — a focused conversation to remove what's blocking momentum.

This is not therapy or motivation.

It is clarity, responsibility, and direction.

"Coming home is not just returning to a place; it's rediscovering ourselves, finding solace in our own essence, and embracing the familiarity of our soul's sanctuary." - Unknown

Introduction:

Welcome Home

First and foremost, I extend my heartfelt gratitude for embarking upon this journey with me. I can only imagine the myriad of experiences, challenges, and triumphs that have shaped your life, leading you to this precise moment now.

Before delving deeper into the pages of this book, I must offer an upfront disclaimer: This is a journey for the brave of heart. It is a voyage that will test your current paradigms and beliefs, and challenge the very foundation of your reality. If you choose to embark upon this path, I urge you to do so with an open mind and a willingness to explore the depths of your psyche. Not only because I share my very real hardships but my triumphs mixed with my supernatural experiences and insights that will seem stranger than fiction.

If you find yourself in agreement with these terms, I encourage you to proceed with an open heart and a curious mind. However, if you harbor hesitations or doubts, I implore you to consider whether another path may better suit your current aspirations and needs. The choice is yours, dear reader. May your decision lead you toward your path of empowerment and self-realization.

I deeply hope that you find a sense of belonging within your own body, heart, and soul as you immerse yourself in the pages of this book. My sincere aim is that my story and authenticity will resonate with you, awakening a profound realization of your own divine essence and you being vulnerable within yourself to evoke change.

Before you embark on this journey, I invite you to set aside any distractions and find a comfortable place to sit. Know that you are unconditionally loved, regardless of the trials and tribulations you may have faced throughout your life.

Take a moment to center yourself, allowing your mind to quiet and your heart to open. Before you begin to read, let yourself sink into a deep, receptive state, fully embracing the words that unfold before you and asking your highest self to reveal to you exactly what you need for your growth and healing.

May you find solace, inspiration, and profound insights within these pages, and may you emerge from this experience with a deeper understanding of your own inherent divinity.

The words within these pages hold a power unlike anything you've encountered before. All I ask is for you to quiet your mind, open your heart, and allow yourself to receive the miracle that awaits within you. You are a cherished soul, far more than just a human being, and every word I've written has been guided by the divine and is imbued with the intention to aid, assist, and educate you upon your very own expansion.

Here, within the sanctuary of these pages, you are safe to explore the depths of your soul and reconnect with the eternal now. If, like me, you have endured unimaginable pain, trials, and trauma, know that you are not alone. I understand the loneliness of feeling like an outsider, of navigating a journey fraught with challenges and hardships.

Yet, despite the trials you have faced, you have arrived here, now, on the threshold of transformation. You have shown incredible strength and resilience to reach this point, and for that, I commend you.

Before we proceed any further, I urge you to take a moment to pause and take a deep breath. Honor yourself and every step of your journey, no matter how challenging or tumultuous it may have been. Yes, you—your existence holds immeasurable value beyond what you may realize.

More importantly, I want you to take a moment to step into a place of deep gratitude and thank every cell in your body. For this body of yours is nothing short of a miraculous feat of nature, a vessel that has weathered the storms and embraced the adventures of your journey. So, pause from the hustle and bustle of life for just a moment and bask in the marvel of your own existence.

If, like me, you've lived a life filled with twists and turns, highs and lows, epic tales, and synchronistic chaos, you might want to offer yourself a little humor and say something like:

"Hot damn, baby! It's the bonus round! How in the world am I still alive and kicking?! What a miracle!"

Give yourself a pat on the back because you, my friend, are a true survivor of the grand adventure called life.

Take a deep breath, and with each beat of your heart, feel the gratitude pulsating through your veins. Now, I want you to say out loud so that you can hear yourself:

"Thank you, heart, for beating for me my entire life. Thank you for always being there for me, even though I have never seen you. Thank you for being there for me, even though I never asked you once to do what you do. Thank you for keeping me alive through all the good, the bad, the ugly, and everything in between so I could experience this miracle of life. This epic journey of self-discovery and adventure on planet Earth. Thank you for being my best friend and someone I have always depended upon. I love you for it."

Let those words sink in, and feel the warmth of appreciation enveloping every fiber of your being. Your heart, your steadfast companion, deserves every ounce of gratitude you can muster.

An intriguing fact about the heart is its possession of neurons, making it one of the few organs alongside the brain and intestines to exhibit this characteristic. Discovered by Armour in 1991, the heart boasts approximately 40,000 neurons, akin to those found in the brain. This revelation unveils the existence of a *"little brain"* within the heart, scientifically termed the 'intracardiac nervous system.'

Recent studies have further illuminated the heart's significance, demonstrating that it transmits more signals to the brain than it receives. This research underscores the heart's role as a central hub of intelligence and intuitive wisdom, intricately linked to all other bodily systems and cells.

Moreover, from an electromagnetic perspective, the heart's electromagnetic field dwarfs that of the brain, measuring up to 5,000 times more powerful. This field extends outward, enveloping us in an aura spanning anywhere from 8 to 25 feet, contingent upon the individual. Remarkably, advancements in technology now enable us to capture and photograph this aura.

So, when we encounter phrases like '*listen to your heart*' or '*follow your heart*,' rest assured, it's not mere woo woo—it's rooted in science. This very day, consider yourself baptized in the name of science!

Seriously, think about it: if our hearts generate an electromagnetic field around us…Aren't we like superheroes? And we didn't even know it!

It's all quite logical when you pause to contemplate it. Numerous studies have highlighted the profound benefits of positive emotional states, showcasing their ability to rebalance the nervous system. When we experience positive emotions, it's akin to giving the green light to our parasympathetic nervous system, which, in turn, fortifies our immunity, optimizes hormonal function, and sharpens brain activity. Additionally, it plays a pivotal role in regulating gene expression through epigenetics and promotes rest through homeostasis, facilitating system repair, regrowth, and healing.

Conversely, adverse emotional states like fear, anger, jealousy, greed, or hostility steer us down a different path. They disrupt the healthy variation in heart rate intervals, known as heart rate variability (HRV), and trigger a heightened response from the sympathetic nervous system—the fight/flight/freeze mechanism. This unleashes a deluge of stress chemicals that, over time, take a toll on our bodies, disrupting their delicate balance and breaking us down.

This enlightening research stems from over 30 years of dedicated investigation at the HeartMath Institute. For those eager to delve deeper, a wealth of knowledge awaits in the book "The HeartMath Solution," penned by Doc Children and Howard Martin.

Understanding the intricate interplay between our psychological state and physiological functions is truly mind-bending. We come to realize how we've been ensnared by droves of internal and external influences. When stress takes hold, our cognitive prowess takes a nosedive, leaving us unable to perform at our peak. Our immune system wanes, making it challenging to absorb new information or retain what we've learned, as our entire being is consumed by survival mode. Frankly, it's no way to live—a grim reality faced by countless individuals worldwide daily, traversing a path strewn with forgotten dreams, shattered hearts, and perpetual turmoil.

You likely know someone—or maybe even find yourself—in a perpetual state of negativity. Everything seems bleak, and the world feels like a dreadful place to inhabit. I can attest from personal experience that being around such individuals or embodying that mindset yourself is utterly soul-draining. While it's true that our world is rife with problems and challenges, their magnitude only grows as we feed them energy and fixate on the problem rather than seeking solutions and acknowledging our role in them. As one of my mentors wisely imparted, *"Make love to solutions, not problems."*

Let's face it: life can be downright tough at times. We all encounter obstacles, but allowing them to fester and linger infiltrates our mindset and eventually molds our character. We've all encountered those shattered souls who seem disconnected and downtrodden or those cantankerous individuals who loathe the world due to past experiences. But have you ever stopped to wonder why?

Because they've allowed those thoughts to dictate their emotions and dominate their outlook, they either lacked the tools to release the pent-up energy resulting from trauma in both body and mind, or they consciously chose not to do so. Consequently, they fixate on these negative aspects, and that fixation shapes their identity. I'll reiterate it once more for emphasis: where attention goes, energy follows, and neurons that fire together wire together.

We are advanced, soulful supercomputers, and we haven't ever really been taught how we operate and function. It's like, *"Welcome to Planet Earth, kid. Good luck. It can be a tough cookie out there. But hey, it is all fair because no one makes it out alive anyway!"* You may have thought, *"What the hell did I sign up for? Wait...remind me why I decided to come here again?"*

We must learn how to master our minds and emotions, develop resiliency, and become extremely aware of how we function individually. Through the art of releasing and dissipating charged energy that resides within our nervous system and is trapped within the limbic system, we begin to change. Likewise, we begin to form new neural connections and associations. The limbic system, also known as the emotional nervous system, is responsible not only for our emotional lives but also for our higher mental functions, such as learning and the formation of memories. This system permeates every facet of our existence, shaping our states of being, habits, and thoughts.

Moreover, dwelling on past grievances pulls us away from the present moment, severing our connection to the universal flow of life and the silver cord to the divine. This detachment breeds unnecessary anguish, torment, and hardship, all contrary to the pursuit of profound peace and tranquility.

Why do you think so many people medicate themselves? We, as Americans, medicate ourselves and anesthetize ourselves with everything under the sun. It varies from drinking, drugs, sex, shopping, gambling, pornography, eating, negative emotions, social media, work, and God knows what. These are all symptoms of not only soul disconnection but a mental/emotional state that is bathed in grief, sorrow, and trauma. Ever evading pain through distraction.

Maladies we seek to escape from that are hurting far below the skin. Only you know how long you have suffered.

We do everything in our power to depart from the pain and hurt existing within the walls of our hearts and the prisons we've crafted in our minds.

The things we use to distract and numb ourselves from the pain within work for a period, but with time, they don't anymore, and they become our captors. We become prisoners of a trapped soul. Then, after trying everything and doing everything we can to numb the pain, we become entirely like a zombie, i.e., motionless and lifeless, losing the brilliant sparks of life and expressions that we had before.

We wake up daily and wear this mask to appear normal and happy to our families, friends, and society. Yet, in all reality, we are crumbling inside. We are broken, tired, and disconnected, and we wish that it would stop once and for all.

We are often caught in this hedonistic material matrix publicized by marketing, advertising, and cultural indoctrination. We buy more, earn more, spend more, and yet it is never enough. It doesn't satisfy the gaping chasm within our souls. A thousand turns into 10,000, turns into a hundred thousand, turns into 1 million, and yet the numbers never end, and the pain never ceases to stop pulsing within our veins. Seeking that which alludes us just around the corner.

Perhaps one day, we might find ourselves in utter despair and feel the need to take our own lives to end the pain, to stop the sorrow, to cease the suffering, and to alleviate the mind that haunts our souls and torments our hearts.

Maybe you have known someone, a friend, or a family member or colleague who has taken their life or tried, and you were quite surprised to realize that the people appeared normal on the outside. Yet, they had these thoughts and feelings and were suffering in silence from the darkness of the human condition. Ever so weary in the hopelessness of a never-ending sea of pain.

In my family, I have had two uncles who committed suicide, two cousins who died from an overdose, and I have nearly lost my life in multiple NDEs (Near Death Experiences). All involving substances of some kind and a very heavy heart. So, when I speak about these things, I speak deep from within my soul that can relate to depression, anxiety, addiction, suicide, substance abuse, and not to mention; mental, emotional, physical, and sexual trauma. A soul and heart that has now found peace and love so profound it is beyond anything I could've ever comprehended or imagined in my mind many years ago.

You are probably thinking, *"Why the hell am I going to listen to someone who has experienced so much pain and sadness and trauma and has nearly died a couple of times?"*

And that is exactly why you will listen; you will be able to relate. I have transcended so much pain and sorrow and have unofficially received a Ph.D. in the school of hard knocks. So yeah!

Welcome to the class! I'm Professor Funk, and school is in session, baby. ;)

I have lived a fast and hard life, and you'll come to learn that as you experience this book.

During my formative years, I found myself navigating the tumultuous waters of existence, grappling with pain and uncertainty, yet lacking the tools to navigate them effectively. I became ensnared in a web of negative cycles, thoughts, and behaviors that I recognized as destructive but felt powerless to escape. It was as if a switch had been flipped, plunging me into a whirlwind of chaos from which I struggled to break free.

In the blink of an eye, I transitioned from being a dedicated student, excelling academically, a champion athlete and upholding a pristine reputation to a veritable maverick.

Previously sober and steadfast, I suddenly found myself careening down a path of recklessness and abandon, my once-steady course thrown into disarray by the tempest raging within.

I'd close down the bars late at night, drink myself into oblivion, crush pills, and smoke massive amounts of weed without anyone truly knowing, and what I thought at the time was "enjoying" parties and being very promiscuous with a lot of lovely ladies. My older brother said to me once, *"You're a slut."* he'd chuckle, and I'd play it off, saying, *"Whatever, you're just jealous. I hang out with beautiful women."* And I did, but as I dove deeper into my healing, I realized and learned from psychology that trauma precedes addiction and, specifically, that hypersexuality, promiscuity and being more risky are after-effects of deep rooted trauma.

As I grappled with the turmoil raging inside me, a grim realization took hold: I harbored an unshakeable sense that I wouldn't see my 25th year. Frankly, I hadn't even envisioned a future beyond that point. My existence felt tethered to the profound sorrow that consumed me, leaving little room for hope or aspiration. Desperate to escape the pain, I resorted to unhealthy coping mechanisms, attempting to outrun the shadows that dogged my every step.

Despite my earnest efforts to heal, I found myself trapped in a cycle of despair, unable to decipher the intricate workings of my own psyche. It became painfully clear that the journey toward healing and transformation was deeply personal and intricate, defying simple solutions or quick fixes.

Enduring a tumultuous upbringing compounded by the challenges of Tourette Syndrome, I found myself harboring a profound disdain for humanity at a tender age. The world seemed overrun with chaos and cruelty, leaving me disillusioned and disheartened. It pained me to witness the callousness with which people treated each other, fueling a simmering resentment that festered within me.

I vividly recall an incident that stirred my early disdain for humanity. It unfolded at a McDonald's in Lander, Wyoming, when I was merely seven or eight years old, freshly transplanted from Utah. It was a day meant for joy - we were fueling up with lunch before heading to my aunt's Quarter Horse Ranch for a day of riding. Yet, amidst the mundane hum of the fast-food joint, a scene unfolded that shook me to my core. A gentleman with Down syndrome sat peacefully enjoying his meal, oblivious to the world around him. Nearby, a pair of callous teenagers took pleasure in tormenting him, their mocking laughter echoing through the air as they taunted him.

Even in my youth, I grasped the profound wrongness of their actions. It was as if a tempest brewed within me, a storm of indignation and fury that surged through my veins like untamed lightning. Fleeing to the shelter of our family van, I unleashed primal screams, my fists raining down upon the seats as my face flushed crimson red with rage. In that moment, a resolve crystallized within me. I vowed to champion the underdogs, the outcasts, and the marginalized to extend a hand of kindness to those deemed different or ostracized. After all, I knew intimately what it meant to be labeled and marginalized, grappling with diagnoses like ADD, OCD, and Tourette syndrome from a young age.

Everyone needs someone; maybe you have someone or don't, but I promise you that I truly have your back. Whoever you are, wherever you are, I have your highest good in mind because I've had to cross through the depths of hell to gain this knowledge and wisdom. I do not share it lightly, and you should not take it as such.

This book is for the loners, the misfits, the outcasts, the weird, the neurodivergent, the outliers, the cooky, the bold, the brave, the loving, the kind in a world that is broken and filled with hate consuming our world like a virus.

On an imperative note, I have to say that I am ONLY alive today by the grace of God, the very creator of my heart, body, mind and soul. An unconditionally loving and miraculous universe that has saved me from the recklessness, debauchery, and suffering I've experienced in this world.

When I mention God, Creator, Universe, or Spirit, I'm referring to the highest truth of existence. The indivisible source light of unconditional, omnipresent love that is God. God created everything, knows everything, sees everything, hears everything, and is always listening to our hearts. It is not just us here alone. There is a force much greater than ourselves and more magnificent than anything we could ever imagine and comprehend.

Additionally, I am most certainly not talking about the perspective of God based on perpetuated dogmatic religious indoctrination and egoic tendencies of God coming from a religious construct that have perpetuated madness and chaos in the name of "God" across the globe. I am speaking of the living God and Creator, that is more loving and merciful beyond anything you've ever witnessed or experienced on this plane. Breathing and moving within your very heart, soul, and every cell in your body that is connected to the infinite galaxy of our universe. Connected in such a grand and miraculous design that it is insane even to imagine.

Just as importantly, I need you to know where I have come from and why I must speak my truth in this book upfront. As I am offering my heart, soul, and whatever wisdom I have been able to learn from the real world. These experiences are hardcore, soul-breaking, and bone-crushing (literally). I have had challenges that have given me deep wisdom that you cannot learn from a class, professor, or college.

These lessons, challenges, and trials that I have synthesized, alchemized, and transmuted, have given me the power to speak on such items. I would have died many times if my life had been in my own hands. Literally, I would have died when I had overdosed on a whole cocktail of pills that was a mix of oxycodone, Percocet, Lortab, Ambien, muscle relaxers, and night quill that would've tranquilized a horse. My heartbeat, at that time, was ten beats a minute. I was on life support until, surprisingly, I came through. I wished at the time to have rather died.

I could have also died when I was inebriated and involved in a high-speed Dukes of Hazard D.U.I. chase at the age of 21 in 2010, raging through the country of Wyoming with four sheriffs in hot pursuit, drunk off my ass on Vodka. Or the DUI I received in Montana a short time later on my motorcycle that almost led to four felonies, but by the grace of God, I was spared. I was suffering intensely from trauma because religion, society, and my family had failed me. Most prominently, I had failed myself.

If I were in charge of my life, I would have died when I blasted head-first into a cement roundabout while on a motorcycle at 30 M.P.H., not even wearing a helmet with alcohol in my system.... Going to get a pizza after getting into a fight with my X-wife. Thanks, Chamaquita, for being amazing when we were together.

Similarly, while living in Mexico with my wife at the time, I would have died partying late at night in the underbelly of Mexico. Drinking myself to near death and inhaling pills like candy to ease my suffering. I could have died from a liver failure while drinking bottles of tequila, vodka, and rum every day for years to anesthetize myself against underlying trauma and many people not even realizing how bad I actually was. I couldn't sleep and had to drink a 5th a night just to pass out to get to bed.

So, I truly have no ego attached to this, only a deep yearning for the truth to be spoken. I long for people to realize the gravity of our situation and where our planet and people currently reside due to cultural indoctrination, religious dogma, and sociopathic governments and institutions promoting scarcity, separation, and manipulation tactics found around the world. Tactics being perpetuated against humanity by a few evil bastards pulling the strings at the top.

Tactics of lack, fear, greed, and division that separate us from our brothers and sisters worldwide who bleed the same blood, breathe the same air, drink the same water, and not to mention live on the same planet that we all co-exist upon. We have been fed bullshit lies for far too long.

There is a colossal awakening upon us, a tidal wave that we can no longer hide from, bury our heads in the sand from, or turn a blind eye to. By doing so, it would only perpetuate our own suffering. We are literally witnessing the fall of the old archaic systems as they tumble right before our eyes, and global awareness of love is rising across the planet.

I don't know you, your story, your background, or your history, but I do know this. If I haven't lost you yet, and you can walk with my vibe, then you're part of the soul tribe. So, I welcome you to our *Ohana*. I also invite you to join me on this journey of healing through the expansion of your heart, mind, and soul. Awakening the dormant parts of your brilliance as you step into your greatest empowerment and arouse all faculties of your existence.

It is all right if you are uncomfortable or if it seems scary. It is a good thing because you are about to cross out of your comfort zone and land in the unknown universe.

Welcome home, warrior!
Welcome home to the tribe of humanity!
We've been waiting for you because now is our time!

"True masculinity is not defined by the strength of muscles, but by the strength of character." - Anonymous

Chapter 1: A Message for the Men

Let's face the harsh reality: The society we inherit, with its norms, behaviors, and standards of acceptance, has tainted our cultural systems at both national and international levels.

The deeper you delve into the origins of our perceptions, thought processes, and the execution of a well-crafted agenda, the clearer it becomes. Disempowering men undermines the strength of a nation. Attacking the family unit and belittling its significance undermines the very foundation upon which numerous great nations and communities have thrived.

For us men, if you are viewed as emotional or seen crying, you are automatically equated with being weak, vulnerable, and not manly. Aka, *"You a lil bitch, bro."* On the flip side if you are a strong empowered masculine male, its frowned upon by garbage propaganda. These lie's have been perpetuated for so long and have created so much suffering for us men that it's absolutely ridiculous. Look at how many men suffer in silence. How many of our brothers end their lives day after day and trudge through the monotony of passionless living and purposeless existence?

Slaving away in a 9-5 job, only to see 1/3 or more of our hard-earned wages taxed, while billions of our dollars are shipped overseas to fuel wars, pay for other countries' pensions, and fund frivolous programs with OUR tax dollars!. What the French toast? Meanwhile, our country's history and culture are under relentless attack, bastardized by evil forces indoctrinating our youth and sedating the masses with endless, debauched pleasures.

It's no surprise that we, as men, are never taught that it is actually the strongest of men who process their emotions and feel them in a healthy way—honoring what is alive within us and moving through it in an empowered way. If we had that, we would have strong, emboldened men and capable, conscious sentient warriors to stand up to the tyranny of our time.

We are both aware of how simple it is to numb ourselves with drugs of all kinds: by having easy access to porn, sedating ourselves with alcohol that is constantly being promoted, smoking weed, gambling, working nonstop, eating to access, popping pills, hooking up with the next girl, or any other way we can to feel okay, loved, and accepted—anything to get that dopamine hit wherever we can.

I have personally experienced each and every one of these issues many times. I spent so much time running away from my feelings and emotions that when I finally stopped and sat with myself, the years of ignoring my feelings and getting sucked into the program left me feeling lost, disoriented, and hopeless.

I constantly thought to myself, *"Once I have X amount of money in my bank account, it'll be perfect. After I hook up with her, I'll be golden. When I travel here, everything will be different. When I get this car, happiness will be mine."* And yet, no matter where we are on the planet, what we have, how much is in the bank, or what girl we are with, That's exactly where we are.

There is no escaping from ourselves; we can drink for years on end, smoke massive amounts of marijuana, hook up with the sexiest women, work nonstop, move to different countries, make a ton of money and yet, at the end of the day, we cannot escape from what is locked within our minds and trapped in our hearts. No matter where we go, That's where we'll be.

We are lying to ourselves and avoiding the inevitable. It's as if we have a hemorrhaging chest wound, but we don't acknowledge it; we just keep throwing a few bandages on it while we are bleeding out everywhere, squirting blood. *"Oh no, it's not there; it's fine; I'm perfectly fine; don't worry about me; I'll make it through; it'll be better tomorrow. I'm good."* Have you *ever* felt like that?

Now I get it. There's a time and place for hard work, being stoic, and kicking ass. Trust me, I know. For years, I spent endless days hiking across the toughest terrain in the country, with temperatures at times in excess of 110° while rucking a 45-pound pack on my back and fighting fire for 16 hours a day. Hopping out of helicopters into raging forest fires, battling the blaze with hand tools and chainsaws, and sleeping in a tent in the middle of nowhere with my crew. But at the end of the day, after all the adrenaline is gone and the tactical operations are over, we still really don't have a place to process and feel what is alive for us.

Identifying, feeling, and processing our emotions in relation to the challenging things we have witnessed or encountered in life is vital, particularly for those of us who are or have served as first responders, military personnel, or veterans. Emotions that are not felt and processed in a healthy way can lead to destructive coping strategies and poison the brilliance of our hearts and souls.

Many individuals believe that traumatic events like war, death, or shocking events are what cause PTSD. In reality, it can happen when our daily experiences—whether they be at work, school, home, or any other place—consistently elicit a stress reaction, arousing our fight-or-flight response over extended periods of time, again and again consistently.

As a former federal firefighter, one of the most disheartening realizations was witnessing the alarming rates of suicide, divorce, substance abuse, and other challenges faced by my fellow first responders and veterans. These individuals, who courageously risk their lives for our communities and nation, suffer at rates three to four times higher than the general population. It's why I'm deeply passionate about sharing my story and advocating for mental and emotional health awareness while spreading a message of strength and hope. Having walked that path myself, I understand the struggles and stand as a beacon of support for those still navigating through them.

When we first begin to open up to the inside world of our emotions and feelings, it can be very frightening. No, seriously, it can be extreme. It's literally like opening up

Pandora's box. We just want to have a little look, and then, boom! Out jumps a scary monster wanting to eat our face.

"Ummm, no thanks; I won't be having any of that today, sir."

This rings particularly true if you've spent years, or perhaps your entire life, avoiding or suppressing your emotions. It can feel overwhelming and terrifying to finally confront them, knowing that a flood of buried feelings might come rushing to the surface. Yet, it's crucial to sit with these emotions, acknowledge them without judgment, and welcome them in rather than pushing them away as if they're something to be feared or shunned.

Delving into the deepest, darkest corners of our psyche, where pain and sorrow have long been buried, requires courage. It means allowing these emotions to surface and feeling them fully. It's about honoring whatever comes up—whether it's the need to rage, scream, or yell—without causing harm to ourselves or others. It's about embracing the intensity of these emotions and letting them flow through us, ultimately releasing their grip on our souls.

They are trying to deliver a message to us; they are trying to tell us something. They only want us to sit down with them, hear them, feel them, have a cup of coffee with them, and get to know them more personally. By now, you are probably thinking, *"What the hell is this guy talking about? He wants me to feel and honor the very thing that has hurt me, beat me, wrecked me, demolished me, and caused massive amounts of pain in my life."*

"Yeah, right, bro, no way in hell am I going into those deep, dark corners and places I have locked away. I'm good; it's cool. I'm just going to go and distract myself with endless amounts of work, watch some porn, smoke some more weed, have a couple of beers, maybe a shot or two, watch a movie, maybe have a Netflix and chill session. Not sure, but I do know one thing: I most certainly will not be having any of that." *Does that sound* familiar at all?

If you're anything like me, I avoided my emotions like the plague and did everything I could to numb myself or occupy my mind so that I did not have to feel them, look at them, or process them. Because when you experience so much at a young age, you become very good at masking and locking things away. And let me tell you from painful personal experience that this is most definitely the absolute worst way to go about it. It's similar to running from a wrecking ball that gets larger with time, accumulating more mass and energy the further and faster we try to run and escape. Then, one day, when we decide to stop for a brief moment, take a breath, and *KABOOOOM!*

This monster knocks us to our knees, kicks us in the nuts, and says, *"Hey, buddy, remember me? You've been running for a minute. Nice try, pal."* Really, though, it's extremely counterintuitive, yet it's what we were taught. It's no fun, and it's considerably difficult to feel the hurt and pain when it happens and be a sentient savage rather than avoiding pain all our lives.

Some quick background information: I grew up in Wyoming, the literal Wild West, steeped in cowboy and Native American culture, on the largest Native American reservation in the United States. Talk about deep cultural and ancestral trauma on both sides. Trauma still pulses through the veins, manifesting in counterintuitive coping mechanisms and a paradigm of hurt and indifference, which is incredibly sad. It's a land where people cry out for healing and understanding, albeit at a painfully slow rate.

I grew up hearing clichés like, *"Strap up your boots. We have work to do!"*. *"You want something to cry about, I'll give you something to cry about,"* and *"Buck up, cowboy."*

As I reflect on toughness now, my perspective has evolved. It's not about burying everything, concealing it, and pretending it doesn't exist. True toughness is facing the hurt and pain head-on courageously navigating through it. It involves doing what's necessary, putting in the effort, nurturing emotional intelligence, and cultivating resilience.

Certainly, there's nothing amiss with embodying toughness, strength, and unwavering determination to accomplish tasks proficiently. It's essential and invaluable. We require resilient men, courageous men, and wise, composed men. However, we also need healed men. We need men who are emotionally accessible. Amidst the backdrop of Cowboy machismo culture and our cognitive performance-driven society, a significant number of individuals are grappling with inner turmoil. They're hurting yet unaware of the source of their anger, frustration, or emotional emptiness, feeling adrift and utterly indifferent.

It's strikingly evident that our repressed emotions accumulate over time, manifesting in their most detrimental forms, especially among individuals like us tough-as-nails cowboys and warriors. Anger often conceals underlying internal anguish or sorrow, resulting in unspoken emotions being bottled up and managed through what I term U3C:

Unhealthy coping through unrestrained consumption, unbridled carnalization, and unchecked conflict.

These themes reflect the use of unhealthy coping mechanisms to deal with stress and emotions. Archetypes and symbolic forms representing the various ways we cope that can lead us to a lot of problems. Unrestrained consumption can be any substance, such as alcohol. It may be marijuana, pills, nicotine, cocaine, food, or drugs of any kind—whatever gives us a buzz or numbs us.

Unbridled carnalization relates to engaging in unhealthy sexual behaviors. Such as pornography, promiscuity, promiscuous behavior, sexting, masturbation, or whatever relates to unhealthy sexuality in a way that we aren't honoring ourselves and using to cope and numb through purely sexual gratification. Unchecked conflict could be anything relating to aggression as a means of dealing with stress or asserting dominance. Recognizing an affinity toward combativeness, violence, conflict, anger, bullying, and or stonewalling our emotions, and just being *"OK"* or *"fine."* In reality, we are crumbling inside.

When we indulge in these behaviors, they give us a short-term hit with a fast burn rate and prolonged recovery. We either numb out completely or get an adrenaline spike and a hit of dopamine. Getting all twisted, we have a fight, meet some ladies, and, with any luck, go and bang one out. No strings attached, no relationship, just someone to fill the void.

In reality, it's the poison coursing through our veins, demanding expression because we've never learned to acknowledge or explore our emotions. We've lacked healthy models to guide us through this process, leaving us with a toxic residue we're ill-equipped to address.

When we take a step back and examine our culture and society from a bird's-eye view, the puzzle pieces fall into place. The reasons behind people's brokenness become clear, requiring no advanced degree to decipher.

A significant portion of individuals have experienced or are currently living within broken family dynamics and environments. Coupled with societal norms that glorify hedonistic materialism and self-indulgent toxicity, as well as the pervasive sexualization of the divine feminine for profit, this creates a toxic brew. These phenomena are perpetuated by cultural engineering, deliberate misinformation, and systematic brainwashing, compounded by the transmission of generational trauma.

Now, let's be clear—I'm not here to pass judgment on anyone, especially not with my own checkered past. I'm simply shedding light on the situation. I understand that people are doing the best they can with the tools, knowledge, and environment they've been given. But let's get real for a moment. The so-called "education" we've received is garbage. It's pure nonsense. We've been force-fed lies, conditioned, indoctrinated, and trained to believe that dysfunction is normal and that scarcity and unworthiness define our existence.

From the moment we are born, we've been bombarded with messages that we're not good enough, that we lack, that we're sinful, and that life is a constant struggle for survival. It's all been carefully crafted through relentless marketing and advertising to keep us feeling small and insignificant. We've been thrust into a world of chaos and confusion, with very few true leaders willing to challenge the status quo or whom have big enough balls to stand up against the madness for what it is, while doing their best to stay in integrity with themselves and be of service.

The most bewildering aspect of all this is that we often fail to recognize just how twisted, inverted, and toxic our surroundings truly are. It's our norm; it's ingrained in our very being. Now, I'm not suggesting it's all black and white or a universal truth, but once you start peeling back the layers and becoming aware, it's downright shocking.

You might have grown up in an environment where emotional regulation, healthy boundaries, self-worth, and emotional processing were foreign concepts due to a dysfunctional ecosystem. That's understandable, so go easy on yourself. Remember, hurt people hurt people, but the flip side is also true: healed people heal people.

When I embarked on my journey of awakening, a profound question surfaced in my mind: Did I have any influence on the construction of society, culture, government, politics, education, history, and my heritage before my consciousness, soul, and spirit inhabited my body on this planet? Was I given any choice or say, or was everything imposed upon me without my consent at birth?

This realization sent shockwaves through me, causing my paradigm to flip upside down. I came to understand that I didn't have to conform to or empower outdated systems that didn't serve my highest good. I began to reclaim my agency, choosing how I operated, what served me, and what didn't. While we may still operate within certain boundaries, we can redefine them according to our values and what holds true meaning for us.

That's the most liberating aspect of awakening: we hold the power to shape our beliefs, perspectives, and actions in the world. It might not align with the mainstream, but that's inconsequential. When we're living from our hearts, in joy, and aligned with our highest selves, why would we concern ourselves with the opinions of others? After all, they don't foot our bills, hit the gym for us, or determine our talents and capabilities—we do! They didn't create us, so they can't define us.

When we fail to address our emotions, experiences, and traumas, we subject ourselves to unnecessary suffering. For years, this cycle perpetuated itself in my own life, fueled by ignorance and lack of awareness. When we're taught falsehoods, we internalize them, leading to a cascade of detrimental effects. Moreover, enduring significant trauma—be it mental, emotional, physical, or sexual—alters your brain chemistry, psychology, and thought processes, casting a shadow over every aspect of your life. It literally changes your brain chemistry and thinking patterns.

Appearances can be deceiving. While someone may seem perfectly put together on the outside, underneath the facade lies a world of chaos, dysfunction, and concealed trauma. It's crucial not to make assumptions based solely on outward appearances. Just because someone has a polished exterior, appears composed, or maintains physical fitness doesn't mean you understand the depth of their experiences, the trials they've faced, or the scars they carry within their soul.

Before I embarked on the journey of healing and processing my emotions, I exhausted every coping mechanism imaginable: drowning it in alcohol, clouding my mind with weed, seeking solace in physical intimacy, sweating it out through exercise, burying myself in work, overindulging in food, and attempting to escape through sleep. Yet, no matter where I turned or what I tried, the pain persisted. It stood before me, an ever-present specter, peering into the depths of my soul with unwavering intensity.

The lesson learned is this: never judge a book by its cover, and understand that perception often holds more sway than reality. Just because something appears one way doesn't necessarily reflect its true essence.

Another profoundly misleading notion we're fed revolves around casual sex and hooking up. Let's be clear: sex is a beautiful experience with the right person in a serious relationship and marriage. However, engaging in intercourse forms energetic soul ties with the other person, intertwining our energy, experiences, trauma, and karmic connections. Often, we have no knowledge of their past, their state of consciousness, or the patterns that govern their behavior.

Engaging in sexual activity with someone we're not emotionally connected to diminishes our self-worth, self-esteem, and self-love. Instead of giving energy, it drains us. Consider this: as men, our seed carries the power to create life. When we disregard or disrespect this power, it depletes us in ways we may not fully grasp. Despite the societal propaganda, this is the undeniable truth.

For us men, semen retention is akin to forging ourselves into superheroes. Many influential figures have advocated for it, from Napoleon Hill in "Think and Grow Rich" to Sadhguru and countless others. Studies have corroborated its benefits as well: refraining from ejaculation for even just a week can lead to a notable surge in testosterone levels. The advantages are vast, including enhanced libido, heightened energy levels and alertness, as well as improved muscle growth, bone density, and cardiovascular function.

If there's one regret I carry, it's my past as a f*ck boy. It's a stark truth. Throughout high school, college, and beyond, I indulged in a lifestyle of promiscuity. Strangely, in our society, such behavior is often glorified among men, earning praise as they notch up conquests.

Upon deep introspection, I uncovered the driving forces behind my actions. I craved companionship and validation so intensely that I continually sacrificed my own worth because: #1, I possessed charm and good looks, making it effortless; #2, I was trapped in a cycle of trauma; #3, it provided an illusory confidence boost; #4, it triggered a surge of dopamine; and #5, it conferred false social status in certain circles, fostering a sense of belonging and acceptance that I lacked within.

When we lack love from our primary caregivers—our parents, family, or guardians—and grow up in a toxic environment, it triggers detrimental responses within us. Whether consciously or not, we may lash out, seek validation, or exhibit reckless and sometimes violent behavior as a result of the dysfunctional dynamics in our formative years.

We often find ourselves seeking love in all the wrong places, resorting to numbing ourselves with substances, engaging in risky behavior, or, like me, diving headfirst into all of them at warp speed and full throttle. It's a cliché, but just as real: women with "daddy issues" have parallels in men with what are often dubbed "mommy issues." When love is withheld within the family dynamic, or when our parents are caught in unhealthy patterns, we instinctively seek to fill the void within us through toxic means, attempting to patch up the abyss within our souls.

In our relentless pursuit, we search in countless ways, yet the void within remains vast and seemingly insatiable. It's a paradox: the more we acquire, the greater the need, yet the less effective the remedy becomes.

Ultimately, what we crave is profound love, genuine care, acceptance, and appreciation, primarily from ourselves and then from those closest to us. However, when we lack these essentials in our formative years within a healthy environment, navigating life's complexities later on becomes a daunting challenge.

During those turbulent times, my actions were a rebellion against the world, a response to years of bullying and mockery stemming from my quirky Tourette's. It was my way of proclaiming, *"Watch me; I'm fearless; I'll do as I please; I can charm any woman I desire. As a handsome, intelligent, muscular firefighter, I am irresistible to women, and they adore me."*

In those wild days, all it took was a smile, some banter, and a casual invitation to capture a woman's attention. And if that didn't suffice, my profession was my trump card. Just utter the words, *"I'm a firefighter,"* and—boom!—game over. Well, maybe not quite that easy, but there's certainly something about women and firefighters.

Every encounter was consensual, and I shared memorable moments with beautiful women. Yet, it stemmed from deep wounds I hadn't acknowledged. In the moment, I believed it was all about having fun. But when the excitement faded and the distractions subsided, I confronted the truth: I was an empty man, desperately clutching at anything to dull the pain and feel worthy.

In those moments, we sought to fulfill our unmet needs through each other, whether in a sexual context or seeking companionship. Initially, I believed I cherished women, only to uncover layers of resentment toward them—particularly toward my mother, stemming from my tumultuous childhood and the anger I harbored. However, as I embarked on my journey of healing and self-discovery, I came to understand that she, too, had endured profound trauma in her own upbringing. She did the best she could with the tools she had, just as we all do, and beneath her actions lay a deep love for me. She was simply grappling with her own unhealed wounds, perpetuating a cycle she herself had endured and her own self-bitterness projecting onto others.

My deeply ingrained traumatic experiences led me to behave in ways that eroded my self-worth and self-love, inflicting further suffering on myself and those in my orbit.

I became a one-man wrecking crew, leaving behind a trail of destruction, shattered hearts, and chaos. Strangely, I found a twisted comfort in this cycle of pain—a bond to the trauma and a rebellious defiance against anyone who dared try to control me. I thrived in this destructive mindset until the fragile facade I'd constructed crumbled in a blaze of reckoning.

When we endure profound suffering, particularly at the hands of our family and society, it can cloud our vision of the future, trapping us in the present moment. I was convinced that I wouldn't live past 25. With every fiber of my being, I believed it, and truthfully, I didn't even want to. The agony within my soul was overwhelming.

What aided me on my path to healing was a genuine grasp of compassion and forgiveness, coupled with earnest pleas to God for mercy, grace, and assistance. Left to my own devices, I would have perished long ago.

Embracing self-compassion allows us to extend the same empathy to others in our world, accepting ourselves with all our experiences and choices. Life is inherently challenging; it tests and challenges everyone, regardless of appearances or circumstances. We all bear scars from life's battles, some more visible than others. Remember, nobody escapes unscathed. Reflect on this: if tomorrow were your last day, how would you approach life differently? How would your perspective shift regarding the challenges and blessings in your life?

None of us knows when our time will come to an end, underscoring the importance of living each day as if it were our last. Near-death experiences grant us a profound appreciation for life. It's about cherishing every moment with gratitude and profound appreciation for our existence.

Awakening in the hospital, my life teetering on the edge after my motorcycle accident I could only blame myself for, I faced a stark choice. I could continue down a path of pain, destruction, and bitterness, or I could embrace accountability, using the experience as fuel for healing and growth. Opting for the latter, I extended grace and compassion to myself and others, recognizing the opportunity for soulful expansion despite the immense challenges. Too much had been endured to surrender to hatred or self-abandonment; it was time to rise, to learn, and to share the wisdom gained.

God spared my life against all odds and I did not suffer paralysis, mental retardation, a traumatic brain injury (TBI), or anything else after the accident with no helmet.

The doctors echoed the sentiment, calling me a living, walking miracle, the luckiest damn guy alive. So, I extend this miracle to you, from one miracle man to another. May it serve as a beacon of hope and healing, awaiting your decision to embrace it with an open heart.

Avoiding the work and denying ourselves the space to navigate these emotions while failing to honor our current state in the journey only fuels a ticking time bomb. The longer we evade, the more potent the explosion becomes.

Eventually, after prolonged attempts to escape by drowning our sorrows in substances or fleeting pleasures, the bomb will detonate with such force that it shatters our world, causing chaos.

Embarking on this journey of self-discovery and healing will undoubtedly be one of the most uncomfortable and challenging endeavors you can undertake. Yet, it will also be among the most rewarding and transformative experiences imaginable.

By embracing the path of the spiritual warrior and embodying the essence of a sentient sovereign being, you step into the realm of true masculinity—one characterized by profound sensitivity and depth of feeling. Society's misconception of masculinity has led to deep wounds in the divine masculine, fostering a culture of emotional suppression and disconnection from the heart. For years, we've been fed lies that equate vulnerability with weakness, perpetuating a damaging narrative that has caused immense suffering for countless individuals worldwide—men, women, and the planet itself.

It's crucial to recognize the need for a safe and nurturing environment to navigate these emotions. Not every confidant or social circle is equipped to handle such delicate matters, and disclosing vulnerabilities in the wrong setting can exacerbate existing wounds. Seeking out a supportive community or trusted individuals who can provide a secure space for emotional exploration is essential for healing and growth.

Contrary to popular belief, the true Alpha Male of the Group (AMOG) isn't the one who dominates through brute force or aggression but rather the one who inspires, uplifts, and leads with integrity and heart.

In today's society, there's a tendency to attribute all problems to "toxic masculinity and the patriarchy," but this oversimplification misses the mark. We don't inhabit a genuine patriarchy; instead, we're immersed in a culture dominated by toxic, immature boys masquerading it as masculinity. This culture is characterized by wounded individuals who, instead of embodying true strength and leadership, resort to childish displays of power and dominance.

Our current culture is fueled by debauchery and decadence, perpetuated by insecure men who prioritize their own self-gratification over the well-being of their communities and the world at large. These individuals lack the capacity for conscious communication and fail to foster healthy cooperation among our people.

In contrast, a true patriarchy would honor the divine feminine and prioritize service, protection, provision, and leadership from the heart. It would foster empowered, heart-centered men who serve as a warrior class of true masculine kings dedicated to protecting their families, communities, and tribes.

We've not only faced poisonous guilt and shame from our fellow men but also from the distorted narratives of femininity. There's a prevailing belief that all the world's problems stem from men, which fails to acknowledge the shared wounds and struggles experienced by both genders. Let's not dismiss or belittle each other's experiences, but instead, let's acknowledge the generational and societal traumas that have affected us all. It's a destructive cycle that only perpetuates harm. We need understanding, compassion, and vulnerability to create a safe space for healing.

Although the journey ahead won't be easy, I hold a steadfast belief in humanity's resilience and capacity for growth. Now, more than ever, it's not just important—it's absolutely vital for the future of our species and our planet. Let's rise to this challenge together, with courage, compassion, and unwavering determination. Opening the door to our collective healing that starts now if we solely choose it to be.

"Youth is not defined by age, but by the spirit of adventure and curiosity within." – Anonymous

Chapter 2: The Early Years

The doctor's office was cold, with pale lighting illuminating the patient waiting room, which evoked a sense of hollowness. As I sat there with my mother as a young boy, the doctor entered the room in his white coat and stethoscope around his neck. I had always hated the doctor's office. I was part of a number of experiments in which my blood was drawn numerous times, vials and vials for *"Tourette's Syndrome Studies"* at the University of Utah.

This time was different, though. I remember the doctor speaking with my mother and him looking over at me and then back at her, saying, *"He won't be able to read or learn well. He'll have extreme difficulty in school as he won't be good at math or science. I'm sorry to say that he'll have a very difficult life."*

Even at the young age of six or seven, I thought, *"No, not true, not my life. That's not going to be my life. I'll show him. I'll show the world. I'll do great things!"*

THE MIRACLE MAN

I was born in Salt Lake City, Utah, and raised in Kaysville, UT, until I was seven years old. I was raised in a Mormon family, or the Church of Jesus Christ of Latter-Day Saints, as people call it. It certainly has life-shaping standards and ideals in accordance with its faith, but it also has a certain dichotomy to it that can result in deep-seated religious trauma.

Religion in Utah, much like in many other states and regions globally, creates a distinct bubble. If you're part of the religion, you're inside the bubble; if not, you're an outsider peering in. This exclusivity breeds a culture where conformity is prized, and deviation is met with ostracization and judgment. For example, families often enforce strict boundaries, only permitting socialization among children who belong to the same faith.

I've personally witnessed families disown their own kin for deviating from the expected norms, such as not embarking on a missionary journey. Siblings, cousins, sons, daughters and relatives have been cast aside and deemed unworthy simply because they chose a different path. This rejection, carried out in the name of religion, is nothing short of heartbreaking and hypocritical. It flies in the face of the very principles of compassion and acceptance that these religious communities claim to uphold, yet have succumbed too.

Growing up in such an environment, I couldn't help but recognize the toxicity and destructiveness of this mindset. It bred a culture of judgment and superiority, where adherence to dogma was valued above genuine human connection and empathy. It's a sobering reminder that within the folds of religion, the essence of true spirituality and compassion can sometimes be lost.

In my youth, Tourette's syndrome manifested prominently in my life, particularly in challenging family and school environments. The condition, characterized by uncontrollable repetitive movements or sounds known as tics, had a significant impact on my daily experiences. These tics, ranging from blinking excessively to making involuntary noises, made me stand out and subjected me to ridicule and bullying something fierce.

Despite my genuine kindness toward others, I found myself targeted by peers who failed to understand or empathize with my condition. One vivid memory stands out: a bus ride home from school where my facial tics were particularly pronounced, drawing unwanted attention and further exacerbating feelings of isolation and frustration.

While quietly observing the passing scenery on the bus ride home in Wyoming, I was abruptly confronted by an older kid's hostile accusation: *"Stop winking at me, faggot."* The venom in his words pierced through me, and with a mixture of defiance and frustration, I retorted, *"I am not winking at you. I have Tourette's, asshole."* It was a difficult daily struggle being a loner, misunderstood and bullied relentlessly.

Despite the challenges of navigating a world where my quirks made me a target, I found solace in my connection to nature and animals. From a young age, I felt a deep spiritual bond with the natural world and the grand mystery of life, often misunderstood by my family and community due to its unconventional nature. My authenticity and openness to my spiritual experiences sometimes led to misunderstandings, such as the time my brother, startled and frightened, misconstrued my connection with the divine as something sinister.

At the age of nine, while engrossed in prayer and meditation, my brother's sudden intrusion into my room led to a misunderstanding that echoed through our household. Startled, he dashed out of the room, exclaiming to my mother, *"Mom! Kye's talking to the devil again!"* Unbeknownst to them, my connection with the divine was a deeply personal and natural experience, guided by an internal impulse that flowed effortlessly from within. Regularly encompassing love and profound experiences.

Growing up in an environment where metaphysical exploration was not purely uncommon, thanks to my father's influence, I was a hyper-aware and spiritually attuned child, prone to glimpses of the unseen and the mystical. You can't even imagine the things I've seen, witnessed, and experienced during my life - everything from paranormal to extraterrestrial: angels and demons, spirits and ghosts, entities, orbs, mystical lights, alien spacecraft, and stuff that leaves you in absolute awe. Mind you, none of these experiences were facilitated by the use of any psychedelic plant or animal medicine. Those came later in life... Hallelujah for psychedelics utilized properly.

After many of my early childhood experiences, I suppressed everything because I started to believe that I was demonic. I thought I was becoming a bad kind of person and was crazy. This hyper-religious perspective and construct created trauma that really limited my perspective of myself and how I connected with the world because I was cultured to perceive everything through an immensely strict religious lens.

If one deviated from that viewpoint of the religion, you were considered out of line, misplaced, misguided, and a lost soul.

That is why I had so much opposition in regard to religion; it was as if religion was shoved down my throat, and I didn't have any other option. I had to do what everyone did and never understood how someone could preach about one thing and do the exact opposite. How I was an innocent child and yet a sinner at the same time. Everything felt so phony, like a shallow game of country club where everyone turned up to compare themselves to the person with the nicest house, car, or larger bank account.

Of course, I'm grateful for what it taught me: discipline, faith, and belief in community, but it had some detrimental aspects to it, which made it look like a cult.

That's one of the reason's I don't cling to organized religion anymore. We don't have to look too far into history and realize what has been done in the name of "Religion" across the globe. I believe in a direct relationship with God, the divine, our creator, where I don't need to have an intermediary between myself and God. That intermediary is Christ, the Christos frequency, and that eternal truth of unconditional love. I believe that our relationship with God is uniquely ours and ours alone. We don't have to explain it to anyone, justify it, or prove it. How we connect to that truth is ours alone. Nobody can come in between that, and it exists within us all, but only if we choose to connect with it and activate it. While there is benefit in community and structure, it becomes blemished when one sect believes they hold "ALL" the truth and are the only way to God. Further creating more separation and division.

Organized religion operates within a legalistic framework, akin to that of the Pharisees and the Sadducees, where adherence to strict rules supersedes spiritual connection, relationship, and personal transformation with God. It externalizes our divinity, fostering a sense of separation from our inherent connection to the divine within us, as we are created in Gods image. This stark contrast left me feeling like the odd one out for many years, perplexed by the disrespect and hypocrisy I witnessed among adherents.

When I was nine years old, I reached a point of despair so profound that I contemplated ending my own life. The turmoil within my family was relentless; my parents were locked in constant conflict, my mother oscillating between absence and explosive outbursts, and my father often absent except for fleeting weekends. School was no refuge; I endured relentless bullying and found myself without any friends. In the depths of my despair, the prospect of carving myself up and bleeding out seemed preferable to enduring the perpetual torment of my existence.

Amidst all this suffering and sorrow, one day, my brother caught me masturbating in my room. In my religious upbringing, this was a big sin. I thought I was going to be thrust into hell and that I was an evil person who had brought great damnation and sin upon me. He said that he was going to tell our mother just to spite me, and he called her at work. I remember pleading with him and begging him as he picked up the phone, dialed her work number, and said in a pleased voice, *"Mom, I caught Kye masturbating in his room."*

This threw me off the rails and put me in a very dysregulated spot. I remember my mom coming home from work to pick me up and take me to the ER. I was sobbing and crying, solely wanting support and love, and nothing was said… Just silence from her as we drove half an hour down the road. With my dad in another state working as he regularly was.

She took me to the emergency room as I said I wanted to kill myself, and I was given a sterile hospital room to myself until the doctor arrived. No one else was around. There I was, this young boy, all alone weeping, feeling like I was going to hell and was an evil person. The doctor came in, approached my bed, and asked in a friendly tone, *"What's going on here today?"*

I responded while blubbing and crying, *"I'm so bad. I'm evil, and I'm going to hell. My brother caught me masturbating. Now my life is over."*

He looked at me, pausing in astonishment, and said, *"That's normal....People masturbate. You're figuring your body out and how it functions."*

At this point, I was extremely confused and responded bewilderedly, *"What do you mean... I'm sick. It's a sin. I'm going to hell."*

Again, he was baffled at my thinking and said kindly, *"It's a normal part of life and a human experience."*

I recall seeking solace and support when I left the hospital, but I never got any. My brothers and parents remained silent. The only response I got was my family's need to hide every knife in the kitchen because *"Kye is suicidal and the problem child."*

Nobody could relate to how I was feeling, and the constant shouting, screaming, and frequent fighting at home only intensified my sadness. However, this experience has been one of my greatest teachers. It fostered a deep trust and relationship with my creator and my own heart.

Being in Wyoming, away from the city, surrounded by the open country, was truly wonderful and healing. My brothers and I could embrace our wild and carefree spirits. I rode horses and dirt bikes in the vast expanse, climbed mountains, fished and hunted, and shot guns off our back porch – experiences that were impossible in the congested and confined city.

Wyoming held a serene charm and breathtaking beauty that captivated me. One of our neighbors, Lex Burton, a rancher and farmer who was also part of our church, became a significant influence in my life. He even taught himself how to read by reading the Bible. A very humble, loving and epic human being I am eternally grateful for. He took me under his wing, imparting invaluable lessons on ranching and farming. From mastering the art of driving a stick shift while unloading hay for his cattle to welding repairs, I absorbed every skill he shared. Under his guidance, I learned to operate a tractor and assist in moving coal, all before the age of twelve. I can vividly recall navigating the country back roads in that tractor, basking in the warmth of the sun on my back and the invigorating scent of freshly cut hay lingering in the air.

Throughout my early teenage years, my time outside of school, sports and church was dedicated to assisting on his ranch and farm, honing my skills in welding, farming activity, cattle drives, driving trucks and tractors. I experienced exhilarating cattle drives across the red desert and mountain terrain, often spending several days beneath the vast expanse of stars. This immersion in nature, particularly with horses, proved to be a lifeline during bouts of depression. It fostered a deep connection to the beauty of the natural world and to God himself. Lex Burton, a respected figure in our community, played a pivotal role in my life, leading me toward spiritual enlightenment, self-empowerment, and a profound appreciation for the bond between humans and horses.

Lex Burton was known for his jovial demeanor, always wearing a smile and filling the air with laughter. His wife, Goldie, was equally warm-hearted, preparing delicious turkey and ham sandwiches for us before our workdays. One time, Lex tricked me into crossing the electric fence, assuring me it was turned off. *"Go ahead,"* he said confidently, *"just cross over and grab me that piece of twine over there."* As I firmly grabbed the fence, I received a shocking jolt. Lex couldn't contain his laughter and teasingly said, *"Hurts, doesn't it? Great for keeping them cows in."*

Some of my fondest memories were of herding cattle and riding for hours on end on a horse named 'Lightning' in the middle of nowhere, with the golden sunshine bathing the plains and the smell of sagebrush in the air. I had a connection with the horse and the natural world that words cannot express; it was like being in a Western movie, a force in the union of animal and human freedom. It was heavenly. You know if you know. If not, sucks to be you.

From an early age, wrestling became a significant part of my life. We were a large wrestling family that spent every Friday and Saturday traveling to compete in Greco-Roman and freestyle events around the state and the Rockies. After putting in a lot of practice, I became really good at it, winning many matches and tournaments eventually winning a state championship in Greco-Roman and Freestyle when I was younger. Strengthening my body, mind, and soul as I began maturing into a young stud.

During my junior year in high school, I was 19-0; every match but two were pins with a few technical decisions; I won so many points they called the matches. I was on my way to be in the running for a state championship, then I got mono…. Da Da Da… It wrecked me, going 0-2 to people I had beaten with ease previously in the year. In all honesty, I probably got it because I was kissing all the girls. *SMH*

During a tournament in my early teens, I remember when all the brackets were released. The wrestlers would flock to the walls, looking at who they were matched with. These two kids in my weight division were reading the bracket in front of me, and I heard one say, *"Dammit, man, I have Kye in the first match."* His friend replied, *"Oh, sorry, bro,"* and *laughed.*

I watched this unfold from behind, then moved my way forward between the two. I guided my fingers down the bracket and then looked over at the one I was going to have my first match with. Looking him directly in the eyes like a hungry lion, I said, *"Good luck,"* and walked away, smirking. Knowing I was going to throttle him and win the tournament. I have an entire shoebox filled with gold medals mixed in with a few silver and some bronze from the tournaments I won over the years.

At one of my final tournaments, during the last match of the 8th-grade wrestling season, where I won first place, an accident occurred. I inadvertently caused injury to an opponent, resulting in a broken neck. The sight of the emergency medical team rushing him away on a stretcher filled me with profound remorse. However, my older brother, perpetually provocative, chose to exacerbate the situation by casting blame upon me: *"Wow, Kye, way to go break the kid's neck. You're a terrible person."*

Adding insult to injury, the fact that the injured individual happened to be black was immediately seized upon by my brother, who attempted to paint me as a racist. His hurtful words cut deep, as he often wielded them as weapons in our sibling dynamic.

It's a curious twist of fate how I endured so much childhood bullying for being weird and quirky and receiving unwarranted criticism about my appearance. Beauty-shaming, believe it or not, is a real phenomenon. If I had received a dollar for every instance I was labeled "Pretty Boy" and subjected to mockery simply for being myself, I'd likely be comfortably retired by now. Admittedly, the impact was deeper than I care to admit. However, a pivotal moment arrived when I realized that people's hurtful words were not a reflection of my worth but rather a manifestation of their own internal battles and insecurities.

This revelation granted me a sense of liberation. Being deemed physically attractive and being the embodiment of societal standards comes with its own set of challenges—a double-edged sword if you will. Oftentimes, individuals project their own feelings of inferiority or inadequacy onto others, treating them differently based on appearances. Those who have encountered similar experiences can undoubtedly relate to the complexities of navigating such dynamics.

As I matured, my resolve solidified—I was determined to chart my own path. No one would dictate my capabilities or define my identity, particularly after some dope of a doctor's early prognosis foretelling a bleak future in reading, writing, academics, and life in general. Their limited expectations couldn't have been more off-base. I've evolved into a globetrotting adventurer, fluent in foreign tongues, and presently engaged in chronicling my extraordinary escapades in this book. Remember this: never allow anyone to confine you within the boundaries of their perceptions or underestimate your potential!

One aspect of human behavior that I found intolerable was bullying—especially when it targeted individuals who were different or faced challenges. I intimately understand the sting of mockery and discrimination due to my own experiences with hyperactivity and Tourette's syndrome. My inability to focus or sit still led to my placement in what some might label as "special classes" alongside peers with various challenges. As I grew stronger, I found myself compelled to confront bullies not only on my behalf but also on behalf of fellow underdogs. Their cruel actions baffled me, as their behavior seemed devoid of any logical reasoning.

When I say I grew up in a small town, I mean minuscule—a place devoid of even a single stoplight. From third grade to eighth grade, I attended Wind River School in Pavilion, Wyoming. It was the epitome of a western town, populated by a mix of hicks, rednecks, Native Americans, and good old-fashioned God-fearing country folk, all nestled in the middle of nowhere. At the time, its population hovered around 485 souls, though that might even be a generous estimate. But it paints a vivid picture of the isolation and tight-knit community that characterized my upbringing.

Interestingly enough, I attended the same school as Matthew Fox, known for his role in 'Lost.' If we ever desired a taste of urban life, the nearest big city, Riverton, Wyoming, boasted a population of 10,000—requiring nearly 40 minutes of travel each way. For those familiar with rural living, this journey would resonate deeply. In small towns, everyone is intricately woven into each other's lives, privy to the minutiae of one another's affairs, whether welcomed or not. Indeed, small-town drama often serves as the primary source of entertainment.

During my fifth-grade year at elementary school. We were engaged in a game of Red Rover during recess—a classic pastime familiar to many, but if not, well damn, I guess you'll have to google it. This particular incident emphasizes my status as an outlier, as I liked to read the dictionary for fun. It seems a fondness for language acquisition runs in my blood; after all, one of my great, great, great uncles was among the co-founders of Funk and Wagnalls Dictionary. There was an undeniable allure in learning words and vernacular that resonated with me deeply.

It was my turn, and I yelled, '*Red rover, red rover, send a homosapien over.*" I thought it was hilarious and very clever, but it was the wrong crowd. No one knew what it meant. 5th graders, sheesh. The teacher thought I said something else and yelled, *"Kye! You can't say that word!"*

I thought to myself, it's a human...Send a human over... Other times I got in trouble were when I would say to a classmate, *"Ewwww, your epidermis is showing. That's gross."* And I would laugh and laugh and laugh. They had no clue what I was talking about and would get offended and tell the teacher, and then she would come and talk to me and say, *"Kye, you can't say that word. It's very offensive."*

Growing up in the countryside afforded unparalleled freedom; you could unleash your wild side, be as loud as you pleased, and revel in the simple joys of childhood without a care in the world. Pity was reserved for those locked in the urban hustle and bustle—trapped amidst ceaseless traffic, perpetual noise, and throngs of people. In our neck of the woods, a traffic jam typically stemmed from cows or livestock leisurely crossing the road or Farmer John chugging along in his tractor.

Transitioning to Riverton High School in the BIG CITY marked a significant change. Suddenly, I found myself navigating a sea of new faces, forging fresh friendships, and exploring unfamiliar social circles. The contrast was stark compared to the cozy familiarity of my small class of thirty students over the past six years. Yet, amid the excitement of novelty, there was an undeniable sense of adventure.

High school was a whole new ball game compared to the days of elementary and middle school where I was bullied . I was hitting my stride, both physically and socially, excelling in wrestling and academics and gaining recognition through my travels.

While I was attending the 9th grade orientation night to familiarize myself with the school, I remember walking down the halls and overheard these two girls chatting. With one of them saying, '*Omg is that Kye? Is he coming to our school now?*' As the other girl giggled Yes.

Let's just say I was a bit of a Casanova. I reveled in flirting with the ladies, always ready with a joke or a laugh. So, imagine my delight when the senior yearbook rolled around with its prestigious awards. Who's going to be famous? Who's the most popular? Who's destined for success? And guess who snagged the coveted title of "Biggest Flirt"? Yep, you're looking at him. Ah, what a proud moment that was.

When I started high school, my parents laid down the law: if I wanted a college education, I had to earn it myself. So,

I rolled up my sleeves and focused on academics. I excelled, earning a 3.98 GPA and a spot in the National Honor Society. Besides wrestling and football, drama became my sanctuary, where I discovered a passion for acting and earned the title of All-State in my senior year.

My efforts paid off handsomely with numerous scholarships, turning college into a profitable venture. I pursued a general studies AA followed by another in English, graduating with high honors and joining the Phi Theta Kappa honor society.

My love for academia led me down an unexpected path —I unearthed a genuine passion for media production and film. Transitioning into a radio and television broadcasting degree program, where I found myself in the heart of the action, with Wyoming PBS production studio right on campus and our very own radio station.

Directing and filming live TV thrilled me, as did the rush of being live on the air, broadcasting to audiences far and wide. Under the DJ Name of 'The Captain,' I manned the airwaves at 88.1 Rustler Radio. The hands-on experience I gained was invaluable, laying the foundation for my future adventures.

After hearing horror stories from friends who attended pricey film schools but hardly touched the equipment until their junior year, I made the decision to extend my stay in my community academia. Staying longer allowed me to accumulate abundant hands-on experience, all while getting paid to attend school. Along the way, I had the privilege of being mentored by remarkable individuals like Amanda Nicholoff, John Gabrielson, and Jeremy Neilson. Their guidance was invaluable, and I owe them a debt of gratitude for shaping my journey. Mahalo Nui Loa to you all.

However, at the tender age of 21, a heartbreak shattered my world, propelling me onto a destructive path. From the moment I took my first sip of alcohol at 21, everything changed. It was like a switch had been flipped, and I found solace in the numbness it offered. Before I knew it, I was caught up in a whirlwind of parties and heavy drinking, convinced that alcohol was the answer to escaping my emotions.

In 2010, I found myself caught in a downward spiral, culminating in two DUIs within a short time—one in Wyoming and the other in Montana. The Wyoming incident unfolded like a scene from 'The Dukes of Hazzard,' complete with a high-speed chase through the boonies involving four sheriffs.

Meanwhile, the Montana mishap nearly resulted in felony charges. With no prior record to speak of, I suddenly found myself immersed in a whirlwind of destruction and chaos. I had unwittingly morphed into the quintessential 'bad boy' straight out of the movies.

The trauma I had buried since childhood, compounded by the high-stakes environment of being a federal firefighter, when not in school, had triggered PTSD, causing my suppressed emotions to erupt. I felt constantly on edge, grappling with a deep pain and sorrow that seemed to consume me from within. To cope, I immersed myself in superficial distractions—flings with beautiful women, excessive drinking, and constant marijuana use. Yet, despite the facade I maintained, no one truly comprehended the turmoil raging beneath the surface.

Validation became my drug; if a woman found me attractive and our interaction turned sexual, it momentarily filled a void within me. Yet, despite my outward friendliness, I maintained a strict emotional barrier, keeping everyone at arm's length. Deep down, I harbored resentment toward the world and women, stemming from the tumultuous relationship I had with my mother in my formative years. While I understood she grappled with her own demons, the scars left behind were deep, painful, and fueled my inner turmoil.

I vividly recall days spent holed up in my house, subjected to the relentless cacophony of my parents' yelling and fighting—a manifestation of their own unresolved childhood traumas. It was a cycle of generational trauma, perpetuating itself endlessly. As I matured, I gained perspective, empathizing with the struggles my parents faced— caring for three boys while grappling with their own unhealed wounds and lacking the tools for healthy coping mechanisms. In hindsight, their journey was undoubtedly fraught with challenges.

It took me years of introspection and self-discovery to unravel the complexities of my own psyche. But now, armed with this understanding, I'm grateful to be able to share my journey and help others navigate their emotional landscapes. This newfound clarity has empowered me, fostering a deeper connection to my soul and purpose.

Depression was a constant companion throughout my life, and I sought solace in anything that offered escape: drugs, alcohol, pornography, relationships, food, work—anything to numb the pain. Before turning to substances, I chased adrenaline-fueled thrills, engaging in daredevil escapades like hopping out of helicopters into forest fires, tearing down country roads at breakneck speeds on bullet bikes, and stepping into the ring for cage fights. To the outside world, I embodied the archetype of the Wild West bad boy, but beneath the bravado, I was simply a man grappling with his own brokenness and a profound sense of not knowing how to navigate life's challenges.

Unbeknownst to me, I carried a heavy burden of pain, yet I actively avoided facing it. This trauma was buried deep from within, a dichotomy of being unaware of its existence and choosing to ignore it, all stemming from childhood experiences exasperated by high-stakes life on the line firefighting situations around the country. One particular incident from my middle school years remained locked away in my psyche, hidden from my conscious awareness for decades as a method of self-preservation. The depth of the pain was so profound that my mind had sealed it off entirely, preventing me from unraveling it or healing until much later in life.

For the longest time, I couldn't understand why I felt so unsafe and foreign in my own body. A stranger in my own skin and an outsider looking into my own heart and mind.

It wasn't until coming to hawaii that it unlocked within me. Long story short, I was taken home by one of my athletic coaches at the time, making an unscheduled stop in a secluded, remote mountain location where he brandished a silver pistol revolver and raped me at gunpoint, saying if I told anyone, *"He'd blow my *bleeping* brains out."* Years later, he did just that to himself.

The crux of the matter is that you can't heal what you don't know happened. An ever illusive enigma compounding the suffering within my soul. Through all my unhealthy coping mechanisms, I was attempting to shield myself from my emotions and quiet my racing thoughts. In hindsight, I realized this coping mechanism was far from healthy. Suppressing emotions is akin to bottling up a volcano; eventually, the pressure builds until it erupts, causing more damage than if it had been addressed earlier.

Instead of addressing my emotions or the underlying trauma, I threw myself into reckless behavior. While I won't deny that there were moments of enjoyment, it was ultimately a distraction—a temporary escape from facing my inner turmoil.

The societal expectation for boys to embody a macho, stoic persona—the tough soldiers, warriors, providers, and protectors—dictates that shedding a tear is unacceptable. This programming instills a deep-seated anger within men, stemming from unhealthy dynamics. We're taught to prioritize action over emotion, a mindset that is inherently inhumane.

It's this very stigma that urgently needs to be dismantled. Instead of encouraging young boys and men to suppress their emotions, we must acknowledge and address them through healthy outlets and mechanisms. Experiencing and expressing emotions in response to life's challenges, traumas, and tough circumstances is normal—something every individual goes through. However, it must be done in a healthy, safe manner for ourselves and others. Emotions are universal; they are not unique to any one person.

Emotions are the threads that weave the tapestry of life, encompassing its countless experiences and undulations. My mission is to impart the message that it's perfectly okay to not be okay; life can be a relentless challenge. It's raw, it's real, and it's often difficult. Through my own trials, I've come to understand the importance of embracing authenticity and acknowledging where we stand in our internal landscape.

There's no shame in embracing our emotions and seeking out healthy coping mechanisms, enabling us to operate at our highest frequency and truly thrive. I see myself as a spiritual warrior, having journeyed through the darkest depths to emerge with wisdom to share with others. My aim is to guide others toward the light, offering insights gleaned from my own transformative journey marching through hell.

One of the most empowering acts we can undertake is embracing authenticity and vulnerability, both within ourselves and with others, within a supportive community. By refusing to hide from our true selves and our emotions, we honor what needs to be seen and witnessed. It's akin to freeing our souls from the grip of black tar, allowing expression to release us from our inner prisons. As a mentor once told me, "*Secrets keep us sick.*" It's by bringing our struggles into the light of consciousness that they can be illuminated and ultimately transformed.

So, I encourage you to delve into those aspects of yourself that you've been avoiding, masking, or numbing. On the other side of this journey lies freedom, joy, and bliss, once these emotions have been processed and released from our bodies. While there are countless modalities that can aid in this process, it's important to remember that healing is not one-size-fits-all. Each individual's path to healing is unique, and it's essential to find what works best for you.

I've discovered a wealth of transformative tools along my journey, each offering its own unique benefits. From EMDR and EFT, psychoanalysis, emotion codes, to somatic release, reiki, acupuncture, and acupressure—these modalities, when approached with intention and guided by skilled practitioners, can facilitate profound healing. Additionally, practices such as prayer, fasting, breathwork, cold therapy, and even psychedelics have played pivotal roles in my personal growth.

I'm excited to share these resources as part of the program associated with the book, offering readers a comprehensive toolkit for their own journey toward healing and self-discovery. Precisely for the reason that you DO NOT have to suffer decades like I did. These are vetted resources, tools and modalities that can truly change your life in the online course on my website.

I proudly embrace my true emotions and share my vulnerable experiences without regret or shame. I am not a victim in any sense of the realm. I am a champion; I am a brave leader guiding the path with the fire of hope. Every hardship I've endured has shaped the person I am today, and that's the very essence of this book. Literally building myself up from scratch, and through sharing my journey, I hope to inspire healing and empowerment in others.

It's about transforming tragedy and trauma into triumph, refusing to be defined by our past but instead rising as victors. By transmuting pain into wisdom and growth, we shift our perspective—recognizing that challenges happen for us, not to us. Your mess becomes your message when you choose the path of empowerment and embark on your soul's journey to greatness. The divine can take trash and make a masterpiece, turning garbage to gold.

With the power of my heartfelt words, I am privileged to offer the world a glimpse into the authentic experiences that have molded me into the person I am today. This is my unique story, one that only I can truly tell. So, let's unite on this journey of empowerment and growth together.

"Service to others is the rent you pay for your room here on earth." - Muhammad Ali

Chapter 3: Battling the Blaze: Fire Fighting

When I was around six years old, my younger brother was celebrating his birthday party at Chuck E. Cheese's in Utah. It was getting late at night, and I wanted to leave and go outside. All of the front doors of the building were locked except for one or two on the far side.

"That's the door opener," I said to my brother confidently, pointing at the fire alarm with my index finger.

My older brother replied animatedly, *"That's not the door opener. Don't pull it. It will sound the fire alarm."*

I looked at him in jest, thinking he always messes with me, so I replied, *"You're just lying to me. I know it's the door opener."*

Without hesitation and with all my might being right, I pulled it, and the sound of the fire alarm blared. Sirens and lights echoed in the night as they started to evacuate the whole building. The birthday party abruptly stopped, and it made me feel terrible.

I was so embarrassed that I ran to our family van and hid under the seats crying, thinking, *'I did something so terrible. Oh my gosh, I'm gonna be in so much trouble.'*

The city's firefighters arrived and quickly determined there was no fire, swiftly shutting off the blaring alarm. When they learned it was me who had pulled the alarm, they found me cowering beneath the seats, terrified. One of them crouched down to my level and reassured me, *"Hey, little man. It's okay. We know you didn't mean any harm. Just don't do it again."*

Their gentle words calmed my racing heart. They kindly offered to give me a tour of the fire truck. With their help, I climbed out of the van, and they walked beside me, holding my hand as we approached the impressive fire truck. They pointed out the intricate rigging with pumps, hoses, ladders, and all the tools of their trade. My eyes widened in admiration and awe.

In that moment, they became heroes in my young eyes. As they drove away in the fire engine, they seemed to be surrounded by a golden halo waving at me, leaving me feeling a hundred feet tall and igniting a burning desire in my heart to become a firefighter.

From the tender age when I gazed up at those heroic firefighters, I vowed to follow in their courageous footsteps. In the early months of 2005, fate granted me that very chance. It was then that I seized the opportunity to join a fire cadet program, spurred on by none other than Craig Haslam, our valiant Fremont County Fire Chief, who urged me with a spirited, "*Hey, you should join the cadet program. I think you'll really like it.*"

Still, just a high schooler bursting with energy and curiosity, those words ignited a fire within me. With a history of sports and an insatiable thirst for adventure, it was precisely the encouragement I needed.

Thus began my journey, balancing school days, sports, clubs and with weekends ablaze in training. As a junior, I delved deep into the realms of structural and wildland firefighting, embracing the challenges of emergency medical services and exhilarating ride-along. With each passing day, I absorbed knowledge like a sponge, eagerly soaking up every lesson and technique.

Before long, I was equipped with my own emergency pager, clad in my personal set of fire gear, and proudly sporting my SCBA (self-contained breathing apparatus)—my lifeline in the midst of danger. It was a thrilling initiation into the world of firefighting, a world where every moment was a test of courage and intellect, and every challenge was an opportunity to prove myself.

The thrill of sliding into my bunker gear, strapping on my SCBA, and charging into the heart of the burn building was an adrenaline rush like no other. In those electrifying moments, I couldn't help but think, *"Holy shit, this is intense... I LOVE it!"* Fire and fun intertwined—there was no greater calling for me.

With tools in hand—chainsaws roaring, pikes at the ready—I reveled in the exhilarating chaos of ripping through buildings. And when fire class wound down, we'd unleash the fury of 2" hoses straight from the hydrant, engaging in epic water battles that left us drenched but grinning from ear to ear. We truly had a blast, and I was all in—until, well, the sobering reality of EMS crashed into view.

Bearing witness to the aftermath of accidents, the sight of people left mangled and broken, served as a stark awakening. Amidst the exhilaration and adrenaline of firefighting, I came face to face with a somber truth: alongside the rush of heroism lay a solemn duty to confront the grim consequences of a disaster.

As the weight of this realization settled upon me, I found myself recoiling from the medical aspects of the job— the blood, the guts, the rawness of it all. It dawned on me that a staggering 80-90% of the city's firefighting efforts revolved around these very elements. The prospect of working amidst the mangled, bloody aftermath of emergencies became something I simply couldn't stomach.

With clarity, I made a decisive shift. Opting for a path free from the visceral challenges of urban firefighting, I pivoted exclusively to Wildland Fire operations. Earning my red card certification, I embarked on a journey aligned with my newfound focus. Immediately after high school, I immersed myself in the rugged landscapes of the Forest Service, ready to confront the challenges of nature with a sense of purpose and determination.

Being a rookie on the crew was no easy feat, as is the case in any demanding field, but every challenge was aimed at ensuring our physical and mental readiness for the moment the call came. When that call does come, it's all systems go—there's no margin for error, no room for mistakes, for lives hang in the balance.

I vividly recall my first fire call. Fresh from a grueling PT session in the Sinks Canyon, we received word of smoke rising along the loop road. My adrenaline surged as we swiftly donned our Nomex fire gear, laced up our boots, and piled into the rig, lights blazing.

After a tense thirty-minute journey, we rounded a bend in the road, emerging into a forest clearing. And there it was—the smoke, a tangible sign of our impending battle against the flames. In my excitement, I blurted out, *"I smot the folk,"* inadvertently mixing up the words *"smoke"* and *"spot."* The resulting laughter from my comrades echoed through the forest, a light-hearted moment amidst the seriousness of our mission. Needless to say, I didn't live that one down for a minute.

On another occasion, while up on Loop Road preparing to park the engine for some tree-cutting and project work, a routine task took an unexpected turn. Working for the Forest Service on a fire crew means there's always a plethora of trees to be cut and roadside clearing to be done to enhance visibility on forest roads.

As we maneuvered the engine into position, a simple adjustment turned chaotic. I opened the passenger door to ensure clearance on the side of the road, only for a canister of bear spray, nestled behind the seat, to suddenly roll out and come to rest right in front of the tires. As we parked, with the weight of the vehicle, it triggered a thunderous BANG, leaving us momentarily stunned, thinking a tire had blown out.

In the midst of our confusion, the wind carried a wave of bear spray into the cab, engulfing us in its acrid cloud. Coughing fits seized us, tears streaming from our stinging eyes and our noses running as if in protest.

Amidst the chaos, we frantically shouted, *"Get out of the damn engine!"* scrambling to escape the noxious fumes. Rolling out and tumbling down the hillside, we fought to catch our breath. If you've ever experienced the sting of mace, bear spray is a whole different beast—it hits like a ferocious kick in the face from a donkey.

It took us some time to flush out our eyes and regain our composure while passing cars slowed down, undoubtedly wondering, *"What the hell is going on down there?"*

In 2007, we received orders for a Severity Detail in Rock Springs, Wyoming—a precautionary measure where resources are strategically positioned due to severe weather, lightning, low humidity, and other factors. It was my first time on the road for such an extended assignment, and about a week into the detail, I found myself in a predicament. Despite my best efforts, I hadn't packed enough clothes, and I was starting to feel rather crusty.

Late one night, nearly 10 PM, I seized what seemed like a safe opportunity to tackle the laundry situation. With a sense of determination, I gathered all my fire gear—pants, shirts, socks, even my skivvies—and stuffed them into the washer. As the cycle began, I settled in with a magazine, passing the time at the KOA, where we were stationed for the duration.

Just a few moments later, Dan rushed in, *"Kye, we got a fire call! We have to go now!"*

I replied, *"Bro, all my gear is in the washer! I don't have anything. I can't even open it, Once you start the wash, it locks!"*

He chuckled and said, *"You're shit outta luck, man. Better figure it out."* At this point, I was literally in shorts and sandals with no shirt. I quickly replied to him as he ran out the door, *"Let me use your pants!"*

I was in a predicament because I knew we would be spiking out since it was so late (staying out on the fire line), and all my laundry was in the washer. Luckily, I'm a quick thinker and have some charm. There was this cute girl who was working at the front office right next to the laundry room. I walked in and knocked on the counter without a shirt. She came up and said, *"Yes, can I help you."*

At this point, I was a little embarrassed. Nah,...just kidding. I was actually grinning as I replied, *"This is going to sound weird, and I am sorry, but I have to ask. We just got called to a fire, and all my fire clothes are in the washer, and we won't be coming back tonight. Is there any way you could just take it out and throw it into the dryer for me? I can pay you for your time, but really, it would be a lifesaver!"*

She chuckled and responded sassily, *"So you're telling me you want me to finish your laundry? What do I look like? A maid?"*

At this point, we were both chuckling, and I said, *"Not at all! I think you're someone awesome who wants to give back and help a firefighter in need."*

She grinned, chuckled, and agreed to help me out.

As I was about to leave, she said, *"Umm...do you have a shirt? You can't go to a fire without a shirt looking all sexy like that..."*

I replied, *"Why do you have one for me?"*

While she was blushing, she said, *"I have a gym shirt that you can use. It's my ex-boyfriend's. It's clean and might be a little small for your frame, but you can use it."*

I was laughing at the whole situation and knew I needed to leave right away, so I agreed.

As I ran up to the engine, Dan tossed me a pair of his Nomex pants and socks as our fire engine was about to leave, and we shot off into the night, hot to the fire.

When we finally arrived at the scene, guided by GPS coordinates from dispatch, we discovered a rather underwhelming sight—a tiny brush fire sparked by lightning, barely more than 1/8 of an acre in size. There wasn't much action, but it was enough to warrant a bit of Hazard Pay, so hey, no complaints there.

After some initial confusion locating the fire, we managed to get our bearings and deal with the situation, felling a few small trees to contain the blaze. With the immediate threat addressed, we started to wind down for the night. As we headed back to the rig, engaged in idle chatter, one of our seasoned female firefighters, Heidi, couldn't resist commenting on my shirt.

"Wow, talk about a shmedium," she quipped, eyeing my snug-fitting attire. *"That shirt is way too small for you."* She exclaimed.

I laughed and said, *"It's not mine. It belongs to the girl from the KOA. My laundry was locked in the washer, and I couldn't get it out. These are Dan's pants and socks, too."*

She shook her head and replied, *"Damn, Funk, you're telling me you left all your clothes with some random girl?"*

Replying confidently, I said, *"Not some random girl. She works there. I left my red bag (our clothes gear bag) as well, so she could put my clothes in there when she finishes my laundry."*

At this point, she was laughing and shaking her head in disapproval, *"Rookie move, Funk, rookie move. You think she's going to finish your laundry, huh?"*

I replied, *"Yup, she said she'd take care of it."*

By now, everyone was chiming in, saying that my gear was going to get stolen and I would never see it again, or the girl was a freak and probably smelling my underwear.

By the next day, in the mid-morning, we made it back to the KOA to get our stuff and head to another location. I told everyone, *"Watch! My clothes are going to be nice and folded, and everything is going to be fine."*

Dan replies, *"Uh huh, I'm sure. Everything is stolen, I bet.."*

While they went and parked, I walked into the office and knocked on the front desk, and the cute girl came up. She smiled and said, *"So.... I had to wash your clothes two times because they smelled so bad and I took the liberty of cleaning that red bag, cause it was terrible as well. How can you work in such a smelly outfit?"*

I chuckled and said, *"In my defense, I've been fighting fire, but damn, you didn't have to do that. That's awesome.*

Thanks so much! Can I pay you for the time and money you used for the wash?"

She shook her head and said, *"No, you don't have to pay. It's not every day I get to wash clothes for a cute firefighter."*

Boy, what an experience! I thanked her and gave her a hug. As I made my way back to the engine, I glanced in the bag and noticed that everything was neatly folded, washed, smelled amazing, and had a small piece of paper placed on the top. Right then, I knew it was her number. I reached into the bag and pulled it out, seeing her name and number on it as it read,

"Call me. You're hot.

Sarah."

As I got to the engine, I laughed and chuckled like a little kid, and everyone was curious about what had happened. I told them the story and said,

"I even got a number, baby. Funk the Hunk strikes again!" Everyone was baffled and was like, *"What the hell... That's crazy."* Ahhh, a great memory indeed.

My first out-of-state adventure took me to the Cub Complex in California back in 2008. When the call came in, we had just a few hours to mobilize. I can still vividly recall the sensation of cruising across the country with my fellow firefighters, our engine roaring as we journeyed to confront the inferno.

It felt like we were straight out of a superhero movie, you know? Picture the scene: the theme music swelling as the heroes gear up to take on the villain. You can't help but feel... EPIC. And let's not forget about the allure of being a firefighter. I mean, seriously, it's like catnip for the ladies. They'll even offer to do your laundry and slip you their number, no questions asked. And when you're out on the road or battling flames, dressed in your uniform, you can practically feel the eyes on you. But if you happen to be a good-looking fireman... well, you might as well have a neon sign on your back screaming, "HUNK ALERT."

Sure, it was tough work, but hey, someone had to do it, right? Anyway, back to the story…

As we arrived on the scene, we were met with the sight of two fires merging into one, and our task was clear: to assist in holding the line during a back burn operation alongside one of the divisions. Now, for the uninitiated, this tactic is all about preventing the main front of the fire from advancing by removing any available fuel along the line. Essentially, we create a buffer zone where the fire can't gain traction.

After a thorough briefing on operational procedures and safety protocols, we got to work staging ourselves, strategically spaced about a hundred yards apart, with a long line of fire engines stretching over half a mile. On one side, the plan was to ignite the controlled burn, while on the other side, our mission was to defend the line and prevent any stray embers from jumping across.

With the burn team at the helm, armed with drip torches and flares, they began laying down fire in a coordinated effort, marching three people deep. But here's the kicker—the relative humidity was so low that practically everything caught fire with a vengeance. By the time the burn team reached their designated endpoint, a towering wall of flames erupted, roaring to life like a squadron of F-16s taking off. The trees ignited with a ferocity that seemed to shake the very earth, as embers and sparks danced across the line, a mesmerizing yet perilous spectacle unfolding before our eyes.

In that moment, I found myself face to face with a force of nature unlike anything I had ever encountered. With my fire gear on and Pulaski gripped tightly, I stared into the heart of the inferno as if confronting a mythical dragon, its flames consuming everything in their path. It was a humbling reminder of our own mortality, highlighting just how minuscule we are in the grand scheme of the universe, pitted against the awesome power of Mother Nature herself.

The smoke was so thick that visibility was reduced to a mere 8-10 feet ahead of us. I dashed from one spot to another, tirelessly battling small fire spots to prevent them from gaining a foothold across the line. With each swing of my Pulaski, coughs escaped my lips, mingling with the crackling of flames. Yet amidst the chaos, there was a thrill coursing through my veins, a sense of exhilaration that whispered, *"Holy S*&%, this is nuts… I LOVE it!"*

PS… I have a sneaking suspicion that quite a few Wildland Fire Fighters are closet pyromaniacs. There's just something undeniably primal about fire—it's alive, it breathes, and it grows like a living, breathing monster, stirring the deepest parts of our souls. Once you've been bitten by the firebug, it's hard to shake off because, let's face it, it's downright addictive.

And then there's the camaraderie of being out in the great outdoors with your crew, who become more than just colleagues—they're your family. It's an experience unlike any other, giving you this profound sense of connection to nature itself. To be a part of something so vast and powerful, to be able to give back to the very environment that has nurtured us for generations—it's an incredible feeling.

After two years with the Forest Service, spending countless hours on the engine and tackling local forest protection with a few brief excursions out of state, not to mention endless months of chainsaw work for various projects, I found myself craving more action. Don't get me wrong, I had an absolute blast and learned a ton during those early days of my fire career. But deep down, I knew I was meant for something more. I needed to spread my wings, travel further, and immerse myself in even more fire action, and that just wasn't happening where I was.

An exciting opportunity arose through a local tribal elder, a friend of mine, who offered me a chance to join the helicopter attack crew and fly on an A-star B3 sponsored by the tribe. This bird, operating under the DOI (Department of Interior), traveled far and wide, supporting not only tribal lands but also lending aid to federal fires and collaborating with agencies nationwide.

Eager to prove my mettle, I threw myself into preparations with unwavering determination. I tackled the pack test—a grueling 3.5-mile hike/duck walk with a 45lb lead vest strapped to my chest—and clocked one of the fastest times, completing it in less than 45 minutes. I even aced it wearing steel-toe boots, a last-minute improvisation when I forgot my running shoes. My performance earned me the possibility for an interview to attend S-271 HECM – Helicopter Crew Member training, and I prayed for the opportunity to be part of the crew.

It felt like ages, waiting for that fateful call. I'd spend evenings on my porch, gazing up at the stars, offering up silent prayers to God, thinking, *"It would be beyond incredible, Lord. To soar across the country, battling blazes. I'll make you proud, I swear."*

With each passing day filled with eager anticipation, countless prayers, and a hefty dose of patience, the phone finally rang. *"Kye, you're in. Report for training on Monday,"* came the electrifying voice on the other end. I erupted into a frenzy of hoots, hollers, and wild jumps, a man possessed by the thrill of his ongoing fire adventures.

Wildland Fire operations are already a beast unto themselves, with a multitude of rapidly shifting variables—topography, terrain, fuel types, moisture levels, weather patterns, geography, and vegetation. And let's not forget the ever-present wildlife and available resources. Adding aviation into the mix was a whole new ballgame, one that initially left me reeling. But as days turned into weeks, I found my confidence soaring. Not only did I hone my firefighting skills, but I also discovered leadership qualities within myself that I never knew existed. And before I knew it, I was head over heels in love with this exhilarating new dimension of my fire career.

The integration of aviation into our firefighting efforts brought forth a realm of heightened sophistication and risk, demanding flawless execution in every facet. We grappled with a multitude of factors: payload calculations in accordance with elevation, the impact of temperature variations on lift capacity, fuel reserves meticulously mapped against mission distances, and the intricate balancing act of load distribution. Safety briefings, aircraft capabilities, pilot expertise—each element added complexity to an already intricate operation.

We stood poised, ever vigilant, primed to spring into action at a moment's notice, with the ability to spool up the helicopter within a mere ten minutes. There exists no parallel sensation in the world to the electrifying moment when the call crackles through from dispatch, signaling the commencement of our mission.

The adrenaline surges through your veins as the helicopter's engines roar to life, the heady aroma of Jet-A fuel enveloping the air. With the swagger of cinematic heroes, we stride purposefully toward the waiting bird, each step a testament to our readiness for the challenge ahead. Climbing into the helicopter, clad in our fire gear, we ascend into the skies, a tangible sense of invincibility coursing through our veins. In that moment, we feel like true badasses—masters of our domain, ready to confront whatever inferno dares to cross our path. Feeling like a big swinging D baby.

I consider myself immensely fortunate to have traversed the breadth of the United States, venturing into some of the most remote and pristine territories—places that many may never have the privilege to witness. Amidst these vast expanses of forest and tribal lands, where civilization fades into the distant horizon, my crew and I descended like modern-day warriors, our eyes ablaze with anticipation for the battles ahead.

I am profoundly grateful for the invaluable lessons in respect and connection to the land that I gained from the tribes I collaborated with across the nation. This experience transformed my entire existence, weaving me into the fabric of my fire family—a bond I hold dear to my heart for eternity. It's a camaraderie that defies description, one that civilians who haven't treaded the line cannot fathom. To stand shoulder to shoulder, risking our lives for people and places unknown is a calling that resonates deep within our souls.

Engulfed in the relentless heat of 110-degree days, burdened by a 45lb pack, we toiled tirelessly for 16-hour stretches. Chainsaws roaring, sweat dripping, we carved through burning trees, bushes, and shrubs, our hands calloused, our spirits unyielding. For fourteen consecutive days, we etched lines in the earth, a testament to our unwavering commitment to the mission at hand.

The possibility of being out on the line, battling the blaze for up to 21 days straight, pushes you to your mental, emotional, and physical limits and beyond. It's your crew, your family, that becomes your lifeline—filling the air with laughter, fostering camaraderie, and embracing a "let's get this done" attitude to protect the lands, the people, and the communities we hold dear. It's a journey that challenges and tests your character yet fuels an insatiable desire to return for more.

But once you've weathered the firestorm, once you've been there and felt the flames sear your soul, you're forever changed. You're baptized by fire, welcomed into a select group of individuals who've shared this extraordinary experience. And in that transformation, you find yourself becoming something better, something more—a testament to the resilience of the human spirit.

The best leaders I've had the privilege to work alongside didn't just lead—they lifted others up, imparted wisdom, fueled passion, and inspired excellence. They instilled in us the belief that we were capable of greatness, nurturing our growth and standing as beacons of integrity and guidance.

One of the most impactful figures in my life, forever etched as my soul brother and a legendary figure in the realm of firefighting, is George Violante. I've never encountered someone who embodies hard work, genuine care, and exceptional skill to the extent that he does. His influence continues to shape my journey, even to this day. I owe him an immeasurable debt of gratitude for his leadership, guidance, and unwavering support, which have far surpassed any expectations.

You know, a truly exceptional leader is someone who elevates everyone around them. They don't just talk the talk; they walk the walk, inspiring others to rise to their fullest potential because they believe in them. They invest in their growth, forging genuine connections and guiding them toward a brighter path.

From this journey, I've learned the invaluable importance of surrounding oneself with the right kind of people. It's crucial to assess how those around you contribute to your life—do they uplift and empower you to excel, or do they weigh you down? These are the pivotal questions we must ask ourselves as we inevitably become reflections of the company we keep.

Firefighters are the epitome of selflessness, dedicated to serving others and risking their lives without a second thought. While most people flee from danger, we're the ones springing out of helicopters into the heart of raging forest fires. The rush

I felt was akin to the adrenaline surge I experienced in cage fighting or riding motorcycles and horses at breakneck speeds.

But it wasn't just the thrill of the action that left me in awe. Through this journey, I've had the privilege of exploring countless breathtaking locations across the country—a true marvel that I'm profoundly grateful for.

One of the most unforgettable moments was soaring over the Grand Canyon at a staggering 13,000 feet with the helicopter doors wide open. Strapped in, peering down into the vast expanse below, I couldn't help but feel humbled by the sheer magnitude of the world around me. It's moments like these that remind us of our place in the universe, instilling a deep sense of reverence and gratitude.

Firefighting has been a profound teacher in the realm of leadership, imparting invaluable lessons along the way. It's not merely about commanding authority but rather about embodying service and fostering the safety and well-being of others while striving for loftier ideals.

In my role as a PIO (Public Information Officer) during the wildfires in California in 2020, I stumbled upon a troubling statistic: wild-land firefighters had one of the highest rates of suicide and divorce among emergency service personnel.

Intrigued, I delved deeper into the data, only to uncover a stark reality—the rates of depression, anxiety, and substance abuse among firefighters, police officers, military members, and EMS personnel were three to four times higher than the general population.

Upon deeper reflection, it became clear to me why those in high-stress professions, like firefighting, often grapple with unseen battles. The constant exposure to fight-or-flight scenarios alters both their physiology and psychology, setting a baseline far above that of the average person. Yet, when the shift ends, or the tour wraps up, we return home to our families, expected to seamlessly transition from chaos to calm. There's little time to decompress, and many of us simply bury our stress, allowing numbness to take hold.

For me, the root of many near-death experiences lay in a blend of firefighting trauma and childhood wounds, a cocktail of PTSD I hadn't even recognized. Sadly, this struggle isn't unique to me; countless individuals in emergency services and the military battle in silence. Fear of being perceived as weak or unfit for duty often silences their cries for help, leaving them to suffer in solitude, fearing the repercussions of speaking out.

Therefore, I've embarked on writing this book, driven by the desire to destigmatize and normalize discussions surrounding mental and emotional well-being. I want to reassure people that it's perfectly okay to not be okay. You're not flawed; you're not weak—rather, you're experiencing a wholly human response to the challenges and hazards inherent in our line of work. My journey has been arduous, but I stand here today because of the grace of God.

Experiencing intense stress, shock, and trauma is nothing to be ashamed of, particularly for those in emergency services or the military. It's a natural reaction to the trials we face. Yet, there's an added layer of stigma for us, as those meant to be the rescuers often find themselves in need of saving. Through this book, I aim to shine a light on mental health awareness and share the foundation I've established—Frontline First Responders™—to provide knowledge, awareness, and resources to our courageous first responders, military personnel, and veterans nationwide.

They are the true warriors on the frontlines, tirelessly serving our communities, families, and nation day in and day out. Now, it's our turn to rally behind them and offer our unwavering support.

A portion of the proceeds from each book sale will be channeled back into the foundation, ensuring that vital resources reach those who are silently battling their demons or have tragically succumbed to the burdens they bore alone. Your support, in any form, is deeply cherished by those who need it most.

Perhaps you have a loved one—a family member, a friend, a neighbor—who serves as a Frontline First Responder™. This book presents a wonderful opportunity to show your support and care by spreading the message, volunteering your time or resources, or contributing to our cause financially. Together, we can advance our mission across the nation.

To all my brothers and sisters in arms, past, present, and future, I hold you in the highest regard. Your sacrifice, dedication, and resilience do not go unnoticed. You are the unsung heroes, bearing the weight of our families, communities, and nation on your shoulders. I salute you with the deepest respect and gratitude.

"In the end, it's not the years in your life that count. It's the life in your years." - Abraham Lincoln

Chapter 4: Returning From Death's Doorstep

There I lay, sprawled across the unforgiving pavement, bleeding out fast and suffocating in my own blood. Lifeless and in shock, my body and face mangled in what seemed a murder scene. Blood everywhere at the edge of asphyxiation and death. Drifting in and out of consciousness after colliding with the concrete roundabout at 30 mph—no helmet, and my head taking the brunt of the impact, launching into it like a rocket. It all began with a heated argument with my ex-wife, prompting me to impulsively hop on the motorcycle to fetch pizza despite having alcohol in my system. *In full disclosure, it wasn't even my bike; it was my buddy Adams who let me borrow it at the time.* *(Thanks, Adam, for being a great man.)*

As I cruised down Hollywood Avenue in SLC, a false sense of invincibility washed over me. The pizza was securely strapped to the back rack, but my judgment was clouded by intoxication. Despite my years of motorcycle experience, I was in no condition to ride. An ill-fated glance over my shoulder behind to check on the pizza proved disastrous. When I refocused on the road ahead, a roundabout materialized—no lights, no signs, no reflectors—just a silent, ominous obstacle waiting to shatter my illusion of control. Launching into it head first, with my face taking the brunt of the impact.

Lying there in a mutilated pool of bloody destruction, I knew I was about to die. Gasping for air with every blood-soaked breath. At that precise moment, I prayed with all my heart and soul to God for a miracle to save me. Thinking to myself, *"I really messed up, I'm sorry, I'm so sorry God, please help me I pleaded."*

In that instantaneous moment, I left my body and transitioned into a realm of existence that was pure white and pure bliss. There was an overwhelming sense of love, peace, and tranquility unlike anything I had ever experienced before; nothing in my entire life could match the sensation I felt when I first arrived in that beautiful place. Imagine the best moment of your life and multiply it by a million! That's where we come from.

Feeling enveloped in a sense of peace, warmth, and love unlike anything I'd ever known on Earth, I thought to myself, *"Oh my God, this is incredible. I want to stay here!"*

A powerful yet tender voice responded, *"You can't stay here. Your time isn't up yet. You have to go back."*

Appalled by the notion, I retorted, *"No way! There's a bunch of chaos down there, and it's incredibly tough. I'm not going back."*

God chuckled softly—his sense of humor shining through. *"I know,"* he replied. *"That's precisely why I need you to return. You have a mission to fulfill."*

Disheartened and reluctant to leave behind the divine bliss, I pleaded to stay.

"You must return. It's not your time," He reiterated *gently.*

As time stood still, I watched from above as my broken body lay on the pavement, a gruesome sight of blood and carnage. Bones shattered, head bleeding profusely, drowning in my own blood.

Summoning my negotiation skills with God, I pleaded, *"Okay...If I HAVE to go back, you HAVE got to ensure I'm not*

*paralyzed or a vegetable. I won't be much use to you otherwise.
I promise to share my testimony worldwide."*

God responded with a deal, *"Agreed. I'll give you
another chance, but you must share your story, the truth, and
how I saved you."*

In a sudden surge, I plunged back into my broken body
on the pavement - returning to the blood-soaked wreckage of
flesh and bone. Each breath was agony, every heartbeat a
thunderclap of pain echoing through me. With mere moments
left before the abyss claimed me, Dr. Cameron, a trauma doctor
who just so happened to live right across the street, dashed to
my side with lightning speed.

My injuries were a symphony of agony: three shattered
ribs, a shattered scapula, and internal bleeding ravaging my
brain, kidney, and spleen. My left arm hung broken and
mangled, impaled by some unseen force, while my left leg bore
two fractures and three torn ligaments, its foot torn asunder, a
gory tableau of destruction. Blood flowed freely, painting the
ground crimson in a macabre display.

Hemorrhaging profusely from the laceration on my
face, my shattered eye socket leaked life's essence, while my
jaw lay in ruins, broken in half and separated from my skull.

Every breath was a struggle, drowning in my own blood, the shadow of death looming ever closer.

Doctor Todd sprang into action with lightning speed. Concerned about a potential spinal injury, he hesitated to move me, but the urgency of the situation demanded action. If he hadn't acted swiftly, I would have suffocated on the pavement, drowned in my own blood. With the instincts of a seasoned professional, he carefully cradled my head and spine, gently rolling me over to clear my airways, allowing precious breath to flow once more.

Utilizing his years of training and expertise, Doctor Todd initiated lifesaving measures, taking off his very own shirt to try and stop the bleeding. Amidst the chaos, he managed to call 911 and summon emergency services, and miraculously, an ambulance was dispatched, passing by a mere two blocks away, racing to our aid. Covered in my blood, he spared no urgency, directing the responders with fierce determination, warning them that every moment mattered, that my life hung in the balance.

As the paramedics worked feverishly to stabilize me, my father arrived at the scene. Despite our recent estrangement, guided by the hand of God, he found his way to the exact location in the sprawling expanse of the Salt Lake City Valley. Stepping out of his car, he was met with a grim warning from a concerned paramedic, a stark glimpse into the severity of the situation unfolding before him.

The paramedic saying to him, *"Sir, you don't want to see this. This is nasty. It's really bad. He's probably going to die."*

My dad glanced over at his nearly-dead son while they were working on me and responded with 100% assurance to the EMT, *"That's my son."*

The paramedic, in astonishing disbelief, replied, *"How in the hell could you know that."*

My dad then responded, *"God told me and directed me here, right to this spot."*

The most interesting thing my dad told me later on was that he knew that I was going to be in an accident that night. When they were loading me into the ambulance, my dad was over on the corner, praying the whole time that I would stay alive and be given another chance at life, calling in the angels.

After nearly 11 hours of intense surgery, the doctors managed to save me. They worked tirelessly to repair the damage to my face and various other parts of my body.

Through God's miracle, the internal bleeding in my brain had ceased, and they were able to address the bleeding in my kidney and spleen with stints.

After the reconstructive surgery on my face, a day later, one of the doctors remarked, *"While we were in there patching you up, we noticed your nose was a little crooked, just slightly. So, we went ahead and straightened that up for you."* Having a slight crook in it from wrestling and cage fighting back in the day. I couldn't help but chuckle at the irony of it all and responded, *"I nearly kick the bucket. God saves my life, and I get a nose job out of it. What a trip."* The doctor, with a hint of amazement, replied, *"You're the luckiest man alive. In all my years, I've never seen anything like this. "*

Never meeting the man who saved my life until four years after the accident, God brought in another miracle.

After my workout at the gym, I felt this strong pull, a spiritual nudge, guiding me to the exact spot where that miraculous event had unfolded. Looking up to the heavens, I asked, *"Okay, what's the plan?"* And it became clear—*"Start knocking on doors. You're going to find the man who saved your life."* After three unsuccessful attempts at various houses,

I paused and scanned the area. That's when I spotted it: the house across the street as chills ran down my spine.

I approached and knocked. A teenager, around 15 or 16, answered. I asked him, *"Have you been living here for long?"*

With a confident nod, he said, *"Yeah."*

I then asked if he remembered a motorcycle accident that had happened outside their house some time ago. His eyes widened, and he replied, *"Yes."*

Taking a deep breath, I said, *"Well, I'm that man."*

His expression shifted, registering a mix of shock and disbelief. *"Oh my God,"* he exclaimed, *"I need to get my dad!"* And with that, he hastily closed the door.

I heard shuffling behind the door and faint voices conversing as the door opened again. I saw a middle-aged man appear before me in an apron from cooking dinner and ask, *"Can I help you?"* in a firm manner.

I asked him the same question, *"Do you remember a motorcycle accident a few years back?"* He responded with a hesitant *"yes."*

I paused, letting the weight of my words sink in, and then I said, "*I am the man that was in the accident.*"

His eyes widened in disbelief, frozen in shock as if he'd seen a ghost. He scanned me up and down, realization dawning on him that I was the one he had encountered on the road, the one he had saved from the brink of death.

Locking eyes with him, I could sense his astonishment as he stammered, "*I thought you died... You lived... you lived. No way you're alive! You cannot be that man. That's impossible.*"

With a calm resolve, I replied, "*You're right. I am not that man. That man died that night, and I was reborn.*"

As we drew closer and embraced, tears streaming down our faces, the depth of our connection spoke volumes. Without uttering a single word, we both knew he was the one who saved me, and I was the one he saved. He then invited me into his home to meet his family and tell me all about that night as I only remembered small blips of details. By the end his son said, "*When my dad returned to the house late that night, he was covered in blood. His hands and arms and body looking like a murder scene.*"

Attempting to convey the profound emotion of meeting the man who pulled me from the brink of death, guided solely by the spirit, is beyond words. Unless you've experienced the profound gratitude of being saved, it's impossible to comprehend the sheer magnitude of such a miraculous gift— one that can never be repaid.

After enduring everything, I want you to understand this: whether you're in the midst of hardship, emerging from it, or have already triumphed over it, know that you are cherished. It's a privilege to share my testimony of God's divine love and the undeniable miracles that exist in this universe.

As I regained consciousness the day after the harrowing motorcycle accident, I confronted a stark reality: the fault lay squarely with me. With this realization came a pivotal choice: succumb to bitterness and resentment, allowing it to consume my being, following a similar path of pain and destruction or embrace full accountability and transform the experience into a catalyst for profound growth. Recognizing the sheer "luck" and miraculous nature of escaping paralysis or severe head trauma from the crash swiftly humbled me.

As I lay in that hospital bed, I made a conscious choice not to harbor resentment or bitterness. Instead, I embraced the reality of my situation with a sincere sense of acceptance and determination. I understood that while I couldn't alter the circumstances, I had full control over my attitude and mindset. It was a simple decision, albeit not an easy one, to replace frustration with compassion and empower myself to grow from the experience. And with unwavering resolve, I sent out this intention to the universe, knowing that both God and the cosmos were listening attentively.

Despite the pain and discomfort, I maintained a positive outlook. I engaged with others in the hospital with kindness and empathy, recognizing that our interactions not only impacted them but also reverberated within me. This understanding, rooted in the interconnectedness of human experiences, fueled my actions with love and compassion, both toward others and toward myself.

In the face of near death, I realized that as long as I'm alive and breathing, there's still room for growth and development. It's only when we surrender to failure and give up that our journey truly ends. During my arduous recovery, the support of my former wife and family was invaluable. I found myself enveloped in gratitude, hope, and love, both for myself and those who stood by me.

I embarked on a journey of healing, not just physically but mentally and spiritually as well. Through what I termed "PMP" (positive mental programming), I directed golden light to my cells, willing them to repair and regenerate at an accelerated pace. It was a practice fueled by compassion, patience, and profound gratitude.

Amidst my own struggles, I encountered Mary, a woman grappling with her own adversity. Despite breaking her back for the second time, leaving her confined to a wheelchair, she remained resilient, cradling her body with unwavering strength. Witnessing her fortitude served as a reminder of the indomitable human spirit and the power of perseverance in the face of adversity.

Reflecting on Mary's suffering, I couldn't help but acknowledge the stark contrast between her circumstances and mine. It was nothing short of a miracle that I escaped the motorcycle accident without a spinal injury or a traumatic brain injury. Considering the severity of the crash and the absence of a helmet, I could easily have been paralyzed or worse. Yet, here I am, bearing only a scar on my face and profound testimony to share after emerging from the depths of the hell I had inadvertently created.

As I conversed with Mary, learning about the challenges she faced, I was struck by a profound sense of gratitude. Despite the hardships she endured, including her husband's abandonment during her hospitalization, I couldn't help but count my blessings. My own wife stood by me during my darkest hour, a support I recognized as nothing short of divine intervention. It was a stark reminder that even in the face of death's looming shadow, God had a plan for me—one that spared me from the brink of oblivion that fateful night on the pavement.

Through a blend of mantras, affirmations, prayers, meditations, and visualizations, coupled with a steadfast commitment to rapid healing, divine intervention commenced. Embracing a state of profound acceptance, I refrained from resisting or judging my circumstances, allowing the healing process to unfold naturally. Remarkably, my recovery progressed so swiftly that I was discharged from the hospital after just two weeks.

This experience underscores the power of acceptance over resistance in facilitating healing. By fostering a state of homeostasis and relaxation within the body, we enable its innate capacity to repair and regenerate. By quieting the mind, engaging in deep breathing, and cultivating internal sentiments of elevated emotions and trust in the divine within us, we open the door to miraculous healing.

Our bodies function as intricate supercomputers, constantly processing the thoughts, feelings, and emotions we feed into our subconscious mind. Like sophisticated programs, our cells respond to this programming, shaping our overall well-being. When we cultivate gratitude, joy, and resilience in our thoughts, our mind, body, and spirit align harmoniously. It's crucial to recognize that our bodies are attuned to our inner dialogue, carrying out commands without discrimination. Therefore, it's imperative to program ourselves positively.

Remarkably, just three months later, I resumed working out, much to the astonishment of my neurologist. Perplexed by my rapid healing, he marveled, *"Kye, how are you recovering so quickly? It's unprecedented!"*

In response, I simply stated, *"I've learned a few things."* I delved into a wealth of resources on healing, delving into topics such as metaphysics, psychology, mind-body medicine, biology, and the quantum realm. Influential figures like Dr. Joe Dispenza and Dr. Bruce Lipton became my mentors, guiding me on my path to understanding the intricacies of healing.

In moments of adversity, embracing gratitude and joy can serve as powerful catalysts for healing, regardless of the circumstances or who may be at fault. Through my journey, I gained insight into how the intricate workings of my body's physiology and psychology converged in a divine symphony, offering a pathway to tap into the inherent healing potential we all possess. This universal truth transcends individual experiences and extends to each of us.

The motorcycle accident occurred in 2017 during my time residing in Salt Lake City, UT. At that juncture, I found myself entrenched in corporate finance yet deeply discontented. My belief system equated money with ultimate happiness, viewing it as the solution to all problems. However, this flawed ideology placed my value and worth solely in numerical terms—a perpetual chase with no end in sight, leaving me perpetually feeling inadequate.

Upon returning from Mexico with my then-wife, I confronted my struggles with alcoholism head-on and sought rehabilitation. The relentless pursuit I had been on had left me devoid of the ability to simply exist and find solace within myself, unable to navigate life's complexities without resorting to escapism.

In 2010, when I overdosed, my mindset was entirely different. I was engulfed in profound despair. Death didn't seem like a tragedy; rather, it felt like a welcome relief from the relentless agony of my soul and mind. I harbored a deep resentment toward everything—the world, my family, myself, and most certainly religion.

Even in the depths of despair, there was divine intervention. Despite my heart rate plummeting to a perilous ten beats per minute from my OD in the hospital after ingesting a lethal cocktail of pills, my initial reaction was one of bitterness and resignation. Narrowly escaping death once again. Waking up in the hospital, I found myself restrained to the bed, surrounded by a mix of sorrow and relief in the eyes of my family and church members. The overwhelming sense of embarrassment washed over me, compounding the physical and emotional distress I was already experiencing.

After regaining consciousness, I muttered under my breath, *"Back in this hellhole, FML."* All I craved was an escape from the excruciating spiritual and emotional torment I was enduring. Every fiber of my being longed to escape the pain of existence. I couldn't shake the relentless grip of suffering on Earth. I grappled with profound questions about my own nature. Why was I consumed by bitterness, sorrow and anger? Why did every emotion feel like a tidal wave threatening to drown me? I demanded answers from the divine, challenging God to produce the contract that bound me to this earthly existence.

Little did I know, underlying this turmoil were undiagnosed PTSD and unresolved childhood traumas. Additionally, undiagnosed food sensitivities were exacerbating my mental and emotional instability, further complicating my already tumultuous state. Many people overlook the significance of food sensitivities, often mistaking them for allergies. Allergies typically manifest with obvious symptoms like facial puffiness or swelling of the throat, while sensitivities are subtler. Over time, consuming foods that trigger sensitivities can lead to a myriad of symptoms, ranging from brain fog and fatigue to mood disorders like anxiety and depression and even more severe conditions like Alzheimer's disease and dementia.

Recognizing the impact of food on my health was a pivotal moment for me. It underscored the importance of self-awareness and understanding our individual complexities. I always advocate for thorough testing to identify allergies and sensitivities, as it lays the foundation for tailored dietary approaches.

Moreover, steering clear of processed foods is paramount. Our current food system prioritizes profit over health, perpetuating inflammation, weakening immunity, and fostering widespread illness. It's essential to be vigilant and prioritize whole, unprocessed foods to safeguard our well-being.

It's truly remarkable how deeply interconnected our gut health is with our mental and emotional well-being. I recently discovered that a staggering 90% of our serotonin, a key neurotransmitter linked to mood regulation, is produced in the gut. When our gut microbiome is disrupted due to factors like processed foods, tap water, and chemical additives, our entire system can become dysregulated if not properly detoxed.

Before the overdose, I endured a heart-wrenching breakup that compounded my mental anguish. She was the first person I had ever truly connected with, and the depth of that bond was staggering. It was my inaugural foray into romance during my college years. Fearful of being hurt, I abruptly ended the relationship, believing it to be a prudent decision to shield myself from future pain. Little did I realize, my attempt to safeguard my heart only intensified my suffering. In hindsight, what I deemed as wisdom was, in fact, a tragic mistake born out of the fear of love. This realization only deepened the abyss of my mental torment.

Each time I regained consciousness in the hospital after brushing with death, it forced me into deep reflection. Mortality became a stark reality, a reminder that none of us are immortal. We all have an expiration date, a finite span of existence, and we must confront our own mortality. Life offers no guarantees; what we have today may vanish tomorrow. It's a lesson in cherishing every moment and finding gratitude even amidst hardship.

It's easy to compare our lives to others', but appearances can be deceiving. Someone may seem to have it all or appear worse off than us, but we never truly know their struggles. They might just be better at hiding their pain. Gratitude for our own existence empowers us, lifting us from despair and sadness.

In the face of adversity, maintaining gratitude transforms us from victims to victors. Instead of dwelling on the negatives, we focus on what we can control. We remind ourselves that tough times are temporary, and we will persevere. *"This too shall pass"* becomes our mantra, guiding us through life's storms.

Life is a journey of varied experiences, each presenting its own challenges and lessons. By refraining from judgment and embracing each experience, we unlock a greater sense of empowerment. Through adversity, we cultivate resilience, foster growth, and deepen our appreciation for life. It becomes a testament to our character and inner strength, reflecting our beliefs, hopes, and determination.

When we resist the urge to succumb to our limitations, we open ourselves to endless possibilities. Excuses and self-imposed limitations only serve to confine us. It's a reminder to choose empowerment over stagnation, to reject complacency and embrace growth.

True fulfillment transcends material possessions. While we may strive for success and abundance, true wealth lies in gratitude, purpose paired with passion and contentment. Without appreciation for what we have, material possessions lose their significance. Like hedonism, the pursuit of material wealth is insatiable; it's never enough.

It's unfortunate how society conditions us to prioritize material possessions and external validation. We're bombarded with messages that suggest happiness is synonymous with wealth, status, and possessions. The truth is such external sources of fulfillment are fleeting and often leave us feeling empty.

Consider the state of our nation – despite being hailed as prosperous, we're grappling with a profound mental and emotional health crisis. Our first responders, police, and military personnel endure alarmingly high rates of suicide, substance abuse, and depression. Teen suicides and mental health issues have skyrocketed, particularly following the challenges of 2020. Despite technological advancements and material abundance, many people feel stressed, disconnected, and unfulfilled.

It's evident that true well-being transcends materialism. We must challenge societal norms and cultivate inner fulfillment through meaningful connections, purposeful living, connecting to the divine and holistic well-being.

Because folks, the truth is, we're facing a crisis – a crisis of disconnection, misinformation, and manipulation. We're being fed lies, fake news, fake history, poisoned food, all while our consciousness and spirituality are under attack. This isn't just about materialism or consumerism; it's about the very fabric of our humanity being torn apart.

We're in a battle for our minds, our spirits, and our souls. It's a war on consciousness, on spirituality, on our very essence as human beings. And if you follow the money, you'll see just how deep the corruption runs.

That's why I'm writing this book. Because the so-called "American Dream" is nothing but a facade. A mirage of the past. It's a trap designed to keep us docile, complacent, and disconnected from what truly matters. We're encouraged to consume mindlessly, poison ourselves with toxic food, become enslaved in debt and bastardize ourselves through noxious media, all while staying silent and obedient, chasing after the almighty dollar.

But it's time to wake up and see through the lies. It's time to reclaim our power, our autonomy, and our humanity. It's time to break free from the chains of deception and forge a new path based on truth, connection, and love. And that starts with speaking out, rocking the boat, and refusing to be silenced any longer.

Before my life-altering motorcycle accident, I was living what seemed like the perfect life. I had married a beautiful woman, fulfilling a prophecy I had made years earlier while in middle school, saying, *"I am going to marry a Mexican beauty queen!"* And my friends and family would laugh and dismiss it as ludicrous. I was engaged and successful in corporate finance, physically healthy, and in great shape. Yet, despite appearances, I was internally crumbling, so very sad beneath it all. Drowning in pain.

I felt trapped in my career and marriage, unable to accept the love my wife offered. I was broken, pushing her away, acting out of character and projecting my pain onto her. Unbeknownst to me, I was suffering from PTSD and still had deeply rooted trauma. Despite seeking help through rehab, counseling, and talk therapy, I found no lasting relief. I was coping negatively because I was unaware of the root causes of my suffering and simply didn't know.

It took soul-crushing experiences for me to learn that which I know now and offer to you freely. In 2010, although I wasn't trying to end my life, I was indifferent to death. Then, in 2017, waking up in the hospital again gave me a better understanding of myself, but it took years to fully grasp. Much of my inner healing happened in Hawaii, where I discovered modalities that could have saved years of suffering if I had known earlier.

Initially, my finance firm assured me they'd continue working with me, even planning a lunch. When two of the managers showed up at my house to pick me up for food, they fired me on the spot. My reaction was, *"Wow, That's pretty f****d up."* Later, I learned they fired my whole sales team. It left me bitter, but I realized we can't entrust our destiny to others. We must craft our own lives, believe in ourselves, and allow God to lead. Life's not fair, but the stronger we are in our faith and action, the more miracles flow through us once we accept the lessons and scars and move forward boldly.

The medical bill from the motorcycle accident shocked me - nearly $500,000. Since I had alcohol in my system, the insurance denied coverage, leaving us with the full cost. To worsen matters, my Cobra insurance, which I had been paying for months at $1,500/month after my work separation, was also denied, and they kept all the money. *"Sorry, no refunds here."* All this added stress to my marriage, knowing I was the cause. I was fired under the guise of a lunch invitation. Only later did I realize that the managers loathed me as I had formed a marketing committee with the owners, CEO, CFO and other higher-ups, and they weren't apart of it. Having someone young in the firm come in and create such a thing was a slap in the face. It was their way of getting back at me.

Now, here I am, drowning in massive debt, my body broken, my marriage falling apart, and I couldn't blame anyone but myself. Life is already hard, but it's even harder if you're stupid, thickheaded, or don't know how you operate because you're traumatized. It was a major junction where I had to turn my ENTIRE life over to God. I remember saying to Him, *"Hey, I've always thought I could do anything and everything, but here I am. I need help. I don't know how I am going to make it out of this situation."*

That's why I urge you to never relinquish control of your fate to anyone but God. God has a plan for your life, far grander than you can ever imagine, and he resides within us and all around us. Separation from our God-connected self leaves us vulnerable to manipulation.

Connecting with my faith and higher purpose illuminated the light within me and guided me through turbulent times when I couldn't see a way out. It forced me to consider what true happiness was, who I was and what was truly valuable in this short life. Realizing the marketing culture had programmed me to strive for the American Dream, but it wasn't my dream. It's a painted facade. Realizing this sparked a deep awakening. I understood that God wanted me to be happy and fulfilled, to flourish and share blessings. Not wrapped in guilt and shame and surrounded by materialism that I'd made my God.

Forcing me to acknowledge that my worth is not based on the accumulation of things. It's my character, my heart, my faith and moving forward through the trials and challenges in life. Celebrating the small wins that make life valuable. The little things that all add up – the 1% every day. Changing my thinking slightly, eating a bit healthier, walking in nature, adopting more appreciation and action and valuing every little thing fills us with gratitude that grows into love.

In Mexico, my former wife and I had a two-bedroom apartment near the boardwalk. Our air conditioner leaked into a bucket, filling it every few days. Every drop counts. Every action counts, adding up to the whole. We often want massive change immediately, but that's not realistic. Recalibrating just 1%, celebrating small wins, and being grateful for little things empower us. A 1% change in trajectory compounded over time can lead to entirely different destinations.

Mixed with slowing down is crucial; otherwise, we miss out on life's intricacies. We become distracted and disconnected, overlooking life's beauty. It's not easy since everybody has their own struggles and challenges. But no matter what we have faced or experienced, our trials can become our triumphs. God always has a plan, and the universe is for us and our growth and expansion.

Right before I had my motorcycle accident, one of my colleagues in the finance firm said to me, *"Get out while you still can before you get the golden handcuffs."*

I pondered the concept of the golden handcuffs, representing my job and how I was chained to it. I couldn't leave my clients and the amount of money I was making. I was literally bound to my desk in a corporate building with people I didn't care to be around. You think it's great because you're making a ton of money, but you're tied up to this money, which you can't even afford to leave.

Similar to many relationships that have lost their spark, people find themselves chained to the wrong person, wrong habits and wrong mindsets. Everyone's yearning for something or someone else to fulfill and complete them, but that's just Hollywood propaganda. Needing someone to complete you implies that you're not whole and are lacking, fostering a recipe for disaster and codependency. We need God, ourselves, our purpose, and mission to complete ourselves before anyone else.

Thinking that somebody else will fix us or that a relationship will make us happy is a misconception. Placing such expectations on another person or relationship is immature and selfish. Many individuals remain in unhealthy relationships out of fear of loneliness or self-discovery. They're afraid to confront who they truly are and look deep within their heart and soul. Had I maintained healthy boundaries with myself and others, I wouldn't have found myself in those relationships. I ignored my gut instinct, seeking acceptance and validation from others to love myself.

Our culture has programmed us to be codependent. But no one else can fill that void except for you, your purpose, and your connection with God. Expecting someone else to fix you will only leave you disempowered and vulnerable to manipulation. It's essential to find empowerment and stability within yourself and ask: How can I honor myself and my path?

It may sound harsh, but I took the ring back after proposing because, deep down, I knew it wasn't the right decision for me. However, the aftermath was intense - she was shattered, calling her mom, then mine, and everyone was in tears until I caved in and returned the ring.

So many people are trapped in relationships, jobs, or careers that only serve their monetary or selfish needs, draining them of their vitality. Even those in long-term marriages often find themselves locked in constant conflict.

By following our hearts, we discover our path because each of us possesses unique talents, abilities, and perspectives. With over eight billion people on Earth, no one has experienced life exactly like you, shaping you into a truly individual soul. Every person holds a distinct viewpoint. Once we realize there has never been anyone like us or ever will be, thats when we discover the super power of being divinely unique. Following a one-size-fits-all blueprint for happiness leads to nowhere. Instead, it's crucial to explore your preferences, dislikes, and aspirations to honor your true self.

It's like this, why heed financial advice from those with shaky financial stability? If I aim for wealth and empowerment, I won't listen to those who haven't achieved it themselves. People offer unsolicited advice when it's not needed. Instead, honor your path and assert, *"This is my journey. This is what I want to pursue."* Don't let others deter you or dictate what you can or cannot achieve.

When I was younger, doctors diagnosed me with ADHD and Tourette's syndrome, predicting my academic struggles and limited achievements. However, I refused to let their words define me. I took control of my journey and excelled in everything I pursued. Had I listened to their discouraging forecasts, I would have lived a vastly different life, disempowered and disconnected.

In the grand tapestry of life, success isn't merely about achieving milestones or amassing wealth. It's about honoring our essence, staying fiercely true to ourselves, and marching forward with unwavering determination. It's about finding joy in the journey, celebrating even the smallest victories, and embracing gratitude for life's myriad blessings.

For it is in our gratitude and faith that the divine universe responds in kind, showering us with boundless opportunities and unforeseen miracles. With each step we take, fueled by faith and gratitude, the universe conspires to manifest our deepest desires, propelling us toward our dreams with unwavering certainty.

This, my friends, is the true magic of life—an enchanting dance between faith, action, and divine providence, where every moment is imbued with the potential for greatness. So let us embark on this wondrous journey with hearts full of faith, minds ablaze with possibility, and souls aglow with the knowledge that we are co-creators of our destiny. Embrace the magic, for it is within us all.

"Experience is simply the name we give our mistakes." - Oscar Wilde

Chapter 5: Mistakes or learning lessons?

Mistakes are an inevitable part of our human experience, integral to our journey of growth and expansion. Rather than viewing them as failures, we must embrace them as opportunities for learning and development. It's essential to cultivate self-compassion in the face of mistakes, as self-judgment and shame only hinder our progress.

The misconception that mistakes equate to failure is widespread, but the truth is that success often arises from numerous failures. It's not about avoiding mistakes but about resilience and perseverance. Each time rising after a fall, inching closer to success.

The journey is uniquely ours, and comparing ourselves to others only detracts from our joy and inner peace. Taking away what we can do with what we have now. Instead, let us focus on our individual path, embracing each stumble as a stepping stone toward growth and fulfillment and taking massive action.

Success is the art of transforming mistakes, tragedies, and hardships into catalysts for personal evolution. Just as physical growth requires breaking down muscle fibers, mental, emotional, and spiritual growth demands resilience and perseverance. In my view, success is synonymous with significance, measured by the positive impact we make on the world. It's about leveraging our unique blend of experiences, talents, and passions to contribute meaningfully to the tapestry of life.

Embracing our story, both the triumphs and the tribulations, empowers us to learn, adapt, and chart a new course. Each setback then becomes a stepping stone to wisdom and self-discovery. Our greatest lesson lies in realizing that we hold the key to our own liberation. By prioritizing our own perception over the judgments of others, we break free from the shackles of societal conditioning and reclaim our autonomy. It's time to rewrite the narratives that confine us and embrace our true potential as sovereign divine beings of God.

The powers to be have constructed a rigid mold of what's considered "normal," and deviating from it brands us as weird, outcasts, or outliers—essentially, not accepted into 'The Program.' This stifles our authenticity, leading to depression, anxiety, and disconnection as we suppress our true selves to fit into a sick system.

A quote I will forever remember from a friend is this: if we are truly following God and the divine in our lives, *"Doors that open are direction and doors that close are protection."* Knowing this changed a lot for me and gave new light on how life unfolded for me and the results of my decisions to honor my path

Through personal trials, I've come to realize that we are always with ourselves, 24/7, 365 days a year, regardless of circumstances. If we're not compassionate, forgiving, and loving toward ourselves, we create a personal hell of endless self-judgment and criticism.

A crucial tool I offer my clients is the life audit and thought state assessment. Without the awareness of our thoughts and where they stem from, we cannot change them. Our patterns derive from our formative years, and unraveling them requires shining the light of consciousness into our subconscious realms without judgment. It's a journey of self-discovery, peeling back the layers to reveal the true essence of what our beliefs and values are unique to us.

Allowing us to enter into forgiveness, which isn't really about others; as much as it is primarily for ourselves to release that which is not within our true alignment. Holding onto resentment and anger only weighs us down, like dragging around a suitcase filled with past hurts. Brandishing them as *"badges of honor"* for the victim mentality. It's a burden we impose on ourselves, and only we can release it. By practicing forgiveness, we cultivate compassion and grace, essential qualities for moving forward into a brighter future.

For too long, I ran from mistakes, my past, and even myself, unable to cope or forgive. Growing up without a stable blueprint, I lacked the tools to process or cope, leading to anger and negative patterns. Many, especially men, share similar struggles due to societal dynamics. Yet, running away is never the answer; facing our challenges head-on is. With a mindset of resilience, we confront our adversities, knowing we are stronger than anything we're enduring as it forges us into our greatness.

As divine beings, our souls transcend the physical realm's limitations. Despite our body's constraints, our souls are eternal and cosmically resilient. Animating that which would otherwise be defunct allows for perpetual progression and growth. Like the buffalo facing the storm, we can be bold, brave, and courageous, knowing that challenges will pass once confronted and embraced.

There's always room for growth when we're willing to analyze ourselves honestly. After my motorcycle accident, instead of playing the victim, I saw it as a miracle—a necessary journey for my soul's expansion. It forced me to confront life and love in profound ways, shaping my understanding of both. Placing me on a plateau of consciousness previously unknown.

History often repeats itself when we fail to reflect on our mistakes and maintain healthy boundaries. When we allow ourselves to be swayed by external pressures and expectations, we often make decisions that aren't authentic to our true selves.

In my very own experience, I knew deep down that getting married wasn't right for me at the time, despite external influences urging me otherwise. In spite of my reservations, I succumbed to the pressures of religion, family, and friends, ultimately convincing myself it would bring happiness. However, it only highlighted the areas that needed the most work within myself and my deep-seated trauma in the relationship.

Even after proposing, I felt a deep unease, leading me to take back the ring later that evening. Yet, I ultimately caved again under the weight of drama and external expectations. It was a messy situation, highlighting the importance of staying true to oneself amidst external pressures.

It can be incredibly challenging to maintain firm boundaries and say no, especially when faced with the emotions and expectations of others, including family. In my own experience, I failed to uphold healthy boundaries, resulting in pain for myself, my partner, and those around us simply because I couldn't assert my truth. As I didn't know how. Ultimately, it was another profound lesson along the way.

When we neglect to set boundaries and remain authentic to ourselves, we invite unnecessary pain into our lives. However, life doesn't have to be as painful as we make it out to be. By fostering an empowered connection with ourselves and understanding our purpose with our God creator, we can navigate life's challenges with greater clarity and resilience.

Many are held back by the fear of making mistakes or being ridiculed. This fear stifles growth and prevents new experiences. But everyone starts as a beginner. If you're hesitant to act and risk making mistakes, you're missing out on life's potential for growth and learning. Staying within your comfort zone only leads to stagnation and a loss of creative power. The comfort zone is where dreams die, and people relinquish control of their marvelous creator-ship.

Instead of dwelling on the fear of failure, consider the opportunities for learning and growth. What if every action led to valuable lessons and personal development? What if failure was not an option, and every endeavor became an epic adventure? Rather than seeing challenges as daunting, view them as opportunities for greatness. Don't surrender your power to fear—embrace the unknown with courage and curiosity.

One of the most epic adventures of my lifetime began with a simple "yes!" My fire fighting friends from California, who owned property in Mexico's Baja region, had been urging me to join them for years. Each time, I hesitated, citing school or work commitments. But in 2013, after our fire season finished, I finally agreed.

Just after the season ended, I invested in new camera gear, eager to document our adventure. Armed with a brand-new Canon 6D and new lenses, I embarked on a journey from Wyoming to San Diego, then across the border into Tijuana, bound for their home in Baja.

What followed was a thrilling 500-mile quad trip through Baja's backroads, ocean vistas, mountain passes and part of the Baja 1000 race trail. Accompanied by a convoy of side by sides, razors and a support rig. We camped on beaches, savored fresh fish tacos, and immersed ourselves in the breathtaking scenery of the Sea of Cortez.

After the 7 day four-wheel adventure, my buddy proposed another adventure: a solo bus ride to La Paz, Mexico, to meet his friends and stay a few days with them. Despite my initial hesitation, I embraced the opportunity, knowing it would add another chapter to our incredible journey.

The very next day, I found myself at the bus station, purchasing a ticket for a twenty-one-hour ride down the Baja to La Paz. As the only white guy on the bus, surrounded by locals and military checkpoints with soldiers brandishing machine guns, I couldn't help but think, *"Damn, bro, you're a long way away from the 307."*

Arriving in La Paz just days before Dia de Los Muertos, the town was alive with anticipation. I met up with the group I was staying with and set out to explore the city. The Malecon, stretching for miles along the bay, was a sparkling gem surrounded by the azure waters of the Sea of Cortez.

One afternoon, after indulging in too much tequila, I found myself wandering down a back street in the barrio, far from downtown. Two men approached me in a threatening manner, one wielding a stick and waving it menacingly.

Without a moment's hesitation, I ripped off my shirt and squared up with him, ready to defend myself. As I glanced at his buddy for a split second, the other guy swung at me, cracking me across the back with the stick. Letting out a primal roar, I unleashed my inner berserker and lunged at him like a panther, raining down blows on his face with my fists before delivering a decisive elbow strike to his head. He crumpled to the ground like a sack of potatoes, his friend fleeing in panic, leaving his companion in a sorry state.

After the ordeal, I walked into a bank atm room with my shirt off, all sweaty and bloody, huffing and puffing, only to get more cash and go back to partying. What a wild, broken man I was at the time.

Two days later, on Dia De Los Muertos, I ventured out to explore the vibrant nightlife. Dining at a spot called "The Jungle," I noticed two Katrinas casting glances my way from a nearby table. It felt as if a magnetic force compelled me to rise from my seat and approach them, locking eyes with the stunning woman among them.

Arriving at the table, I confidently said, *"Hola chica bonita, como estas?"*

She replied, giggling, *"Estas hablando a mi?"*

I just nodded and smiled, not fully comprehending her words. My Spanish was rudimentary at best, and her English wasn't much better. But as our eyes met, words seemed unnecessary; our gaze spoke volumes. Fortunately, her friend, who spoke English, bridged our linguistic gap. We ended up hanging out all night, enjoying the festivities, dancing, and partying the night away. After they drove me back to my accommodation, we kissed and said goodnight without exchanging contact details or planning to meet again.

The very next day, I woke up realizing what had happened with black lipstick stains smothered on my face and a black kiss on the side of my neck. All I remembered was that she was in a beauty contest, and I couldn't remember her name. I then went on a scavenger hunt across Facebook and the internet searching everywhere I could to find out who this mysterious Katrina was that captivated my heart. Days and days went by. I looked but couldn't find her. Even reaching out to people whom I thought were here, but to no avail, I didn't find her. Relinquishing control, she added me on Facebook as I had a screenshot my name in her phone without remembering. We then planned to meet on a date for sushi the next day.

Over the next few days, our connection deepened through multiple dates and shared experiences. Thank God for Google Translate, which we used to communicate in the beginning. I even had the privilege of meeting her family. It was then she revealed that she was a contestant for Belleza Mexico International and had won the local competition at her college. She invited me to join her in Cabo San Lucas for the prestigious event.

It was such a tough decision: to go or not to go with this beautiful Mexican beauty queen to Cabo for Belleza Mexico International… Yeah, right, I was like, *'um duh, of course I am going!'*

The next day, we hit the road to Cabo with her mom and uncle, ready for adventure. The opening ceremony awaited us at a private parlor in the marina, exclusively for judges, contestants, and the press.

Always thinking ahead, I came prepared to capture every moment, bringing all my camera gear. Like a boss, I donned my chest harness and expertly secured both my cameras with their lenses and lights. One camera rested on my front breastplate, while the other hung confidently at my right side hip. I then delegated tasks to her mom and uncle, enlisting them as my trusty support crew to carry my pelican cases.

With confidence oozing from every pore, I breezed past security, swinging open the door to the parlor as if it were my own domain. Not a single eyebrow raised. (Confidence truly is the key.) With her mom and uncle in tow, carrying the cases, we made our entrance, poised to make an unforgettable impression.

As the contestants strutted up when their names were called, I locked eyes with Ade, and her grin stretched from ear to ear, beaming like the Texas sun. I shot her a wink and then turned into a photo-taking whirlwind, capturing the magic of the moment with every click of my camera, effortlessly navigating the room.

After the opening ceremony, Harley Davidson, one of the sponsors, treated the contestants to a tour of their showroom, showcasing their impressive bikes. Seizing the opportunity, I struck up a conversation with the sponsor and orchestrated an impromptu photo shoot with the ladies and the bikes. It was a moment of pure exhilaration, and we all loved the energy of the moment.

Later, as we dined by the water in the marina, a director from the event approached us and extended an invitation for me to join them in capturing the event. It was an offer too good to refuse, and I knew this adventure was only just beginning.

Another extremely tough decision which I made reluctantly…. I mean, who wants to follow around and photograph and film some fifteen beauty queens in a national beauty contest and escort them around paradise. I was like, *'f**k yeah, put me in coach.'*

In a nutshell, they treated me like royalty - covering my hotel stay, meals and even slipping some cash into my pocket. I found myself cruising around in a Mercedes Sprinter van alongside these stunning 15 beauty queens, visiting sponsors and attending events. Here I was, a firefighter from a small Wyoming town, embarking on this grand adventure in the heart of Mexico, all while barely speaking a word of Spanish. Talk about epic!

Not only did I capture stunning event photography, but I also crafted a video that left a lasting impression at the final ceremony, attended by hundreds at a luxurious resort in Cabo.

It just goes to show that when we embrace life with a resounding 'yes' and exude enthusiasm and confidence, miracles unfold, and incredible experiences come knocking.

Following my unforgettable trip to Mexico and a chance encounter with my former wife, I made a bold decision to sell off everything in Wyoming, close down my media production office and relocate to Mexico. Despite the naysayers warning me of danger and uncertainty, I forged ahead, driving 40 hours straight from the frozen tundra of Wyoming to La Paz, arriving just in time for Christmas Eve. Immersing myself in the language and culture, I embarked on a journey of exploration and discovery. Looking back, it wasn't a mistake; it was the adventure of a lifetime.

If I had listened to my family and friends, I would have missed out on so many epic adventures around Mexico that I'll save for the second book.

Many folks shy away from exploring new paths due to fear of the unknown and making mistakes. But here's the truth: there are no accidents in life. Every step we take is divinely guided, whether we realize it or not. I firmly believe that God and the universe are on our side, not against us. It's us who struggle against the natural flow of life, clinging to the past or future instead of embracing the present moment for what it is—an opportunity for growth and expansion.

Think of it like lifting weights: your muscles tear and repair themselves to grow stronger. Mistakes work in a similar way; they tear us down to build us up better than before if we CHOOSE it. That's why it's crucial to have compassion for yourself. Guilt and shame only poison your journey. Remember, missteps are part of your unique path, not anyone else's.

It's essential to honor your own journey and not compare it to others. Regret is a joy killer, and we don't want to look back on our lives with a sense of missed opportunities. So, let's embrace every experience, learn from our mistakes, and keep moving forward with courage and conviction.

On your unique journey, you'll witness truths that others may overlook. It's perfectly fine to stand apart and refuse to conform to societal norms. The so-called "norm" isn't necessarily what's best for us as individuals. It's merely a construct fed to us through media, movies, and cultural standards—a fabricated "CULT-ure" that doesn't necessarily align with our true selves.

Just look at how mainstream media glorifies drinking, drugs, and violence, distorting the divine balance between the feminine and masculine energies. It peddles satanic and demonic imagery, normalizing what is, in reality, anything but normal. We're amidst spiritual warfare, whether we acknowledge it or not. Without connection to a higher power, navigating this battlefield can be an arduous and lonely journey.

Those in power profit immensely from keeping us in a state of fear, illness, and submission. But we mustn't succumb to their manipulative tactics. It's time to raise our guard, connect with our spiritual essence, and defy the forces that seek to control and diminish us. Knowing that we ARE divine creators and most assuredly can provoke change in our realms.

A single decision has the power to alter the entire trajectory of our lives, whether for better or for worse. It all boils down to our free will and the choices we make. Despite warnings about alcoholism running in my family and witnessing the devastating effects firsthand, with my grandfather dying from cirrhosis, I still succumbed to that first sip of alcohol at 21. It was like a temporary escape from reality, a numbing sensation that momentarily silenced my inner turmoil. Little did I know it would lead to years of turmoil, addiction, and suffering.

Society glamorizes alcohol and drugs as if they're essential ingredients for a good time, but for me, they became chains that bound me to a cycle of destruction. It was a harsh lesson, but it taught me the profound impact that one mistake can have on one's entire existence. Yet, through the darkness, I found enlightenment through God. Emerging stronger and wiser, determined to share my journey with others through this very book. You see God reconditions that which was meant to destroy us and repurposes it for the highest good.

I firmly believe that people must honor their own paths, aspirations, and visions for the future, irrespective of societal pressures or external influences. Too many are trapped in a system designed to benefit the few at the expense of the many. It's time to break free from these shackles and forge our own destinies, guided by our inner truth and authenticity, and preserve what we hold dear and love.

The resilience and brilliance of the human spirit are truly remarkable, but sadly, many grow up with the false belief that they are inadequate or unworthy. They lose sight of the enchantment woven into the fabric of life. Yet, as we delve into

our spirituality and recognize our divine essence, we unveil the truth: we are spiritual beings navigating a human existence. Embracing the magic of God and the cosmic intricacies of the universe opens the door to boundless miracles. However, attempting to impart this wisdom to those closed off to the possibility of such wonders is futile. Let the skeptics remain in their world while you revel in ours.

It's imperative for individuals to stay authentic to themselves, for that is the vein that manifests genius and greatest, unshackled from the chains of societal conditioning and indoctrination. When I awoke to this consciousness, I found myself questioning the systems that predated my existence. I realized that I had no hand in their creation, yet I was expected to conform to their outdated ideologies. I chose to discern what served my highest good and humanity's collective evolution, discarding the rest without hesitation.

Many are awakening to the harsh reality that we've been misled for far too long by global manipulation. The fear-mongering tactics employed only serve to deepen the chasm of separation, division, and scarcity, perpetuating a cycle of suffering and disconnection from ourselves, each other, and the world at large.

During my time in Mexico, I witnessed a profound dichotomy. Despite having less material wealth, the people seemed genuinely happier than the majority of Americans. They embraced a simple yet fulfilling existence, finding joy in the richness of culture, life's simple pleasures, and the bonds of family. Upon returning to America, I was perplexed by the pervasive discontent, despite the abundance of material possessions like luxury cars, expansive homes, designer clothes and the likes. It became evident that our disconnection stems from a lack of rootedness in our divine ancestry, history, and communal identity. In America, being American often equates to being homogenized into a singular, disconnected entity.

For me, the path forward involves not just personal betterment but also collective evolution, ensuring a brighter future for generations to come. Upon relocating to Hawaii, I delved into agriculture, planting, and gardening. As I planted my first papaya tree, a revelation struck me: while it would take nine months to yield its first fruit, it would continue to bear sustenance for years, nourishing future generations long after my time.

We must introspect and ask: What seeds are we sowing today? Our measure of a day shouldn't be the harvest we reap but the seeds we plant. Moreover, how are we nurturing the soil of our minds and hearts to ensure healthy thoughts, habits, and patterns to flourish? When negative patterns and thoughts entangle us, it's tempting to numb ourselves rather than tend to our inner garden. Yet, neglecting this cultivation leaves us with barren soil.

To heighten awareness, we must increase our consciousness. But how do we achieve this heightened awareness? We perceive the world through our lens, much like a self-fulfilling prophecy. Our lens, whether it's tinted with judgment, anger, or gratitude, shapes our reality and becomes the only perspective we know.

Once we grasp this concept, how do we expand our view? We start by recognizing our lens—how we perceive the world, ourselves, and our beliefs. Then, we consciously shift our perspective, altering the lens through which we interpret reality. Instead of viewing the world through a lens of disempowerment, why not choose a lens of possibility and growth?

The essence of awareness lies in curiosity—it sparks a dialogue within our minds, shaping our perspective. For example, when we wonder how to cultivate more self-love or forgiveness, or envision what confidence feels like, we begin to explore our consciousness. By posing such inquiries, we navigate the depths of our awareness. Specific questions yield specific insights, allowing us to discern how our beliefs shape our worldview. These questions create the canvas upon which our awareness paints its masterpiece.

Indeed, questions are the catalysts for transformation. To shift our perspective, we must scrutinize our behavior, for an unexamined life lacks depth and purpose. Without active engagement and conscious awareness, we merely exist, devoid of joy and passion. This detachment extends beyond the individual to encompass families, communities, and nations.

It's disheartening to acknowledge that today's youth are growing up amidst a materialistic and technologically saturated environment unprecedented in human history. In this digital landscape dominated by social media metrics like likes, followers, and status, it's no wonder that young people feel increasingly isolated and despondent. Their minds, psychology, and modes of communication are being reshaped by this digital era, leading to a disconnection from authentic human interaction and a sense of belonging.

Amidst our obsession with technology, social validation, and consumerism, we often overlook the essence of living. The essence of life itself is to be alive, to experience, to breathe, to love. The greatest mistake is failing to appreciate the gift of life itself. Life is unpredictable, and none of us are guaranteed tomorrow. Despite numerous close calls, I'm here today because a higher power deemed it necessary for me to share my story through this book, even when I didn't want to come back.

Speaking from visceral experience, I once followed society's prescribed path to happiness, chasing fleeting pleasures through alcohol, drugs, womanizing and material pursuits, only to find myself drowning in unhappiness and despair. Locked in an endless cycle of discontent, I sought solace in external sources, hoping to fill the void within my heart and soul. But no material possession or worldly pleasure could fill that void. It wasn't until I turned inward, reconnecting with God and embracing my purpose through service and love, that I found true fulfillment.

As humanity, we've made our fair share of mistakes, but the crucial question now is: How do we move forward? How can we support each other and ourselves? How do we unleash our unique gifts, our individual melodies, and our enchanting magic into the world? Each of us holds a divine blueprint, a sacred mission to fulfill. Yet, if we remain trapped in self-blame, consumed by guilt and shame over past perceived mistakes, we risk missing out on the richness of life, shackled in a state of victimhood and disempowerment.

We are all walking miracles, each and every one of us. Within us, 80 trillion cells harmonize seamlessly to create the intricate masterpiece of a human being. They know their role instinctively, without our conscious effort. It's a marvel beyond comprehension. How do we think, feel, speak, and connect with one another? It's a testament to the miraculous nature of existence itself.

When we embrace gratitude for life, we begin to forgive ourselves, opening the door to miracles. With belief, faith, and hope, even the seemingly insurmountable obstacles can be overcome. Conversely, dwelling in guilt and disempowerment only hinders progress.

Life's journey can indeed feel isolating and challenging. A wise mentor once asked me, *"Why are you so harsh on yourself?"* This question forced me to reflect on the burdens I had shouldered from others, realizing they weren't mine to carry. These projections dimmed my light and robbed me of my very joy.

We've heard that life is merely stimulus and response but consider this: if I were to slap five people lined up in a row, their reactions would vary greatly. Some might retaliate, others might retreat, all based on their individual beliefs. If it was simply stimulus and response, each action would be the same, but its not. It's this space between stimulus and response, filled with our beliefs, that shapes our reactions. The smallest of thresholds between stimuli and response illicit the greatest change in that notable moment.

We must examine our beliefs, not those imposed by culture or society, but our own. What do we truly believe? How do we perceive ourselves and our experiences? And how can we glean wisdom from our perceived mistakes?

As I've admitted, I've made numerous "mistakes." For a long time, I tormented myself, drowning in anger, condemnation, and substance abuse. It was a vicious cycle. But through healing, reconnecting with God, and self-forgiveness, I committed to improvement, even if just by 1%, as emphasized in "Atomic Habits."

Change starts with acknowledging mistakes without self-condemnation or judgment. It's about saying, *"I forgive you. I can do better."* We don't need to perpetuate cycles of *shame and guilt. Life is already challenging."* We must face ourselves honestly, asking tough questions to find real answers. We can't change what we refuse to confront.

As I reflect on my journey, I'm speaking not just to my younger self but to all those facing tough times and feeling like they've made irreversible mistakes. But remember, things can always improve. Don't lose faith in yourself and NEVER lose faith in the Divine.

In my previous marriage, I wasn't ready, but my wife's love was unwavering. I struggled to accept it due to my own inner turmoil. Ultimately removing myself from the situation, as I was only perpetuating suffering. Constantly engaging in behaviors I didn't want to engage in. Yet, through healing, I've learned to love and accept myself. I want the same for you.

When it feels like God isolates us, it's often a preparation for a brighter future. Embracing our challenges can lead to profound growth and expansion. Trust in the journey and in yourself. You've not been forgotten; you've been planted and it takes some time to reach through to the light and be born again.

At first glance, my motorcycle accident might seem like a colossal mistake. It left me broken, jobless, bankrupt, and divorced. But let me tell you, those events are my badges of honor, my greatest victories. Without them, I wouldn't be the resilient force I am today, nor would I have penned this book or experienced the miraculous healing I'm now sharing.

They rescued me from a mundane existence, breaking free from a soul-crushing corporate job and an ill-fated marriage. Picture this: your entire world crumbling around you, chaos and ashes at every turn, all caused by your own hand. Yet, you muster the strength to smile, to be kind, to keep moving forward. That's legendary! It's no walk in the park, but I always knew that with God on my side, nothing was in vain. Deep down, I knew things would get better.

If we embrace these challenges, they become our stepping stones, not stumbling blocks. They propel us forward like rocket fuel. But it all starts with owning our mistakes, fully and unapologetically. Once we do, we can transform our experiences into invaluable wisdom to share with others.

This wisdom isn't theoretical; it's earned through gritty, real-life trials. Tough times reveal our resilience or our fragility. By seeing them as opportunities for growth, we reclaim our power from victimhood.

Let's stop the self-judgment and self-bashing. Let's forgive ourselves and craft a new narrative, one that's uniquely ours. It's time to decide: will our story be an epic adventure filled with love and miracles or a lament of victimhood? The choice is ours. What kind of book will you write?

Life's essence lies in transforming tragedies into triumphs by learning from them, embracing them, and empowering ourselves through them. When we stop resisting and judging our trials, we open the door to growth and self-discovery. These are the lessons that taught me my true values and desires in life.

Our mistakes may seem like missteps, but in the grand scheme, they're part of a divine plan. God doesn't err; he orchestrates. When we shift our perspective to see the universe as working for us, not against us, everything changes. We begin to shape our destinies and circumstances, empowering ourselves in the process. With God on our side, who can stand against us? We're not mere bystanders in this cosmic play; we're active participants, co-creating our realities with each thought, word, and action.

I often say, *"We are gods,"* but with a lowercase "g." Little g's as we are not the Alpha & Omega in the omnipotent sense, but rather, we're learning to tap into our co-creative power within ourselves and God. God isn't distant; he resides within us, supporting and guiding us as we navigate this journey of existence, one step at a time.

Here's the profound truth: Each person possesses a gift, a unique offering meant for the world. It's something intrinsic, something only they can bring forth. Despite the trials, tribulations, and moments of doubt, remember this—you are invaluable. Your existence is not a coincidence; it's imbued with purpose and significance. You hold within you the power to make a difference, to shape your reality, and to impact the lives of others in profound ways.

As you journey through the pages of this book, remember that you are not alone. You are loved, appreciated, and cherished. Your presence here is a testament to your resilience, your strength, and your unwavering spirit. Keep pressing forward, keep believing in yourself, and keep shining your light onto the world.

So, my dear reader, I want you to know—I believe in you. I am grateful for you. And as you continue on your path, remember this simple truth: You are a champion, destined for greatness.

"Hustle until your haters ask if you're hiring." - Unknown

Chapter 6: Hustle Game Sales/Business

From a young age, I understood the value of hard work and determination. I knew that to achieve anything worthwhile, I had to roll up my sleeves and put in the effort. There's no shortcut to success; it's all about dedication, trusting God and making things happen. This mindset was ingrained in me through my passion from wrestling, shaping my approach to life from an early age. It's as simple as this analogy, God is the boat and rudder, and we are the oars and paddles. He'll guide us and buoy us, but we must put in the effort and footwork.

My journey into the world of work began in elementary school, clearing snow from the sidewalks of our local post office. Wyoming's unforgiving winters meant plenty of early mornings, trudging through the snow before school even began. But I was determined to earn my own keep. I hustled around town, seeking out odd jobs from local businesses, eager to make a buck before classes or on weekends for spending money.

As I stood there in the post office, asking for work, the lady behind the counter leveled her gaze at me and asked, *"If I give you a job, are you going to show up and be responsible? You get one shot, and if you don't show up, you're fired."*

Without skipping a beat, I replied with unwavering confidence, *"I won't let you down. I'll show up and do the best job."*

Showing up day after day when it snowed, shoveling it all before school even started. Looking back at it now, I realize she didn't truly need the help, as she could have had a plow take care of it in less than a minute. But my determination, tenacity and vigor sparked an opportunity for her to help.

There's no room for laziness in my book. If you're willing to put in the work and take responsibility for yourself, there's nothing that can stand in your way.

In my 8th grade year, while my friends were out tearing around town on their dirt bikes, I couldn't help but feel a pang of envy. I wanted one, too, desperately. So, I marched up to my dad and pleaded, *"Dad, I need a dirt bike. I must have a dirt bike!"*

He met my plea with a stern gaze and a simple truth, "*If you want a dirt bike, you'll have to figure it out. I don't have the money to buy you a dirt bike. Sorry, bud.*"

I left his office a little deflated but determined to find a way to make it happen.

From a young age, I learned that putting my desires out into the universe could manifest through unexpected avenues, but only if I put in the effort. When a friend mentioned his uncle, who was battling cancer and needed assistance, I saw an opportunity.

He gave me his number and said to give him a call and that he'd be expecting me. I came to find out uncle Brad was a really funny guy with a big heart. Uncle Brad was quite the character, known for running a booth at the Carnival whenever it came to town. His game involved popping balloons with darts to win posters and small framed pictures.

Initially, he didn't want me to come and work with him because I was so young, but I convinced him after a very firm handshake and looking into his eyes saying, "*I won't let you down, and I'll make us a bunch of money. I need a motorcycle and this is how I'm going to get it.*" Small town perks and connections can be life-changing.

For the next two weekends, all I had to do was show up an hour before the booth opened, blow up balloons, roll up posters, put the small glass panes in the cardboard frame, and run the game. It was so easy, and with me being a talker and having the gift of gab, I hustled people like mad.

With a quick wit and a knack for engaging people, I'd call out to passersby at the Carnival, weaving playful banter into every interaction. Saying things like, *"Wow, look at your arms. You must be strong. I bet you're terrible at darts, though."* Or *"You look like a girl that's amazing at darts."* Whether it was teasing their dart skills or complimenting their strength, I knew how to grab their attention and build rapport.

The game was simple but effective: pop three balloons with darts and win a prize. Most people, fueled by their ego, couldn't resist the challenge, even if they were terrible at darts. As they aimed, I kept the energy light and the conversation flowing, turning each interaction into a memorable experience.

In sales and business, confidence and rapport are everything. If people don't like you, they won't buy from you. So, I've always made it my mission to make people laugh, engage in friendly banter, and leave with a smile, ensuring they'd remember me long after our interaction ended.

In just four days spread over two weekends, working no more than 4 hours each day, I raked in a whopping $1,500 for myself. That's right, $93.75 an hour, straight into my pocket, all while in the 8th grade from sales! When Brad handed me a roll of cash, He said, '*You'll do great in anything you do, just remember, always keep your sense of humor!*" I felt like a true baller, rolling out of there with a grin from ear to ear.

With that money burning a hole in my pocket, I wasted no time. The very next weekend, I went and bought myself a Honda XR-125. And let me tell you, with that FMF pipe roaring like a jet engine, I felt like royalty as I cruised down the country roads, the wind in my hair and a smile on my face.

At that time, I was kinda dating this girl. Let's say her name was Tracie. I remember she came up to me while I was working one of the nights and told me that it was over and we couldn't hang out anymore. Years later, I found out that her family had been teasing her that she was dating a Carny, and she was embarrassed. I didn't care at all. I bought my brand-new motorcycle and was like, 'Bye, Felicia.' Girl or motorcycle? Not a tough decision.

In 2014, after moving from Wyoming and living in La Paz, Mexico, with my girlfriend, who later became my wife, I found myself diving headfirst into entrepreneurship. I was hustling, offering photography and videography services to adventure companies, targeting those seeking unique expeditions and fun experiences.

Leaving behind my firefighting career was no easy feat. For years, I had dedicated myself to the noble profession, finding purpose in risking my life to help others and making a positive impact in the communities I served. It was my calling, my identity. But I trusted that everything would fall into place, so I decided to postpone returning to firefighting for the time being.

Then, a family friend from my hometown in Riverton, Wyoming, presented me with an unexpected opportunity: to learn sales by selling home security systems in Texas. It was a departure from anything I had done before, having never ventured into door-to-door sales or undergone formal sales training.

Leaving behind the camaraderie and adrenaline of firefighting culture was a daunting prospect. The bonds forged with my crew and the thrill of flying to pristine outdoor locations in helicopters was hard to let go. Nevertheless, I faced the crossroads with determination, embracing the challenge of stepping into a new realm of expertise.

After deep reflection and prayer, I made the bold decision to step into the world of sales in Texas, leaving Mexico and my girlfriend behind with a resolute mindset: *"If I'm leaving something I love, like flying in helicopters, to pursue door-to-door sales on 100% commission, I'm going to be the best!"*

The shift in culture and attitude was stark. These individuals hadn't experienced the structured command environment I was accustomed to. They hadn't stood shoulder to shoulder with comrades, risking their lives to combat raging forest fires and save entire communities. While performance was still paramount, it took on a different hue. The transition from firefighting to sales was jarring. The sense of brotherhood and shared purpose I had cherished in the fire department felt distant and elusive in the corporate realm.

In this sales role, it was sink or swim—100% commission, no sale meant no income. Each day was a new battle, where yesterday's successes or failures didn't matter. It demanded a laser focus on the present moment and a steadfastly positive mindset. Negativity is a killer in sales, casting a shadow that potential customers could sense. If you failed to sell, there was no one to blame but yourself. It mirrored the world of wrestling in many ways, where success hinged on your mindset, training, and unwavering perseverance amidst adversity.

Amidst all the obstacles, I made an unwavering commitment to rise as the top rookie in the company. No retreat, no surrender. I immersed myself in the art of sales and mastering mindset, determined to excel. Burning bridges, burning boats—I left no room for retreat until victory was mine. Devouring sales books and seminars while practicing and studying our training day after day after day.

Entering a new arena is like diving into the deep end—it's sink or swim. That's why it's crucial to set your sights on your goals, your north star, and hold fast to them, especially in the face of adversity. Without a compelling 'why,' the pressure will crush you. Moving into uncharted territory demands growth; it's an adapt-or-die situation. No one can make that choice for you or put in the effort required for your growth.

We were dropped off in our sales territory by fifteen-passenger vans after obtaining licenses for the town or city. From there, it was on us to work our designated blocks, knocking on doors and making things happen until we were picked up at the end of the day.

Navigating through uncharted territories, we ventured into unfamiliar neighborhoods, engaging in the timeless art of cold-calling, one doorstep at a time. It was about immersing ourselves in the fabric of the community, learning its intricacies, and becoming masters of our domain.

And let me tell you, door-to-door sales is no walk in the park. It's a relentless barrage of rejection:

- 'No!'

- 'Get off my property!'

- 'I don't want it!'

- 'I'm calling the cops!'

- 'Didn't you see the NO SOLICITING SIGN?'

But hey, amidst the sea of 'no's, there's bound to be a 'yes' waiting to be discovered. It's just a matter of persistence and a touch of charm as you're developing your skillset.

In the realm of sales, resilience is key. You've got to armor up with thick skin and unwavering belief in your product or service. Contrary to popular belief, it's not about the salesperson; it's about the client. It's about understanding their needs and their pain points and offering the perfect solution.

And let me tell you, it's not for the faint-hearted. We hustled from dawn till dusk, day in and day out, pounding the pavement, knocking on doors, and facing rejection after rejection. But deep down, I had an unshakable conviction that I could do it, and I wasn't about to throw in the towel.

Day after day, we endured grueling hours, pushing ourselves to the limit in the scorching Texas heat. It was a relentless grind, but with each door knocked each rejection faced, we honed our craft. And eventually, what once seemed insurmountable became conquerable.

Sales isn't just a job; it's a craft that demands relentless practice and constant refinement. With each interaction, whether it ends in a sale or not, there's a lesson to be learned. Every rejection is an opportunity for analysis, a chance to dissect what went wrong and how to improve for the next time.

For me, the breakthrough came when I mastered the art of building need and value, forging deep connections through rapport-building and consistently closing deals with upfront payments. While others faltered, I remained steadfast, refusing to let any opportunity slip through my fingers.

In a cutthroat environment where performance was everything, I stood out. With the highest activation rate and a meticulously clean book of business, I became a champion of sales in the company. In regards to the rookies and many seasoned vets, no one matched my level of determination as I had the cleanest book of business in the ENTIRE company.

Venturing into unfamiliar territory and cold-calling prospects to close deals on the spot is an invaluable skill that I honed through relentless practice. Day after day, door after door, sale after sale, I refined my approach and learned invaluable lessons about mindset, resilience, and effective communication.

The key to success in sales lies in being trained by experts who understand the intricacies of the process. With each repetition, I became more adept at handling objections, managing time effectively, and navigating the sales cycle with finesse. Over time, what once seemed daunting became second nature as I sharpened my skills and gained confidence in my abilities. Like a seasoned warrior wielding a finely-honed blade, I continued to refine my technique, mastering the art of sales through dedication and perseverance.

Living the life of a traveling salesman in Texas was quite the adventure. We were constantly on the move, crisscrossing states like Mississippi, Alabama, and beyond, all in the name of home security. And let me tell you, when you're knocking on doors all day, you encounter some characters.

One memorable encounter took place in the heart of south Houston, aka "H-Town." I approached this house and gave a firm knock. From behind the door, a powerful voice boomed, *"Who is it?"*

Without missing a beat, I proudly declared, *"KYE!"*

The voice shot back, *"Who dat?"*

I matched her tone and repeated, *"KYE!"*

This back-and-forth continued for a moment until she demanded, *"Who are you?"*

With unshakeable confidence, I declared, *"Kye, home security!"*

There was some shuffling and murmuring behind the door as they checked me out through the peephole. Then, I heard it - *"Oooo, it's a fine-ass white boi!"*

With that endorsement, the door swung open to reveal two larger-than-life ladies eyeing me up like I was prime rib. *"Oh hey, suga, how you doing?"* they purred.

And just like that, another day in the life of a traveling salesman took an unexpected turn.

Ah, the adventures of knocking on doors for home security in the hood. Let me tell you, some neighborhoods can make your heart race faster than a caffeine overdose.

Picture this: I knock on this nicer house in the hood near Houston when suddenly, I find myself staring down the barrel of a .45 magnum. Yeah, you heard me right - a freaking magnum. The guy holding it looked like he had a few screws loose and wasn't exactly rolling out the welcome mat. *"Get the F#$% off my land,"* he growled.

I calmly backed away, muttering a polite *"No problem, man."* I mean, who am I to argue with a guy and his big ol' gun?

Later that night, as I'm reflecting on my near-brush with lead poisoning, a cop rolls up, lights flashing like a disco party. He jumps out of his car, eyes wide, and says, *"What the hell you doing out here in this neighborhood at night, white boy? You trying to get yourself shot? Get in the damn car!"*

So there I am, hopping into the seat of a squad car faster than you can say *"getaway driver."* Officer Smith, as I'll fondly remember him, takes me to a safer part of town. And you know what? After a few minutes of heart-pounding adrenaline, we're laughing it up like old buddies, swapping stories about football and the best BBQ joints in town.

So here's to you, Officer Smith, for being my unexpected guardian angel that night. You truly saved my ass, and I owe you one.

Apparently, a concerned citizen had called the cops and told them, *"There's some crazy ass white boy walking around the hood at night."* But hey, leaving behind the open plains of Wyoming for the wilds of Mexico and then landing in Houston for work? That's what you call a ride on the adventure train. And let me tell you, folks, it was a whole different ballgame down there. But amidst the chaos and crazy encounters that I could write a book with alone, I discovered the true meaning of Southern hospitality. And you know what? I made more money than ever before, thanks to my dedication and consistency. Lesson learned: Sometimes, the craziest adventures lead to the biggest rewards.

Each day, I'd dive into my sales journal, dissecting every detail: the wins, the losses, and the areas for improvement. And such dedication paid off big time. I started racking up wins left and right, scoring cruises, TVs, cash, and so much more.

Why? Because I made a promise to myself: I'd be the best. And when you've got that kind of internal fire, nothing can hold you back.

I rose to become the top rookie of the year, boasting the cleanest book of business in the entire company. But there's always a kicker; not every sales outfit plays fair. Some exploit their soldiers on the frontline, withholding rightful commissions in their 100% pay structure.

It's akin to the Roman Empire's success in military campaigns—they understood the importance of keeping morale high. So, they paid their soldiers promptly and fairly, ensuring unwavering dedication to the cause.

Later on, I learned a tough lesson. It wasn't just me; it was practically every rep. Our commissions were getting docked left and right, and it was downright shady. These folks used their Mormon faith as a recruitment tool, promising the moon and stars but delivering less than. *"Wait for the backend,'* they'd say. *smh* Thousands of hard-earned dollars went unpaid, the reps would leave and then they'd keep their book of business.

These same people held up their temple recommends like badges of honor, claiming to be paragons of honesty while pulling off the ultimate con job. They thought they were untouchable, riding high on their self-righteousness. But no deed goes unpunished and Gods see's all and knows all and karma is a bitch.

Well, never again. I won't judge anyone's character based on their religious affiliation or their smooth talk. Actions speak louder than words, and I've learned to keep my eyes open and my guard up around slick operators and trusting my intuition.

After the sales season, I returned to Mexico with my fiancée. We tied the knot in the US before having a spectacular beach wedding in Mexico. However, due to visa restrictions, she couldn't immediately return to America with me.

Settling in Mexico, I was determined to improve my Spanish skills, spurred on by my desire to communicate deeply with her. Love can be quite the motivator! We even developed our own Spanglish language.

Unable to return to the US, we decided to establish a marketing and media production company in Mexico. Recognizing the potential in tourism, I targeted small to medium-sized businesses in travel, resorts, and golf courses, hustling through door-to-door sales and networking in Mexico.

In a daring move, I ventured into a new country, unfamiliar with its language, culture, and regulations. Drawing from my experience, I quickly navigated the system and started generating revenue by leveraging my sales expertise. I began working with small businesses, providing photography, videography, and marketing services. I vividly recall my first client—a small gym—for whom I created multiple photoshoots and a video for a humble fee.

Securing that initial client was pivotal. It served as a launching pad for approaching other businesses and garnering referrals. Armed with a portfolio of successful projects, I showcased my expertise and achievements, enticing new clients with the promise of similar results.

From that humble start with a small gym, I progressed to working with health and supplement companies, then ventured into collaborations with golf courses and travel associations across Mexico. Companies entrusted me with projects that involved travel across Mexico, covering my expenses for flights, hotels, food and wire-transferring payments to my American account. It was an exhilarating journey fueled by my sales acumen, resilience, and ability to craft compelling offers that resonated with clients' needs and aspirations.

While exploring Mexico's diverse landscapes—from Puebla to Mexico City, Culiacán to Michoacán, and Cozumel to Tulum—I immersed myself in its vibrant culture, indulging in exquisite cuisine and pursuing my passions. My work even garnered international recognition, landing me features in magazines worldwide, spotlighting travel, tourism, and real estate. It was truly an epic journey.

However, amid the triumphs, I grappled with PTSD, struggling to acknowledge and cope with it. Unaware of how to address it, I turned to alcohol, finding solace in its temporary relief. Yet, as my dependence grew, it strained not only myself but also my relationship with my wife.

By the end of 2015, I found myself drowning in alcohol, frequenting bars and clubs until the early hours of the morning. Locals dubbed me "El Gringo Loco," a testament to my reckless behavior. On one occasion, in a drunken stupor, I disregarded my wife's pleas and ventured out into the night. Witnessing my descent, she sought help, flagging down the local police—four soldiers armed to the teeth, resembling special forces.

Effectively, what she conveyed to them was, "Give him a scare, but don't harm him, and try to reason with him."

Two of the officers swiftly jumped from their vehicle, bounded up the steps, and forcibly hoisted my drunk ass into the bed of their pickup truck. Their voices thundered in Spanish, berating me fiercely. Though much of their words are a blur, I distinctly recall, *"You're drunk, causing your wife a world of heartache. Stop being a damn fool."* Mind you, that was all in Spanish. They proceeded to drive me around town with sirens blaring, instilling a sense of dread within me for what felt like an eternity. Finally, kicking me out and watching me go up the stairs back home like a little kid with a stern warning to cease my foolishness.

With the unwavering support of my family and wife, I made the courageous decision to return to America and seek rehabilitation in early 2016. My struggles with PTSD had led me down a perilous path, and I knew I needed to break free from the grip of negative coping mechanisms. Though it pained me to leave my wife behind in Mexico, I recognized that it was a necessary step for my survival.

During my time in rehab, I underwent a profound transformation. I focused on healing the broken parts of myself, both physically and mentally. With dedication and determination, I regained my strength, and eventually, my wife was able to join me in America. It was a much-needed respite, a chance to rebuild our lives together.

After completing rehab, I embarked on a new journey in sales, this time as an inbound sales representative specializing in TV, Internet, and home services. Drawing from my past experiences, I approached this role with confidence and determination. I understood the system, and I knew I could excel because it was all about serving people's needs.

Throughout my sales journey, I learned the importance of guiding prospects down a path, demonstrating the value of our services, and addressing objections before they arise. A successful salesman must wholeheartedly believe in the product and the impact it can have on people's lives.

While I was still moving through the company's training program I was able to get sixteen consecutive sales in one day. One after another, bam, bam, bam. On the last day of training, one of the sales managers ran into the room, all stoked, and exclaimed in excitement, *"Kye sold sixteen yesterday! He sold sixteen in a row!"*

The other sales trainer was less than enthused and was extremely insecure with himself, so rather than pumping people up and being positive, he was jealous and rudely said in a nasally tone, *"I don't care. We're in training. You can't interrupt us like that."* I thought, what a joker. We're in SALES training, and I just rocked it! What a punk.

After the training, he came up to me and said, *"Yeah, I could sell to anybody like that if I lied to them, too."*

I replied, *"Man, you're an idiot. You're just jealous that I'm an amazing salesman. I'm doing it practically, and you're just teaching it."* He shut up real quickly and walked off, huffing and puffing.

When you begin to succeed, expect haters and jealousy to rear their ugly heads. There will be those unsettled and unnerved by your brilliance. But despite their negativity, forge ahead. This is your journey, not theirs. Keep excelling, keep shining, and never let anyone dim your light. Be bold, be brilliant, be beautiful, and NEVER EVER DIM YOUR SHINE!

Months later, an opportunity arose for me to be recruited by a corporate finance firm. My cousin's boyfriend, knowing the HR lady, put in a good word for me. Despite lacking a finance background or formal education in the field, I possessed invaluable skills in sales, learning, value offering, and rapport building.

Transitioning into finance was a natural progression for me. While the products and sales cycles differed, the fundamental process remained the same. Instead of assisting consumers or small business owners, I found myself cold-calling C-level executives of multimillion, if not billion-dollar companies—CFOs, treasurers, controllers, and beyond.

Our firm specialized in aiding companies generating over $15 million annually by funding their capital expenditures and providing additional lines of credit, lease options, and innovative financing solutions. This approach allowed businesses to optimize cash flow, directing it toward revenue-generating activities rather than non-revenue-producing endeavors and liabilities.

A notable example of this strategy's success is evident in Sam Walton's approach. He cultivated diverse relationships with banks and vendors, leveraging multiple vendor credits, lines of credit (LOCs), and equipment financing options. This allowed him to continuously expand and grow without being constrained by available cash. However, many individuals overlook this approach, sticking to a single bank for all financial needs. When encountering resistance, I often emphasized the importance of diversifying funding sources to optimize capital allocation for revenue-driving activities, rather than relying solely on cash reserves.

Cash is indeed the lifeblood of any business, reigning supreme in solving a myriad of challenges when combined with the right resources. In today's dynamic market landscape, characterized by escalating interest rates and inflation, prudent cash management and innovative financing strategies are paramount. While many businesses focus solely on the APR and interest costs when considering financing options, they often overlook a crucial factor: the Rate of Return (ROR). Understanding both sides of the equation is essential for maximizing financial efficiency and optimizing returns on investment.

Consider a scenario where company X borrows $100,000 from a lender at an APR rate of 8%. However, their Rate of Return (ROR) on the invested capital is 25%. This means that despite the interest expense, they generate a surplus of 17% on the borrowed funds by engaging in revenue-driving activities. Without access to this capital, they would miss out on valuable opportunities to grow and expand their business.

Reflecting on my transition from a highly structured environment to the business world, I realized the stark contrast in communication and decision-making processes. In my previous role, effective communication and adherence to protocols were vital, as mistakes could have dire consequences in the fire realms. However, in the business world, the culture often prioritizes obedience over critical thinking. Unlike firefighting, where errors could have life-threatening consequences, mistakes in business typically result in financial losses or missed opportunities.

Through my experiences consulting and operating within various companies in both America and Mexico, I developed a philosophy on how the principles of firefighting could be integrated into business and sales practices. As it became very clear to me that many organizations lacked genuine leadership and had haphazard communication strategies. Internally, employees were not being adequately trained, briefed or engaged in a top-down management style. Paired with stakeholders and key leaders, domineering tactics stifling any input or questioning. Resulting in a toxic culture of apathy and competition rather than collaboration and coordination. While externally, prospects aren't being effectively engaged through revenue-driving storytelling.

Today, I assist my clients by emphasizing the importance of fostering a healthy organizational culture through effective communication and pairing it with genuine leadership. While also driving revenue through enhancing the communication effectiveness of storytelling. Successful companies prioritize both their people and their business goals, investing in employee development and ensuring everyone feels included in the business tribe. This approach fosters a sense of belonging and ownership, leading to greater engagement and productivity.

Ray Dalio, renowned co-chief investment officer of Bridgewater Associates, the world's largest hedge fund, highlights a similar principle in his book Principles. He emphasized the importance of keeping employees informed by recording and disseminating board meetings and other company events to the entire workforce. This transparency fostered a sense of inclusion, involvement, and investment among employees, leading to greater engagement and contribution.

In essence, effective communication is a hallmark of good leadership, complemented by comprehensive training programs. This combination creates an environment where employees feel valued, empowered, and motivated to contribute their best efforts.

Based on my experiences, I've discovered the concept of P3, the three P's: Process, Protocols, and Procedures, which are essential components for all businesses and sales operations. Understanding the operational framework (the process), adhering to established rules and conduct (the protocols), and implementing proper training and information dissemination (procedures) are key elements that elevate business performance. Often, deficiencies in these areas can lead to inefficiencies wasting time, resources, and energy.

Furthermore, creating value by crafting unique solutions to identified problems is a fundamental aspect of business success. Increasing value, whether as an individual or a business, requires continuous learning and development. By investing in wisdom and knowledge through training and experiences, individuals can enhance their value proposition. As a result, I've been able to generate revenue consistently, leveraging the skill set I've cultivated over time. This proficiency instills confidence that I can generate revenue regardless of the location or circumstances.

If you hone the skillset of sales and how to increase your value, you can transcend hourly wages of $15, $20, or $30 and instead earn $1,000, $10,000, or even more per hour. The potential in sales is limitless; as you master the process, you can command higher price tags for your expertise. This realization prompts the question: why settle for a nine-to-five grind when you can develop a skill set that allows you to generate revenue both in person and online?

Currently in Hawaii, I work remotely with companies across the nation. The more value I deliver to them, the greater my financial rewards. Sales, I've found, is the most lucrative profession, surpassing even traditional high-earning careers like those of doctors, lawyers, and engineers. With sales, the earning potential is truly unlimited.

This is the essence of my very book, to share the wealth of knowledge and experience I've acquired. It underscores the importance of having a vision for a better life and not allowing oneself to be constrained by the status quo or current circumstances. My background as a firefighter hasn't limited my ability to explore, learn, and grow in new directions. It has most assuredly complimented it.

So many people confine themselves to labels, but the truth is we're multi-dimensional, spiritual beings with unlimited potential. Belief in ourselves and relentless forward momentum can yield miracles—not just for ourselves but for our families, communities, and even the world. It all boils down to consistent effort and adding value.

With 8 billion people on this planet, there's no one else quite like you. So, what's your unique value proposition? What drives you? What are you passionate about? Engage in activities that interest you and explore how you can provide value to others while generating income.

In today's rapidly changing economy, it's crucial to consider how you can diversify your income streams and increase your value. As inflation rises and job landscapes evolve, it's imperative to adopt a new perspective and focus on expanding your skill set and knowledge base.

The power of storytelling is undeniable. It's ingrained in our history, rooted in our tribal and nomadic origins. When you weave a compelling narrative, you create an emotional connection that resonates with people on a deeper level. Stories sell because they engage our emotions and draw us in.

My mission is to empower individuals to recognize their inherent value and potential. Success is within reach for anyone willing to take the first steps, commit to learning, and embrace consistency.

As everything is interconnected, genuine care for others is key to long-term success. Manipulation may yield short-term gains, but true fulfillment and sustainable success derive from genuine empathy to provide lasting value. After all, most of us aren't sociopaths, and our conscience guides us toward authentic connections and meaningful relationships.

In the competitive landscape of business and sales, it's akin to stepping into a modern-day gladiator arena. Your current position doesn't dictate your future; it's about where you aspire to be and the determination to forge ahead for a brighter future—for yourself, your loved ones, and your community.

I share my experiences, both triumphs and setbacks, to inspire others to embark on their own journeys. Resilience is key. Whether you're entering sales, business, or any new endeavor, expect rejection, closed doors, and challenges. But remember, it's all within reach with perseverance and determination.

After months of relentless effort in corporate finance, I successfully engaged with an organization generating $2 billion in net profit in the US and $22 billion worldwide. Leveraging my skills and strategies, I established rapport with the gatekeeper and ultimately connected with the organization's treasurer. This led to obtaining crucial financial information for analysis to explore potential collaboration after the execution of an NDA.

Imagine, with just a phone number and cold calling, I secured a deal with a $2 billion company! No prior acquaintance, no background in finance—nothing but sheer determination and strategic approach.

Cold-calling such high-caliber companies, filled with Ivy League graduates and seasoned professionals, was like diving into the deep end. Yet, I swiftly adapted, learning their language and operational intricacies. It wasn't easy; I faced setbacks and challenges, but each hurdle became a stepping stone to success. The key? Persistence, resilience, and continuous improvement. Keep building momentum, and never stop moving forward.

With a clear vision of my goals and unwavering commitment to my journey, I charted my course toward my North Star. Despite naysayers and doubts, I stayed steadfast, pushing myself to excel and embracing every opportunity to learn and grow. The truth is, there's no one-size-fits-all path in life. We must forge our own, believe in our abilities, and carve out the change we seek.

Life doesn't come with a rulebook; we get to write our own rules and define the game we play. The key is to stay focused on what we can control: ourselves, our mindset, and our dedication to improvement. In the grand scheme, life boils down to birth, death, and everything in between. So, I implore you, may your journey be nothing short of extraordinary, adventurous, and prosperous. Because settling for anything less risks squandering the precious gift of life and living with regret down the line. Let's make every moment count and create a legacy worth celebrating. Trust in your journey, and may God bless your path with abundance and fulfillment.

Begin today by identifying what you want to strive for and the experiences you wish to embrace. Start creating them and taking action. Fear often arises when there's no clear vision when the path ahead seems opaque and uncertain. So, solidify your vision and take that initial step. Then take another, and another, and keep moving forward relentlessly.

Remember, it's an ongoing journey of evolution; remain flexible yet steadfast, adapting to changes as they inevitably occur. Keep your chin up as you navigate through the unknown toward a brighter future. Embrace the journey, embrace the challenges, and embrace the growth that comes with it. You've got this.

"Surrender is not giving up, but letting go of control to allow for something greater to unfold." - Unknown

Chapter 7: Surrendering to the Flow

Withdrawing from the incessant chatter of the mind, surrendering to the flow, and relinquishing control constitute invaluable tools in the journey of healing and self-empowerment. Yet, paradoxically, these are also among the most daunting challenges we face. It's the classic case of what we resist persists, and what we suppress ultimately takes the reins. Our healing and growth becomes stunted when we remain ensnared in the labyrinth of our thoughts - endlessly ruminating, analyzing, and constructing mental solutions, only to find ourselves further entangled in attachments and subsequent suffering.

My perspective shifted profoundly through the teachings of one of my mentors, JF Benoist, whose workshops and book, 'Addicted to the Monkey Mind,' shed light on a revolutionary understanding of our relationship with the nervous system. Unlike our cognitive, rational mind, the nervous system operates in a language of its own, one steeped in symbolism rather than words. Yet, our society, shaped by a culture of performance and achievement, conditions us to believe that rewards come only through performance. This paradigm leaves little room for the language of the nervous system, relegating it to the shadows of our awareness.

Our societal value system has long been entrenched in a rigid checklist mentality: achieve top grades, excel in academia, obtain a degree, conform to societal norms, toe the line, participate in elections, and heaven forbid if you stray from this prescribed path. In this relentless pursuit of the elusive dollar, we often discard our feelings and emotions, relegating them to the sidelines.

This mindset has brought us to the precipice of a performance-driven society, where individuals are driven to extremes, resorting to self-harm and numbing substances just to quell the inner turmoil. Yet, this discontent extends beyond the individual level, permeating our culture, our heritage, and even our planet itself. We find ourselves standing at the crossroads, grappling with the consequences of this unchecked pursuit of performance and productivity.

The nervous system, stripped of complexity, is akin to a simple 5-year-old child yearning to be acknowledged, embraced, and cherished. Yet, we've long ignored this primal aspect of ourselves, severing the connection with our innate innocence and the joyous abandon found in the present moment. Just observe children—they effortlessly embody a state of carefree engagement, unencumbered by the shackles of the mind's judgments.

Our ceaseless mental gymnastics, our futile attempts at unraveling life's mysteries, propel us further into the labyrinth of cognitive performance, distancing us from the essence of true understanding. The crux lies not in overthinking but in surrendering to the realm of feeling. It's in forging a symbiotic relationship with our nervous system, listening intently to its whispers of wisdom, that genuine progress begins to unfurl.

Believing in my intellect, I spent years entrenched in the fallacy that I could outthink my struggles. But as Einstein wisely remarked, *"The thinking that got us to where we are is not the thinking that will get us to where we want to be."* The path to true liberation lies not in the confines of the mind but in the boundless expanse of the heart and body.

You've likely encountered advice urging you to surrender to the universe, give it to God or trust the process. Yet, deciphering what this truly entails can be confounding.

How does one relinquish control when it's all they've ever known? In our society, vulnerability is often equated with weakness, leaving us hesitant to release our grip on control.

Imagine releasing the tight grip of control, allowing yourself to surrender fully to the flow of life. What would it look like? How would it feel? These questions often linger unanswered amidst the plethora of clichés we encounter daily. But fear not, for Dr. Funk is here to guide you through the process, drawing from the depths of my own transformative journey.

There exists a profound disparity between knowledge and wisdom. Knowledge is mere information acquired without application. Wisdom, on the other hand, is the embodiment of experiential learning, the transformative application of that knowledge. It is this wisdom that I now share with you.

My sole purpose is to illuminate the path with the truth I've gleaned from traversing the darkest depths of human experience. If my words can kindle a spark of inspiration, if they can alleviate even a fraction of someone's suffering, then my mission is fulfilled.

Our brains, remarkable supercomputers, have safeguarded our survival throughout our lives. Yet, in their quest for control, they sometimes lead us astray. We become ensnared in the grip of the mind, losing touch with our sovereignty as we navigate on autopilot, oblivious to the present moment.

A staggering 95% of our daily actions, from emotions to habits to thoughts, unfold unconsciously, directing the course of our lives without our conscious awareness. Time slips through our fingers as we drift through existence, disconnected from the rhythms of life.

In this haze, we detach from our hearts, surrendering to the whims of the mind and the suffering it spawns. We lose touch with our inner guidance, numbed to our true feelings and intuition. It's a state of being where we're taught to exist, yet it's far from living authentically.

In the frantic pace of modern life, many find themselves overstimulated, overworked, and overwhelmed. Caught in the cycle of busyness and striving for the elusive "American Dream," we lose sight of our true essence and purpose. We become disconnected from the brilliance within us, numbed by the incessant demands of society.

While not everyone may experience this to the same degree, a significant portion of society grapples with feelings of disconnection and disillusionment. We've been conditioned to believe that success is synonymous with busyness, productivity, and material wealth. Yet, this narrative is a deception woven by cultural norms that promote scarcity and conformity.

In reality, true success lies in cultivating peace and clarity within ourselves. Tuning into the internal guidance within as we embark on our souls journey. Naturally resulting in the significance of our path unfolding. When we quiet the noise of the external world, we tap into the depths of our soul and connect with the divine. It's in this state of inner stillness that we discover our true power and potential.

In our journey from anxiety and depression to a state of flow, we unlock the power of pure awareness. By calming our nervous systems and gaining clarity of thought, we become more effective and authentic to ourselves. In this state, we align with our mission, purpose, and passion, resonating with the vibrant energy of the universe.

Letting go and surrendering the grip of the mind requires practice, like any skill. As we deepen our awareness of our thought patterns and consciousness, we find it easier to release control and allow the natural flow of life to guide us.

When intrusive thoughts arise, we pause and return to the present moment, grounding ourselves in our senses—what we hear, feel, sense, and smell. Pattern interrupting and implanting empowering thoughts.

Nature, with its rhythmic patterns and cycles, offers profound wisdom. From the changing seasons to the ebb and flow of the tides, nature effortlessly adapts and thrives. In many ways, we are not so different. We, too, possess an innate connection to the natural world, a blueprint for growth and vitality. It's simply a matter of rediscovering our true nature and embracing the inherent rhythm of life.

The battlefield of life often lies within the six inches between our ears—the realm of our thinking mind. I've traversed through needless suffering, stranded on the island of my mind, longing for the warmth of my heart's embrace. It's a simple truth: what we focus on amplifies. If we dwell on pain, it multiplies; if we cultivate gratitude, it flourishes. Love begets more love—it's a cycle as old as time itself. And the pathway to this transformation? It's in the practice of presence, of anchoring ourselves in the rhythm of our breath and the clarity of our awareness.

As a seasoned photographer, I've witnessed firsthand the power of perception. Our truth is molded by the lens through which we perceive the world—a lens shaped by our patterns, thoughts, and perspectives. To evolve, we must first acknowledge our blind spots, embracing a heightened awareness of our inner landscape.

In essence, our perception shapes our reality. Regardless of our circumstances or location, the lens of our perception remains constant. It's a timeless truth that beckons us to awaken to the infinite possibilities that lie beyond our limited perspectives.

To shift our perspective, we must first acknowledge the lens through which we perceive the world. This requires a conscious examination of our programming and perspective. If we're operating on autopilot, unaware of our internal programming, the journey begins with questioning and introspection. Only by understanding our current lens can we consciously choose to alter it.

Embracing change is paramount. We must be open to the possibility of viewing the world through a lens of empowerment, prosperity and love. This shift requires effort and intentionality. It involves training our brains to detach from old programming and adopt a new perspective—one that aligns with abundance and positivity.

Central to this transformation is surrendering and detaching from the grip of the mind. When we operate from a place of judgment, criticism, and attachment, we create separation and discord. True peace arises when we shift into love and compassion, aligning ourselves with the universal flow of abundance and harmony.

The mind operates through storytelling, weaving narratives based on past experiences and projecting them onto the present and future. However, these stories are often inaccurate or biased, serving primarily to maintain a sense of control and understanding in an uncertain world.

Many of us have encountered suffering in various forms —emotional, mental, physical, spiritual, or sexual—that leaves a lasting impact on our being. While this suffering may seem unjust, it offers an opportunity for growth and learning, fostering compassion for ourselves and others.

Yet, if left unaddressed, this suffering can leave behind a toxic residue, poisoning our present and future. To prevent this, we must confront our pain, heal from it, and release it, allowing ourselves to move forward unburdened by the weight of the past.

The pivotal step in releasing and distancing ourselves from the mind's grip is realizing that we are not victims; we hold the power to care for ourselves, nurture ourselves, and reclaim control over our lives. Our happiness is our responsibility alone—we are not beholden to anyone else for it. We must consciously choose to better ourselves each day, comparing our progress only to our past selves.

One of the most profound moments of surrender and release I experienced was on the Kona side of the island. While camping in a remote area while my friend Nikki was visiting the island, I borrowed a camper van from a friend and spent several days immersed in nature, far removed from the chaos of everyday life.

As the golden rays of dawn bathed the inside of the van with their comforting warmth, I felt an irresistible pull toward the ocean. Venturing out onto the black, gleaming lava fields stretching for miles along the coast, I prepared myself for a transformative experience.

With my free-diving gear in tow, I navigated the rugged terrain, listening to the rhythm of the waves crashing against the rocky shoreline. Before submerging myself, I paused to perform my breath work, allowing the rhythmic ebb and flow of the ocean to guide my meditation. With a heart full of reverence, I offered a prayer—a humble request for safe passage and a moment of clarity amidst the vast expanse of the sea. It was a gesture of respect, acknowledging the immense power and wisdom of the water that surrounds us.

As the waves rolled gently toward the shore, I gauged the timing just right, leaped off the rocks and plunged into the ocean. It was an unfamiliar spot, yet a sense of ease enveloped me, urging me to venture farther out. With every stroke, I distanced myself from the shore, immersing myself in the vastness of the Pacific.

Glancing back at the towering rocks being washed by the waves, I marveled at the enchantment of my solitude amidst the ocean's expanse. A deep breath filled my lungs as I descended to the ocean floor, around 30 feet below, greeted by a breathtaking spectacle. Rays of golden light danced upon the ocean's surface, illuminating the crystal-clear blue waters, where vibrant-hued fish darted playfully around me. It felt like a scene from a dream.

After an hour of exploration, as I began my return journey, a glimmer caught my eye from below. Retrieving it, I discovered a pair of dive goggles, a serendipitous gift that felt like a sign of spiritual revelation in regards to *"gaining vision."*

The next day, as I repeated my ritual, my prayer shifted to a deeper connection with my pu'uwai (heart). Once again, I offered my intentions to the ocean's depths and embarked on my aquatic odyssey. With each stroke, I felt a profound sense of gratitude welling up within me, acknowledging the privilege of life and the sacred bond with the Aina (land) and Kai (ocean)

Diving down some 35' to 40' in a single breath, it felt as though the ocean itself cradled my soul, guiding me through a threshold into another realm. Suddenly, a palpable presence enveloped me, emerging with an electrifying intensity. I scanned my surroundings, searching in every direction, yet found nothing tangible. Still, I could sense it, pulsating within my very being.

This potent energy defied description, and I instinctively knew it was there. Casting a glance behind me yielded no answers, but as I turned back to my left, there it was —a MASSIVE HONU (sacred sea turtle), hovering just 2 feet off my left shoulder, gliding gracefully beside me. Its sheer size dwarfed me, measuring a staggering 6 1/2 feet in length and nearly matching my own wingspan.

Overwhelmed with joy and gratitude, I was moved to tears behind my mask. Recognizing the significance of the Honu, which had guided me to the island and welcomed me ashore, I felt a deep connection and decided to communicate with it to seek its wisdom.

Stating clearly in my mind and opening my heart, I addressed the majestic creature, *"Brother Honu, it's an honor to see you. Mahalo for this experience. Can you please tell me what the key to life is? What is it you can share with me?"* I realized this might sound unconventional to some, but I firmly believe in our ability to connect with animals, spirits, and our ancestors when we quiet the mind and open our hearts, allowing our intuition and psychic abilities to awaken.

With the radiant sunrise casting its golden light upon us, the Honu seemed to transform into an ethereal being, its flippers moving like celestial wings. In response to my inquiry, it conveyed, *"You see how effortlessly I am gliding. Do you think I am focused on the future or the past, or am I completely in the eternal moment of now with love? You see me riding the wave of life, working with it rather than fighting against it and in the flow. Easssyyyy Bruh."*

Astounded and absolutely baffled by the response I received, I glanced to the right of me off into the blue void, and there was another Honu - a little smaller in size the same distance on my right shoulder. At this point, I freaked out, giggling and laughing, and needed to go up for air. They followed me as I surfaced, staying right below as if waiting for me to come back.

I stayed out there for about an hour, thanking the majestic sea turtles for the profound experience and the wisdom they shared. With a heart filled with pure bliss, I began my journey back to the shore, careful not to be caught off guard by the waves as I climbed the rugged lava rocks. Letting out a loud, triumphant *"CHEEEEEHUUUUU!"* I couldn't help but smile from ear to ear as I gathered my belongings and headed back to the parking lot, feeling utterly alive and connected to the universe.

As I walked, still basking in the afterglow of my ocean encounter, I encountered an Aunty and waved with Aloha. To my surprise, she called out, *"I saw you out there. You had an experience, didn't you?"* Taken back by her remark, considering there was no way she could have witnessed my underwater adventure, I replied, *"Yes, I was with 'Aumakua Honu."* Without missing a beat, she responded, *"The trinity it was, wasn't it?"* Her words left me even more bewildered, as she seemed to recognize that I had been accompanied by two Honu, with myself being the third part of the sacred trio.

Walking over to her, I said, '*Who are you, Aunty? How do you know these things?"* She calmly smiled with a very pleasant demeanor about her as she waded in a tide pool. It was warm, welcoming, and powerful. She looked over at me and said, *"I'm just an Aunty who cares about our future, and I am glad you were called here. You're here for a reason. You are a portal keeper. To show people a better way of being."*

By this point, tears of gratitude were streaming down my face, enveloped in a profound sense of unconditional love and support. We conversed for what felt like an eternity, sharing stories and connecting on a soul level. Just before parting ways, she graced me with a prayer in the sacred Hawaiian tongue, blessing me with her words of wisdom.

However, upon returning to my van, I realized with a sinking feeling that I had misplaced my keys. Frantically searching through my bag yielded no results. My mind began to spiral into panic mode, entertaining thoughts of being stranded. But in the midst of this chaos, I remembered the lessons from my mystical encounters. With determination, I grounded myself on the lava rocks, breathing deeply as I quieted my mind through prayer and meditation.

Less than a couple minutes later, this voice came into my mind, *"What does your name mean, Kye?"*

I responded to the thought, *"Well, Kye originated amongst my Germanic tribal ancestors in the 16th century, meaning the keeper of the key or bringer of light."* (Which I didn't find out till my 33rd birthday on the island.)

At that point, I said out loud, *"Well damn, the keeper of the key doesn't have the key,"* and laughed at myself. The voice then asked again, *"What does your name mean, Kye?"* I knew it was alluding to something deeper, and so I responded again, *"Well, in Hawaiian, Kai is the ocean."*

Right at that second, it clicked. The keys were in the ocean. Without thinking, I said out loud, *"I am going to find them. The ocean will grant me the keys, and I will find them. My name is Kye! My name is Kai!"*

A few seconds later, with a renewed sense of determination, I strapped on my free diving gear once again, let out a hearty, *"Cheeeeehuuuuuuu!"* and plunged into the depths.

For hours, I combed through every nook and cranny, diving down 40 feet, scouring under rocks and through the coral. Despite growing tired and cold, I refused to give up. With a steely resolve, I asked aloud, *"Where are the keys?"*

Suddenly, a thought pierced through my mind like a beacon: *"They are closer to where you jumped in."* Trusting this inner guidance, I made my way back to the spot where I had entered the water. Beneath an overhang, I sensed a cavern beckoning me. With unwavering faith, I declared, *"They are here. I am going to find them."*

Visualizing the keys in my mind's eye, bathed in the soft glow of light filtering through the water, I took a deep breath and descended some 17 feet. Peering into the darkness, I moved with purpose, searching every crevice. Then, as if guided by an unseen force, I spotted them: the keys nestled among the rocks right outside, bathing in the illuminated golden radiance on a rock that looked like a hand.

In a rush of adrenaline, I lunged toward them, cutting my ankle on the sharp lava rocks in the process. Blood mingled with the water as I clutched the keys in my hand, triumphantly emerging from the depths.

Now that I had found the keys, I thought, *'Oh great, now I am going to get eaten by a shark!"* I was so pumped that I launched up out of the water and began screaming, *'YESSSSSS! F%$* YEA! YESSS!!! HOLY SHIT BRO"* and laughed as if I had just won a billion dollars. I floated up the 4' wall of lava rocks and started doing this victory dance on the surface. I was stunned. I was baffled. I was astonished, and yet it happened. The ocean gave me the keeper of the key, the keys.

To all my readers, I understand how audacious this may sound, and yet, it was an adventure of truth and wonder that defies easy description. It was an epic moment that transcended mere words.

One crucial lesson I gleaned from this experience is that possessing something of immense value means little if we lack the means to access it. We must possess the key. And while there may be many keys, the ultimate key to life lies in surrendering to the guidance of a higher power and having unwavering faith coupled with persistent action.

When we surrender, we open ourselves to a state of pure receptivity, flowing with the current of life rather than resisting it. We then declare our intentions, quiet our minds, and listen intently to the wisdom of the divine and our inner selves. Miracles are not reserved for a select few; they are available to us all. Just imagine the wonders that can unfold in your life when you begin to practice surrender and faith. If I could uncover a pair of keys in the vast expanse of the ocean, consider what treasures await you in your own journey. Dare to believe, dare to surrender, and watch in amazement as the universe conspires to fulfill your truest path.

"Our ancestors are the silent architects of our existence,
their legacies echoing through the corridors of time,
guiding us with whispers of wisdom and tales of resilience."
- Unknown

Chapter 8: Ancestral Connections

It is nothing short of miraculous to contemplate how we have arrived at this moment, both as a collective humanity and as individuals. Consider the unfathomable journey of survival and resilience that each of our ancestors undertook, spanning countless generations and spanning the vast expanse of time. From the struggles of primitive existence to the triumphs of procreation, their strength and tenacity echo through the ages.

Think about the sheer magnitude of experiences and challenges they faced, from the untamed wilderness to the complexities of human interaction. Yet, embedded within us is the legacy of their resilience and wisdom encoded in every strand of our DNA. There is no such thing as "junk" DNA; every molecule carries a sacred imprint waiting to be awakened and activated.

Moreover, consider the intricate symphony of cells that comprise our bodies, working tirelessly in harmony to facilitate our every sensation, thought, and action. And beyond our individual selves, marvel at the diversity and richness of ecosystems, climates, and cultures that populate our planet.

We are the living embodiment of our ancestors' hopes, dreams, and aspirations. Their DNA courses through our veins, shaping our identities and guiding our destinies. It is a testament to the interconnectedness of all life, a sublime tapestry woven from the threads of countless generations.

In realizing the profound legacy that resides within us, we awaken to the boundless potential that awaits. We are not merely individuals; we are custodians of a sacred lineage entrusted with the task of carrying forward the torch of life. Embrace this heritage, for it is the foundation upon which our future rests.

Since arriving on the Big Island of Hawaii, I've felt a profound pull to delve deeper into my ancestral roots. The rich tapestry of Hawaiian culture and spirituality that saturates these islands stirred within me a desire to understand my own lineage more fully.

Questions began to swirl in my mind: *Who were my people? Where did they come from? What were their beliefs and experiences?* It dawned on me that my very existence is a testament to the lives and legacies of those who came before me. Their essence courses through my veins, shaping every facet of my being.

In just four months of being on the island, I found myself forming a profound bond with the sacred land of Hawaii, attuning myself to its whispers that directed my path and actions. This intuitive connection blossomed within me, guiding me to the places I needed to be and the tasks I needed to undertake. One day, amidst the lush embrace of the jungle, this inner wisdom spoke to my heart, informing me that I was destined to receive a tattoo. I couldn't help but laugh at the unexpected revelation.

Replying out loud, *"Oh, you think so, huh? If I am going to get a tattoo, here are the requirements: #1, it has to be a traditional stick-and-poke Tebori Tattoo, #2, it has to be done by a Hawaiian local deeply connected with positive mana and profound aloha, #3, I am not going to go and find them; you have to bring them to me."*

Little did I know, a month later, I'd encounter a serendipitous meeting with an aunty named Kazume. She had dedicated her life to the ancient practice of stick and poke tattooing and was deeply connected to Hawaiian traditions, radiating powerful mana like a beacon of light in the darkness. Kazume had even developed and perfected her own methods, incorporating elements from the island into her craft. Among her innovations was an ink crafted from the Kukui nut oil. Highly esteemed for its oil, meticulously extracted and utilized for medicinal purposes, cooking, waterproofing, and even lighting lamps and also only for tattoos.

After a lengthy conversation and a multitude of questions, I finally received confirmation in the form of goosebumps enveloping my body, signaling that this was the right decision.

Her words resonated deeply with me as she said, *"This is not merely a tattoo; it is a ceremony to honor your ancestors and all that you are because of them. You will be transformed by this ceremony and will never be the same again. We'll do a bind rune to honor your ancestors and your lineage."*

Being in both awe and excitement I said, *'When can we do it? When can we have the ceremony?"*

Chuckling at my sense of urgency and excitement she responded, *"As soon as you connect with your ancestors through deep meditation, prayer and preparing a spirit plate for them to honor them."*

Having previously prepared spirit plates for ceremonies like sweat lodges, I was familiar with their significance. These plates serve as offerings to honor our ancestors, recognizing their continued presence in the spiritual realm, as we believe in the eternal nature of our souls.

Telling her okay, *"I'll be ready in three days time and we'll do it then."*

She nodded in approval and said, *"I'll come and pick you up on Saturday and we'll do it then."* As I didn't have a vehicle at the time and was still using my good ol thumb. Thank God for the Aloha spirit to get around the island without a vehicle.

Over the next three days, I embarked on a water fast, mentally and spiritually preparing myself for the upcoming ceremony. Through prayer and meditation, I sought deeper connections with my ancestors, inviting their presence into my life. The night before the ceremony, I thoughtfully prepared a meal reminiscent of what they might have enjoyed: savory potatoes sautéed in olive oil with onions and sausage, accompanied by sliced apples, chocolate, and honey. Placing it in the fridge, I eagerly awaited the morning.

Waking up in excitement and also being a little nervous she showed up right on time and off we went.

As we drove down the jungle road adorned with the beautiful green scenery I knew this day was going to be both a mystical and magical experience and I'd never be the same in the best possible way.

She looks over at me just as we were about to arrive in the dedicated jungle location of her work she said, *"This is a brave thing, you'll know exactly where the tattoo is meant to go once the design is drawn after the ceremony."*

A little confused I said, *"How will I know where it goes? I have no idea where it needs to be or what the design will be?"*

Chuckling as she's probably heard the question a hundred times she replies, *"Trust me, you'll know it'll be so clear to you it will be unmistakable."*

"Alright, I'll trust what you say." I reply even though I had no idea what was about to unfold.

When we arrived we began setting up the space and setting intentions. Intentions are critical in any endeavor as it directs not only your mental and emotional focus but your spiritual focus while moving through the ceremony and experience.

As she began to sage me and the area and light the incense, a profound sense of peace washed over me, reassuring me that I was not alone. I felt the presence of my ancestors, unseen but deeply felt, their love surrounding me. Words fail to fully capture the sensation, but I wish for everyone to experience it someday.

Next, we arranged the food I had prepared in a sacred space, illuminated by candles, for the offering plate. Kazume then invoked the directions with her conch, speaking in the Hawaiian tongue. Standing courageously, I held my buffalo hide drum in my right hand and the mallet in my left, feeling a profound stillness envelop us. As Kazume chanted and blew the conch, time seemed to freeze. Completing a full circle, a surge of energy coursed through my entire being, causing me to collapse to my knees as if struck by lightning.

The emotions stirred within me were profoundly intense, evoking tears and sobs of deep gratitude from the depths of my being and soul. I reflected on the preciousness of life, remembering the night several years ago when I lay bleeding on the pavement, teetering on the brink of death, only to be saved.

In the blink of an eye, the air surrounding us begins swirling fiercely in a counterclockwise motion, creating a miniature tornado within the jungle space. Kazume's eyes widen in astonishment as she gazes down at me, tears streaming down my cheeks as I kneel with drum in hand. The powerful wind whirls around us, enveloping our sacred space with its forceful embrace.

She exclaims, *"Oh my God! Your ancestors are BIGG! They're all here, and they're MASSIVE! I've never witnessed such a powerful presence! You are profoundly loved! OMG!"* Her gaze scanning up towards the sky above the structure that housed us.

Chuckling in delight she says, *"Well, this is going to be an interesting day."*

I begin laughing with her and say, *"Oh man, what did I sign up for."*

We then proceed to the actual tattoo ceremony where I select three runes from a leather bag filled with black stones that she curated from the black sands beach and etched the runic alphabet into.

She then requests that I sit quietly while she enters a meditative trance to craft a unique imprint for the tattoo. As I sat patiently, the scent of incense lingered in the air, as the candles flickered in the warm afternoon sun. Connecting with my breath, embracing the tranquil atmosphere surrounding us.

After a few minutes of silence she then says in excitement, *"Ah hah, here it is, this is what I see is needed."*

At the very first glance of the symbol she crafted from the three runes, I felt an instant recognition. Chills ran down my spine, as if a laser beam had appeared on the top left of my hand.

Blurting out, *"It has to go on the top of my left hand!"*

In a deeply pensive state she peers into my soul and responds, *"Bold, very bold, the left hand represents both your feminine side and your receiving side and also the past. It seems we must bring more light into the past to illuminate the future."*

Placing my left hand on the table she began to transfer the design onto transfer paper and placed it on the top of my hand.

Looking into my eyes she asks, *'Are you ready? This is going hurt, there isn't much meat on top of the hand there?"*

Nervous yet confident, I replied, *"Yes, I am as ready as I'll ever be."* With each tap of the single 2 1/2" thorn from the island, mixed with kukui nut ink, over the next three hours, I faced a test of character and resolve—a process of transformation.

Within the first couple of minutes I was sweating bullets and went into a deep trance state where I left my body and went into this magnificent purple cloud. Chanting words and channeling a language I hadn't heard before, *"Þurhs vanadornis eorðmægen gelōme Þunorhéat hēol andhrīfe, Ádléþan brægan gēapneōd hāligā, Drīfendes ēadig."* I intoned the likes of this for nearly 10 minutes until I returned back into my body.

Drenched in sweat as she tapped away, I said, *"Kazume, I have no idea what I am saying. But I know its from the divine."*

With a big smile on her face she looks up at me as she gathers more ink and says, *"It does't matter, it sounds good."* Tap, tap, tap.

After nearly three hours of excruciating pain intertwined with profound feelings of liberation and mystical encounters, the tattooing process was finally complete. The entire ceremony spanned five hours, excluding the time spent preparing the offering plate beforehand.

"Before we conclude, there's something crucial I mentioned earlier regarding the Kukui nut oil. It serves as a source of light, and your left side symbolizes reception. In the coming days, expect to receive an abundance of light, triggering significant internal shifts. Stay prepared and grounded, and don't panic if you notice changes. Reach out to me immediately if anything feels off." She said right before she dropped me off back home.

Two days later, while in my jungle cabin, I felt as though electricity coursed through my cells, overwhelming me to the point where I couldn't bear it any longer.

Giving her a call I said desperately, *"Kazume what did you do to me! I feel like I am going explode. What is happening?"*

All I hear from the other side of the phone is her contagious laughter and light hearted spirit reply, *"You are being reborn, don't worry about it, just keep breathing, enjoy the ride and everything will be fine."* And hangs up the phone.

During this period, I delved deeper into researching my ancestors, tribes, and heritage, immersing myself in a profound exploration of my roots. This journey became a transformative experience, anchoring me to a newfound sense of connection and identity. With each discovery, I felt an ever-growing sense of pride in who I was and a profound appreciation for the rich tapestry of my origins. It was as though I had unearthed a treasure trove of wisdom and heritage, solidifying my understanding of myself and my place in the world.

Driven by this newfound curiosity, I delved into researching my genealogy, particularly exploring my Germanic tribal ancestry on my father's side of being Danish, Swedish, and German. Having already forged a connection to my Latin roots through years spent living in Mexico and immersing myself in the vibrant culture there, I was eager to uncover more about my heritage.

Then, one day, my friend Deva dropped a cryptic hint that piqued my interest even further. *"Have you heard about the Lion Man?"* he asked, leaving me intrigued and hungry for more. With a mysterious smile, he urged me to google it, refusing to divulge any further information.

That night, fueled by curiosity, I plunged into a digital rabbit hole and Googled it. And there it was, unveiled before my eyes: "The Lion Man" or Lowenmensch Figurine, a staggering 40,000-year-old masterpiece carved from woolly mammoth ivory. Discovered in a German cave in 1939, this ancient relic stands as one of humanity's earliest artistic expressions and the oldest confirmed statue ever found.

A fusion of lion and man, the statue's enigmatic presence cast a spell over me. Intrigued beyond measure, I delved deeper into its origins. The cave, nestled in the heart of Baden-Württemberg, Germany, lies just a stone's throw from Munich and holds the prestigious title of a UNESCO World Heritage Site.

Every detail of this ancient history captivated me, stirring a strange sense of familiarity deep within my soul. A nagging intuition whispered that I had encountered something akin to Badden or its likes before. So, after much soul-searching, I turned to my dad, affectionately known as Papa D, and posed a simple yet profound request: "*Send me our coat of arms.*"

Years ago, my mom had gone to great lengths to procure our family's coat of arms and ancestry, presenting it to Papa D in a carefully crafted frame as a birthday surprise. Now, as I awaited his response to my request, I couldn't shake the feeling that I stood on the cusp of a profound revelation, a discovery that could unlock the mysteries of my ancestral lineage.

When the message finally arrived, I was awestruck. It turned out that my family hailed from the very region where the Lion Man statue was unearthed. With the earliest recorded bearer of the name was a knight called Funke, who was living in the town of RÄ¼desheim in 1218 AD.

"Damn that's epic!" I declared out loud, my mind racing with excitement.

"They found the Lion Man in the same area where my family name originates!" Raising my hands in astonishment as I uttered in delight.

In that moment, a deep sense of connection washed over me. Lions have always held a special place in my heart; I was drawn to them like a magnet as they represent strength, courage and protecting their pride. Everything from *"The Lion*

King" to lion-themed jewelry, my affinity for these majestic creatures was undeniable.

As the realization sank in, I knew with certainty that I had to visit this sacred site someday. Little did I know the next chapter of our divine story was about to unfold. It was October of 2022, nearly nine months after my discovery, when I found myself engrossed in a conversation with Kadi, a dear friend whom I met on the Big Island. She was a mystical soul hailing from Berlin, Germany, and as fate would have it, she was in Germany at that very moment as we spoke over FaceTime.

As Kadi and I conversed, an ethereal blue orb materialized in my room, casting a gentle glow that illuminated the space for a fleeting moment. While such an occurrence might have startled others, I was already familiar with its significance, having encountered it before.

Sharing with Kadi the origin story of the orb, recounting how it manifested following a deeply spiritual prayer experience and how a medium had affirmed its link to the spirit of my unborn child. To me, he was RoyalKye, my yet-to-be-born son, but later on, the very name bestowed upon me by divine revelation from God. This revelation came to me in a vivid dream after a rigorous four-week fast, sustained solely by coconut water infused with mana from the island.

Late one night, as I slipped into the depths of sleep, I found myself immersed in a profoundly vivid dream. Yet, it was more than just a dream; it was an experience too tangible to dismiss as mere figments of the imagination. In that realm of sleep, I believe we traverse different dimensions and realities, fully present and conscious in the depths of REM sleep. Within the dreamscape, I found myself standing amidst an energy vortex akin to the mystical lands of Sedona, Arizona, surrounded by the vast desert expanse. Gathered around me were tribal elders from diverse corners of the globe, convened for a momentous global council meeting, deliberating on the fate and future of our world.

One of the elders, akin to the All Father, beaming in brightness walked to me and gazed deep into my soul asking firmly, *"What is your name?"*

Without hesitation and my soul responding confidently and proud I said, *"RoyalKye Aurelius Fünk."* Uttering the words I've never said or heard before in that form.

Upon hearing my reply, it was as though a key had been inserted into a lock, unlocking a hidden portal within him.

Suddenly, his eyes ignited with golden lightning, and he spoke in a resonant, guttural tone, *"Yes, indeed. You are here for greatness. Remember your true essence."*

In that instant, I felt as if I were struck by a brilliant bolt of lightning, jolting awake and springing from my bed in a flash. It dawned on me—I had just been bestowed with my God-given name. Despite my initial discomfort, the divine message reiterated time and again that this name was now mine to embody and it was not to be taken lightly.

When I first introduced myself with my new name in a group setting, laughter and disapproving looks ensued, accompanied by comments like, *"Who do you think you are?"* However, I chose to disregard their reactions and persist in using my given name. Over time, it became second nature, and I found comfort in it. Eventually, people became curious about its profound significance, affording me the opportunity to share my divine experience with them.

As our consciousness and vibrational frequency elevate, we draw closer to our inherent truth and the resonance of our God-given names—the names we were destined to bear before our physical existence far prior to being formed in the womb. Embarking on this journey demands resilience and steadfastness, for it will challenge every fiber of our being. And to be entirely honest, only those of heroic faith and hope can survive the gauntlet of fire it demands.

We continued our conversation, and remarkably, the orb appeared twice more within a mere span of ten minutes.

It was then that I paused and shared my astonishment with Kadi.

"What's going on? This electric blue orb, 'my unborn son,' has made three appearances," I exclaimed. In our close-knit group, discussions like these were commonplace; many of us were attuned to our heightened senses, capable of perceiving the unseen.

In response, Kadi offered a simple yet profound insight: *"Well, if he's shown up three times, there must be a reason. You should ask him what he wants. Clearly, he's here for something."*

So, I settled onto my bed, took a few deep breaths to clear my mind, and released my grip on control, posing the question, *"Royal, what message do you have for me? What do you seek?"*

In these moments of spiritual connection, our initial instinct or intuitive thought often holds the answer. It's only when our analytical mind interferes that we disrupt this flow of insight, attempting to rationalize or construct meaning. To truly connect, we must let go and embrace the uncertainty, allowing the wisdom to flow effortlessly.

A resolute impression pierced through my consciousness: *"You must journey to Germany."*

I nodded inwardly, then vocalized my query, *"Where in Germany should I go?"*

The response arrived swiftly, a cascade of intuitive knowing untainted by conscious effort: *"You must visit the lands of your ancestors."*

I couldn't help but marvel at the clarity of the message. And then, another directive materialized: I was to conduct a ceremony within the cave.

Eager for more details, I delved deeper, seeking clarity on timing: *"When should I undertake this journey? When must I be there?"* It's crucial to pose precise questions, eliminating any ambiguity from the response.

Again, the message came in clear, *"Before your birthday."*

Mind you, my birthday is at the end of January, and we were nearly in November. I was thinking, 'Are you sure I need to go to Germany in the winter?' I mean the Island here is beautiful with the warm weather, the amazing ocean, warm beach, and the jungle that I love so much... Yet again, it was clear that I MUST go!

When you ignore messages from the spirit or clear signs, you miss out on some of life's most magical experiences and significant opportunities.

Kadi remarked, her voice tinged with amusement as we conversed over FaceTime.

"Sounds like you're coming to Germany," she added with a chuckle.

The idea of traveling to Europe thrilled me, but there was a snag: I lacked the funds to make such a journey. At that moment, my travel budget amounted to a mere few hundred dollars, far from enough to cover a trip spanning 8,300 miles to Germany in the heart of winter.

Nevertheless, the experience left me in awe. It wasn't the first time I'd encountered such mystical occurrences, given my openness to the universe's whispers. Like a closed fist that receives little, a closed mind or heart misses out on both reception and experience.

Despite the financial hurdle, I felt a deep sense of assurance that everything would align perfectly, guiding me back to the land of my ancestors.

As time passed, my mind began to assail me with doubts and worries. Questions swirled: How would this journey happen? Where would the funds come from? The mental chatter spiraled out of control. Yet, in such moments, we must reclaim dominion over our thoughts, redirecting our focus to our breath and bodies, anchoring ourselves in the present moment and asserting our faith over fear.

While our minds crave details, dates, and plans, our higher spiritual self, our connection to the divine, transcends such limitations. We are intricately woven into the fabric of the universe, each of us a fragment of the divine whole. We are co-creators, shaping our reality with our thoughts and emotions and God guiding the way.

The crucial fusion lies in faith coupled with action. We rein in our wandering thoughts, much like guiding a spirited horse, asserting our mastery over them. This is why I often refer to myself as a Cowboy of Consciousness, calling back my roots in Wyoming. It's about taming the wild expanse of our minds, forging a relationship with it through breath, body, and awareness. We must somatically experience our existence, not merely project it mentally.

After centering myself, embracing faith, and expressing gratitude, a crucial realization dawned on me. I recalled my dear friend Shantey, a soul sister I'd connected with on the Big Island, who also hailed from Canada and worked with Air Canada. A spark of hope ignited within me as I wondered if she might be willing to assist me on my ancestral quest.

The following day, I reached out to Shantey, sharing the profound experience I'd undergone and humbly inquiring if there was any possibility of receiving aid with flights. To my relief and joy, she responded with unwavering support. Her words resonated deeply: *"Europe will change you. Once you come back, you won't be the same again. It has so many special places, and the culture is so different."* With her roots in Italy, she possessed a profound understanding of Europe, its diverse cultures, and the intricacies of travel.

Her willingness to assist me was an incredible blessing, a testament to the power of connection and the generosity of spirit. With her guidance, I took another step closer to realizing my goal.

With the flights arranged and faith propelling me forward, the only obstacle left was the question of travel funds. Yet, I held onto the belief that everything would fall into place in the most unexpected and miraculous manner. Life has a way of surprising us with opportunities and positive changes when we open ourselves to the unknown and embrace blind faith.

As I remained focused on my goal, an old friend and colleague, whom we'll call Gabriel, unexpectedly reached out to me about a video project.

"Hey, Kye," he said urgently, *"I need a favor. I have a video project that needs to be completed ASAP. Literally like yesterday!"*

It was a timely call, a testament to the principle that where attention goes, energy flows. We wield the power to shape our reality, either by nurturing growth and life or succumbing to decay and disempowerment. Gabriel's request was not merely a coincidence but a synchronistic occurrence aligning with my journey to Germany.

In a former lifetime, as you know, That's all I did full-time, creating and crafting media productions and business branding videos for many clients around the world.

I replied, *"When do you need it by?"*

He said, *"Next week."*

I chuckled, realizing it was already Tuesday. He asked, *"Can you get it done."*

Confidently, I replied, *"Most definitely, send me what you got."*

For the next five and a half days, I delved into editing, pouring my heart and soul into completing the 10-minute video Gabriel needed urgently for a national convention. Burning the midnight oil, I put the finishing touches just in time. When the entire project was wrapped up, I was rewarded with $10k for my professional efforts. Boom, baby—travel funds acquired! It's astonishing how divinely things unfold when we surrender to our path and heed the signs from the universe and spirit.

Before embarking on my European journey, I returned to the mainland to spend Christmas and New Year with my family. Spirit had advised me not to make any concrete travel plans but to allow myself to be guided to where I needed to be.

The only destinations I felt drawn to were Bavaria, particularly Munich, and Baden-Württemberg for my ancestral roots. Beyond that, I entrusted myself to the divine flow of life.

In all honesty, I had to conceal why I was traveling to Europe. It's not like you can go around telling people you are being called back to your ancestral lands because your unborn son visited you and you're to perform a cleansing ceremony. Hence, the reason I traveled under the guise of "ancestral journey. Keep it simple for the muggles, ya know.

One of the most profound quotes I've encountered, attributed to Einstein, resonates deeply: *"The single most important decision any of us will ever make is whether or not to believe that the universe is friendly."* When we trust in the inherent benevolence of the universe, and God, believing that we are provided for and cared for, miracles unfold effortlessly. It's a belief that accelerates manifestation.

However, this doesn't mean we're immune to difficult situations or fear. As my friend Manu once said, *"Fear is the guardian who resides at the gates of change."* Embracing change and stepping into the unknown can be daunting, but it's often where the most profound transformations occur.

After a few short days in Toronto with my soul sister, Shantey, and her giving me the low down on traveling and some safety pointers, I was ready to go. One Cotopaxi 42L backpack, my computer case, and a fluffy plush metro pink Guess memory foam neck pillow I purchased in Canada, and off I went.

Touching down in Frankfurt, I was practically buzzing with excitement, laughing and giggling like a madman as I stepped off the plane and into the airport. Everything around me felt exhilaratingly unfamiliar—the signs, the language, the accents—like being caught in a whirlwind of lightning-fast foreign words. It was a thrilling sensation to navigate through this new world, discovering each moment as it unfolded, experiencing it all for the very first time. Not a single hotel or Airbnb had been booked in advance, nor did I have a set travel route. But that uncertainty only added to the adventure as I delved deeper into my ancestral roots. Being the first one in my family line in over 100 years to step foot once again in our points of origin.

For Americans who have never set foot in Europe, the sheer richness of its culture and ancient history is staggering. It permeates every corner, the street pulsing with the richness of history. And it's essential to grasp the depth of connection many Europeans have to their lands—generations upon generations rooted in the same soil. Unlike us Americans, the people there have a continuity that stretches back centuries, if not millennia.

Early on in my journey, I came to recognize a profound sense of disconnection from our ancestral heritage—a sentiment echoed by many fellow Americans I've spoken to. While being American has roots in a proud identity, there's often a yearning for something deeper, a missing link to our past. As we have been whitewashed into one thing. And That's precisely what drove me to Europe—to unearth and reclaim that deeper ancestral connection.

After getting some directions in the airport, I made my way to the train station, eager to explore downtown. It was still early morning, the sun yet to rise, and the air bitingly cold, a far cry from the warmth of the island, thousands of miles away from home in this foreign wintry land. As I stood on the platform, waiting for the train, I couldn't help but notice a well-groomed gentleman beside me, clutching his bike.

"Heading to work?" I inquired politely, breaking the silence.

"Yes, I am," he replied in a heavy German accent, eyeing me curiously. *"You don't look like you're from around here."* he stated.

I chuckled at his observation. *"What gave it away? The braids or my sun-kissed complexion?"*

He nodded knowingly. *"Where are you from?"* he asked.

With a sense of pride, I responded, *"I'm from Hawaii. It's home now, but I grew up in Wyoming, the wild west of America. I'm here on a journey to connect with my Germanic ancestors. This is my first time in Europe—just arrived."*

Without missing a beat, he chuckled and quipped, *"Why the hell are you in Germany in the winter, leaving the paradise of Hawaii? You're crazy."*

I paused for a moment, then replied bluntly, *"God directed me here to connect with part of my ancestral lands. I'm on a soul mission."*

He didn't bat an eye, simply nodding in understanding, holding space for my answer. The train rumbled into the station, and as we boarded, the conversation settled into a comfortable silence, the rhythmic motion of the train carrying us along our respective paths.

As our conversation continued, we neared downtown central Frankfurt, which coincidentally was the financial district—and exactly where my newfound acquaintance worked. It was evident I had no concrete plans and was seeking guidance on how to navigate the city.

Glancing at his watch, Stewart paused for a moment before extending an invitation, *"Come with me. I'll show you around downtown before I head to work. We can grab coffee and breakfast at a nice café."*

Everywhere I journeyed, I endeavored to embody the spirit of Aloha—remaining humble, friendly, and open to connecting with my brothers and sisters across the globe. This approach has consistently led me to remarkable experiences and meaningful connections.

Stewart, as he introduced himself, worked with a financial software company that boasted clients worldwide. As we strolled down the awakening streets, our conversation naturally gravitated toward the state of affairs in Germany and the current happenings in his country. I was taken aback to learn that Stewart allocated nearly half of his paycheck toward taxes—a fact that shed light on the unique socio-economic landscape of Germany.

As our conversation delved deeper, I couldn't help but be struck by the somber state of the German spirit. Through my interactions and observations, I discovered that many Germans carried an inherent guilt complex, burdened by a sense of oppression and downtroddenness—largely stemming from events they had no control over, particularly the legacy of WWII and the perpetuation of misguided narratives and lies.

Stefan's words echoed with profound gravity as he remarked, *"If you are a proud German, you are a Nazi. If you fly the flag in your yard, you are a Nazi. If you wear anything with our German flag, you are a Nazi. If you disagree with the government and its overreaching control, you're a Nazi."*

This narrative was a common theme in the nations of not only my germanic ancestors but in the US and countries I visited including; Denmark, Sweden, Norway, the Netherlands, and Austria. You couldn't be proud of your history or culture or people. God forbid you were white and proud. They tout inclusion and diversity EXCEPT if you're white. You're labeled a bigot and racist or Nazi. You must have complete allegiance to the UN and none to your national heritage, culture and history.

How is this even okay? How is it that everyone can be proud of their color and they're history except if you're white? White is beautiful, black is beautiful, brown is beautiful, we ALL have the right to be proud of our color and our heritage and people. If you scream DIVERSITY and inclusion that INCLUDES everyone!

It left me feeling deeply disturbed. To witness people denied their cultural identity and heritage fed a constant stream of lies and misconceptions throughout the years—it was truly disheartening.

In my own research and observations, I've come to understand that a united Germany is a formidable force. Germany's significance in Europe extends far beyond its landmass and population; its economic prowess, cultural influence, and contributions to the arts, sciences, and industry have long shaped not only the continent's trajectory but global endeavors.

To all my Germanic brothers and sisters I say this, "*I want to express my deep love and admiration for you all. I'm inspired by your resilience, your work ethic, ingenuity and your unwavering spirit. You've shouldered burdens for generations, and it's time to release the weight of guilt and shame that is not yours to bear. It's time for forgiveness, for growth, and for pride in your heritage and cultural identity."*

Do not allow others to dictate your worth or define your identity. Reconnect with the sparks within your soul and let your dreams flourish. Reject the narratives of guilt and shame and division and embrace a future filled with hope and unity. Gott Mit Uns.

After immersing myself in the charm of Frankfurt's old town and exploring the city for a few days, I boarded the Euro rail bound for Munich. As the train sped along the German countryside, I marveled at the snow-covered fields and forests, transforming the landscape into a winter wonderland straight out of a postcard. Traveling by train in Europe proved to be incredibly convenient, offering seamless access to breathtaking vistas and historic landmarks.

Upon my arrival in Munich, I was warmly welcomed by my friend Frank, whom I had connected with on Instagram a year prior. Frank, a gifted music producer known for his ability to craft captivating soundscapes, treated me to a tour of the city's historic district. The architecture and history surpassed anything I had ever witnessed before. The craftsmanship, attention to detail, and the palpable sense of emotion evoked by the surroundings felt almost supernatural.

In awe, I couldn't help but think, *"These people were deeply connected to the divine. They constructed incredible monuments and statues, leaving behind a legacy for future generations."* Movies and photographs simply cannot capture the energy and aura of what my ancestors had contributed to creating. It was a humbling and awe-inspiring experience to walk in their footsteps.

The snow gently kissed my face as we navigated through the city lights, each flake glimmering with ethereal beauty. As we rounded the corner, we came upon a statue depicting the Patrona Bavariae, protector of Bavaria (whom I believe is the Goddess of Germania as she told me), the King, and a majestic lion.

As I gazed in awe, I felt as though the statue beckoned me forward, whispering, *"Come to me, my child. I've been waiting for you. Welcome home."*

In a state of veneration, I ascended the stairs toward the statue, marveling at the energy pulsating through me and the exquisite craftsmanship of the columns supporting the structure. Frank remained by my side, silently accompanying me as I embarked on a profound shamanic journey.

Approaching the statue, I was met with an overwhelming presence. The King stood tall, holding a victory banner aloft, exuding regal magnificence. Beside him stood the Goddess of Germania, her grace and strength palpable, while a lion rested majestically behind them at their feet. And then, like a sudden bolt of lightning, it happened—a surge of energy pierced through my heart, opening a portal within my soul.

Tears streamed down my face, a torrent of emotion washing over me as I dropped to my knees before the statue. Unearthly sounds escaped from the depths of my soul, echoing through the silent night. It was as though layers of ancestral trauma and sorrow were being peeled away, revealing raw, untouched parts of myself. A profound transformation was unfolding within me, as if dormant aspects of my being were suddenly awakened.

Throughout it all, Frank remained silent, a steadfast presence beside me. His unwavering support, like that of a stoic soldier, a proper German, holding space for my catharsis, acknowledging the magnitude of the moment.

There's a deep magic in returning to the lands where our ancestors once roamed—a mysterious alchemy that defies explanation. I cannot articulate the intricacies of this phenomenon, but I can attest to the visceral feeling of being swept up in its currents. My willingness to journey into the unknown, to embrace the mysteries of my lineage, had led me to this profound moment of transformation.

After a day exploring München, I felt the call to journey to Baden-Württemberg, so I decided to rent a car and hit the autobahn. I mean, it's the autobahn—we're talking about unrestricted speed here! No way was I going to cruise along like a Sunday driver. All I have to say about that is, *"Das ist gut! I love German engineering. Drive it like you stole it, baby!"*

As I raced along the autobahn, feelings of ecstatic elation surged through me. With each passing mile, I drew closer to my destination. Eventually, I veered off the autobahn, entering the serene embrace of the German countryside. Fields of agriculture and forests dusted with snow stretched out before me, painting a picture of tranquil beauty.

Absorbing every detail like a sponge, I made a right turn and found myself mere miles away from the cave. The road stretched between two snow-capped fields, with a small island of trees to my left. As I continued down the road, a Pueo (owl) emerged from the snowy thicket of trees and began gliding toward me in the car. It flew parallel to me, a mere 20 yards away from the car window.

Slowing the vehicle to a crawl, I rolled down my window and called out, *"Brother PUEO! I see you, I see you! Mahalo, thank you for joining me on my journey."* Tears of gratitude and joy streamed down my face as I connected with this spiritual messenger letting out a battle cry.

In that moment, I couldn't help but marvel at the surrealness of the situation. Here I was, being escorted by one of my 'Aumakua (spirit guides) to the land of my ancestors and the cave. With a sense of exhilaration, I pulled into the dirt parking lot, leaped out of the car, and began sprinting down the snow-covered path toward the entrance of the cave, which lay just over a mile and a half away.

There I stood, 8,300 miles from my island sanctuary, navigating through a German forest blanketed in winter's icy embrace toward a cave unknown to me a mere year prior. The purpose? To embark on a ceremonial journey guided by the hand of God and the spirit of my unborn son. As the biting cold nipped at my face, I couldn't help but laugh in sheer disbelief, exclaiming aloud, *"This is insane! No one will ever believe this. I can barely believe it myself! Bahahaha!"*

Arriving at the mouth of the cave, its depths obscured by snow, I paused, overwhelmed by the magnitude of the moment. *"My God,"* I whispered, *"I am here."* In that instant, I was struck by the sheer miraculous chain of events that had led me to this precise place at this exact moment.

As snowflakes danced delicately to the ground, like celestial messengers descending from the heavens, I encountered a couple from Denmark on their way to Austria for a skiing excursion. They greeted me warmly, and I seized the opportunity to ask them to capture a photograph of me before the cave. With smiles and goodwill, they obliged, then continued on their journey, leaving me alone amidst the silent embrace of the forest and the enigmatic allure of the cave.

Approaching the cave, a primal scent of earth and ancient wisdom wafted from its depths, beckoning me closer. With reverence, I retrieved the tools I had brought: a stick of sage, beads, and a trinket adorned with a silver figurine of a spiritual warrior.

Truth be told, I had no script to follow, no roadmap for this sacred prayer. One must know, in all my spiritual practices, I ONLY work within the realms of the true light through Christ's consciousness of Jesus. So, I settled onto a rock at the entrance, took a deep breath, and entered a state of deep meditation.

In that sacred silence, intuition whispered its guidance: sage, cleanse the cave with sage. Chuckling to myself at the divine absurdity of it all, I ignited the sage and began to purify the space. The fragrant smoke curled around me, weaving its magic into the very fabric of the cave.

Then, as if possessed by some ancient force, a song welled up within me—a melody never before heard by mortal ears. Surrendering to the flow, I embraced my role as a conduit, channeling energies beyond comprehension.

With each verse, emotions surged within me, stirring a tempest of primal fury. I raised my hands to the heavens, a warrior preparing for battle, and unleashed primal scream's that echoed through the cavernous depths. Like a berserker possessed, I tore through the cave, unleashing a torrent of raw energy—a force to be reckoned with in the cosmic dance of creation and destruction.

As swiftly as the storm of anger and rage consumed me, it receded like a crashing wave, leaving behind a profound sense of sorrow. I allowed the emotions to flow through me, like water off a swan's back, until I found myself weeping uncontrollably, my heart heavy with the weight of ancestral pain and suffering. Dropping to my knees and curling into a fetal position, I felt the collective anguish of generations past, aching for redemption and healing.

With only a small remnant of sage remaining, I made a solemn offering within the depths of the cave—a gesture of reverence to God, the Lord of the Skies, the earth, and the spirits of my ancestors and yours.

Offering prayers for a world where forgiveness, love, strength, courage, hope, and faith reign supreme. A world where we honor ourselves and one another, striving to create a future founded on truth, harmony, and love—a world where we protect our families, and our communities from evil filling our world.

What happened next defies logic and rational explanation. As I rose to my feet, clutching the dwindling sage in my hand, a haunting sound echoed from the depths of the cave. It was as if the very earth itself was speaking, its voice resonating with ancient wisdom and cosmic power. Shocked and trembling, I recoiled in fear, stunned by the audacity of the moment and the inexplicable mysteries unfolding before me.

I dropped the sage, its fragrant tendrils dissipating as it shattered upon the ground, and stumbled backward. The sound that emanated from the depths of the cave was otherworldly—a primal roar intertwined with an ancient battle cry, resonating from the very core of the earth. It was as though the cave itself had awakened, acknowledging my presence with a chilling clarity that left my skin prickling with goosebumps and a shiver coursing down my spine.

Exiting the cave, I emerged from the depths of the vortex, enveloped in a profound sense of transformation and inner peace. Bowing down with a mahalo in reverence for the end of the experience.

As I made my way back to the car, the world around me seemed to hold its breath in silent reverence. It was the quietest of places, broken only by the distant calls of a few birds. Climbing into the car, I felt compelled to explore further— these were the lands of my ancestors, the birthplace of the Funk name. I wanted to immerse myself in the landscape that had shaped my heritage, to connect with the echoes of generations past.

Leaving the parking lot, I cruised down the country road, passing quaint historic buildings and what seemed to be a town with a population smaller than my high school graduating class. Then, out of the corner of my eye, I spotted it—a purple Mercedes transportation van parked in front of a residence emblazoned with the words "FUNK TRANSPORTATION."

"GET THE FUNK OUTTA HERE!" I exclaimed, slamming on the brakes in disbelief. I couldn't resist the urge to investigate, so I steered the car into the driveway, parked, and bounded up to the front door, my excitement palpable as I knocked.

A young teen, about fifteen years old, opened the door, giving me a curious look. *"Do you speak English?"* I asked eagerly, unable to contain my enthusiasm.

He chuckled lightly, his heavy German accent adding to the surreal moment. *"Yes, I speak English, of course,"* he replied, his amusement evident.

I couldn't resist the urge to inquire, so I blurted out, *"Are you a FUNK?"* His expression shifted, slightly confused, as he asked, *"What did you say?"*

I quickly clarified, pointing at the van, *"Funk, Funke, Are you a Funk?"*

His eyes widened with understanding, and he chuckled, *"Oh, no. My father bought that from the guy a town over. There are Funks over there."*

I thanked him for his time and flashed him a shaka before hopping back into the car and driving off.

As I cruised down the road, I couldn't help but marvel at the absurdity of the situation. To travel halfway across the world, guided by unseen forces, have a profound mystical experience in a cave, and then stumble upon a Mercedes transportation van bearing my last name. You really can't make this stuff up!

During my epic near-month ancestral voyage, I traversed through seven new countries, including Canada, diving deep into the roots of my DNA across Denmark, Sweden, Norway, and the sprawling landscapes of Germany. And hey, why not swing by Austria and Holland while I was at it?

While exploring Copenhagen in Denmark, I had the pleasure of meeting a group of gentlemen who were coworkers at a tech company. It was their first encounter with the "Aloha" spirit, and they found it both refreshing and intriguing. Eager to share their local knowledge and aid me on my ancestral journey, they graciously offered to show me around town, introducing me to their favorite restaurants, hidden gems, bars and the rich history and culture of the city from a unique local perspective.

After an unforgettable evening of laughter and enlightenment with my newfound Danish buddies, it was time to wrap things up and head back. But, of course, they had one last surprise up their sleeves—a VIP executive club accessible only to the elite "Who's who" list.

As we approached the club, packed to the brim with the city's social elite, one of my Danish pals shouted in his thick accent, *"This guy right here came all the way from Hawaii to witness this! We're on the list, look!"*

The bouncer glanced over, eyebrows raised in curiosity. *"You're from Hawaii? And you came here in the winter...?"*

He checked his clipboard, muttered something under his breath, and then, with a grin, declared, *"Aloha and welcome Hawaii!"*

With a shared chuckle and a nod of approval, we breezed past the velvet ropes and into the pulsating heart of the club. Surrounded by impeccably dressed patrons who could easily pass for runway models, I couldn't help but marvel. *"This is insane. Everyone here is so beautiful and healthy. Not like America,"* I remarked, half in awe and half in jest.

With a knowing smirk, one of my Danish comrades quipped, *"Welcome to Denmark, the homeland of the beautiful people. Consider this your ancestral reunion to your homelands!"*

As I surveyed the room, surrounded by the epitome of Scandinavian beauty, I couldn't help but imagine myself settling down with someone who shared my European heritage. It wasn't just about looks—it was the whole package: the mentality, the mannerisms, the culture. It felt like home!

After bidding my Danish buddies farewell with a hearty mahalo and blessings, I queued up to retrieve my jacket. But just as I was about to leave, a towering figure loomed over me. Standing nearly 6'6" tall with blonde hair and piercing blue eyes, he looked like a Viking straight out of legend.

With a deep, rumbling voice, he remarked, *"I really like your braids. You look like a VIKING!"*

Grinning from ear to ear, I puffed out my chest with pride and declared, *"F%&$ YEAH, I'm a Viking! I'm here on a clan pilgrimage, connecting with my Danish ancestors."*

The giant of a man was thrilled to hear that I'd traveled over 8,000 miles in the dead of winter to honor my heritage.

After a brief but exhilarating exchange, I ventured off into the night, ready for my next adventure. Reflecting on my journey, I marveled at the incredible distances I'd covered—16,500 air miles, 2,000 train miles, and nearly 215 miles on foot exploring cities and towns. And to have been dubbed a Viking by my Danish brother before setting off for Oslo the next day? It was surreal, and it was an honor beyond words.

As I reflected on my journey, I realized that one of the most noble endeavors we can undertake in this lifetime is to honor ourselves and our ancestors. It's about embracing our roots, acknowledging the sacrifices and struggles of those who came before us, and choosing to rise to our highest potential, preserving that which we love.

With each step of my ancestral pilgrimage, I carried within me the spark of life, the spark of hope. I kindled the fire of love and peace, sharing it with the world around me and leaving a legacy that would resonate for generations to come.

As I stood at the crossroads of past and present, I understood that I was not alone. I was the culmination of all those who had walked before me, their hopes and dreams pulsing through my veins. And in that moment, I became a beacon of light, illuminating a path for those yet to come.

So, I ask you: Will you heed the call of your ancestors? Will you welcome them home and embrace the legacy they yearn to impart upon you? For your ancestors are you, and you are them. Together, let us forge a future guided by the wisdom of the past, united in purpose and bound by love.

"Harmony between body and mind creates the melody of wellness." - Unknown

Chapter 9: Body Mind/Medicine

Transitioning from a state of being utterly shattered, where every breath was a battle, to robust health and vitality just three months later confounded the medical establishment. It emphasizes the undeniable potency of faith, determination, and having a guiding light to steer us through the turmoil of healing. Our bodies, far more resilient and extraordinary than conventional wisdom suggests, possess an innate ability for extraordinary self-regeneration – faster than we've been led to believe. From minor cuts to fractured bones, our biological machinery orchestrates miraculous recoveries. When yoked with the transformative power of a positive mindset, coupled with receptivity from the divine and compassion, our capacity for healing transcends mere physicality, ushering in extraordinary transformations and boundless possibilities.

Upon awakening in the hospital following my motorcycle accident, I faced a pivotal choice: succumb to self-blame and the despair of disempowerment, continuing down the cycle of destruction, or actively choose and harness the experience as a catalyst for profound growth and evolution.

Without hesitation, I embraced the latter path, determined to transform adversity into an opportunity for unparalleled expansion. Realizing I'd traveled far too long to give up now and throw away my miracle.

When we steadfastly commit to a decision, drawing upon our inner strength and faith in the divine, miracles become possible. By refusing to let others dictate our healing, empowerment, or life's trajectory, we open ourselves to the miraculous. For without belief in miracles, none shall manifest. Our healing begins with the unwavering conviction that it is indeed possible.

Hence, the power of our mindset reigns supreme. When we dwell in disempowerment, disconnected from our infinite essence, we operate within a false paradigm. It's essential to realign with our true selves to regain empowerment and battle in life's journey. Building momentum one day at a time. Sometimes, hours or minutes at a time.

Western medicine's narrative often undermines our innate power, perpetuating a false belief in our limitations. Yet, luminaries like Dr. Joe Dispenza have illuminated the truth through his remarkable healing journey and being able to quantify and qualify the results. Dr. Dispenza's insights into epigenetics as well as Dr. Bruce Lipton, unveil the profound impact of thoughts, emotions, and beliefs on the body's transformative capacity. Epigenetics is a recent field of study that explores how we can up-regulate or down-regulate our genetic expression through the feelings created by our internal thoughts. As the brain truly does not know the difference between an inside event and an external event.

When we embrace a mindset brimming with joy, gratitude, and inspiration, we flood our bodies with potent chemicals that catalyze rapid repair, regeneration, and growth.

Merely four days of dedicating 20 minutes each day to cultivating gratitude, joy, and inspiration can initiate profound rejuvenation within our bodies. Researchers have substantiated these findings through blood plasma analysis. Reflecting on this, we must recognize that the healthcare system and government thrive on our disempowerment. They prefer a populace dependent on medication, as it ensures profit. True healthcare, not sick care, entails empowerment and connection with our highest selves, rendering unnecessary the majority of medical interventions unless it's trauma related. It's time to shift from "sick care" to genuine healthcare.

The ultimate outcome lies in preventive care. Our dietary choices, thoughts, consumption habits, and social connections profoundly impact our health. Therefore, we must vigilantly monitor what influences our mindset. It's evident that we face relentless propaganda and media manipulation aimed at severing our connection with our true selves—the divine within us and our fellow beings.

We wield immense power when we acknowledge that we are created in the image of God and are inheritors of His kingdom through Christ consciousness. By embracing this truth and aligning our mindset with the omnipotent power of the supreme creator, we unlock the ability to heal and experience greater empowerment, engagement, and purposeful action. This understanding is pivotal because, as previously mentioned, our energy follows our focus.

Our perspective shapes our reality, even if it's flawed. Real change only occurs when we shift our viewpoint, altering our lives, outcomes, and destinies. Our perception of ourselves and the world dictates everything. It's unsettling to dismantle false personal and global paradigms rooted in limiting beliefs, poverty, division, and manipulation. However, the awakening that follows makes the journey worthwhile.

We needn't embrace someone else's viewpoint if it feels inauthentic or misaligned with our true selves. Whether it's from friends, family, religion, institutions, government, or education, we have the power to reject perspectives that don't resonate with us.

As I experienced understanding the power of my mind, it became evident that we've been conditioned to adopt a very finite mindset. This narrow perspective leaves individuals disconnected, disengaged, and susceptible to manipulation and control.

Throughout history, we have witnessed the pattern unfold repeatedly. Consider the Roman Catholic Church not so long ago—actively suppressing education, forbidding literacy, and punishing those found with a Bible by burning them at the stake. Why? Because an educated populace poses a threat. By keeping people uninformed and disconnected, authorities maintain control and wield manipulation. Their aim? To seize authority from God and impose their distorted version upon the masses. All in the name of 'GOD." Well, that God is most certainly demonic, not a vibe I conform with.

I reiterate the importance of assessing our mindset. Only when we align with our truth, our North Star, our higher self, and the spirit of God's creation can we discern reality from deception. Miracles manifest when we wholeheartedly believe in their occurrence, even when the path forward remains unclear.

Furthermore, when we hold steadfast in our conviction and unwavering faith that an outcome will materialize, it invariably does. This is because our perception directly influences reality. The findings of the double-slit experiment in quantum physics illustrate this phenomenon, indicating that particles, particularly subatomic particles, transition from a denser particle state to a higher frequency wave state based on the observer's perception of the event.

What the heck does that even mean?

This implies that the observer holds the power to influence the behavior of subatomic particles and the nature of reality through mere observation. It underscores the concept that each of us is a universe unto ourselves, as our perception dictates where our power lies. How we perceive a situation determines our state of being — whether empowered or disempowered. Therefore, it becomes imperative for us to understand how our faith, belief, and understanding shape the focal points of our attention.

Our beliefs controls our perspective, our perspective controls our reality, and our reality controls our outcomes and how we operate in the world.

Without question, individuals devoid of formal education, financial resources, or extensive networks have wielded remarkable influence on a global scale. They've catalyzed transformative shifts in various domains, be it by establishing organizations, enterprises, or advocacy platforms or by instigating change in political, cultural, or economic landscapes, all empowered by their connection to the divine and a desire to bring forth that which wants to emerge from them. Their achievements stem from a steadfast belief and unwavering certainty in their ability to effect change through faith-driven action, embodying the timeless adage that where there is determination, a pathway invariably emerges.

These trailblazers possessed a vision that transcended conventional understanding, honing their focus on that singular, elusive goal. With unwavering conviction, they invested their entire being — heart, mind, and soul — into their pursuit. And as they aligned their beliefs with action, propelled by intentions devoid of harm, the response from God and the universe was resounding. For, in the intricate dance of existence, we emerge as co-creators of our reality, as affirmed by the revelations of quantum mechanics.

Furthermore, gratitude stands as the universal key, unlocking the abundance that awaits us. If we fail to appreciate the gifts already bestowed upon us, why would the benevolent forces of the cosmos bestow more? Visionaries like Tesla and Einstein illuminated the truth: everything resonates with frequency, pulsating with energy. Thus, we must perceive the universe as a symphony of frequencies and waves, for even the seemingly solid dissolves upon closer inspection. Delving into the intricate fabric of matter, from compounds to subatomic particles, reveals that 99.99999% of our surroundings is but empty space.

When we embrace gratitude, we unlock the vast potential of the universe. Gratitude becomes the cornerstone of body-mind medicine, guiding us to a state of profound appreciation for our present circumstances. In this state, we nurture our bodies and minds, cultivating resilience and empowerment for the journey ahead. Rather than dwelling on past limitations, we anchor ourselves in the transformative power of the present moment, shaping a future brimming with vitality and possibility.

If you look at the programming in our news media or entertainment culture, a vast amount of it is to keep people distracted and in a fight or flight response.

Why though? Why would these power structures be so concerned with our collective minds and energy?

It's simple once you realize how we operate. If we're in a fight or flight/freeze response, four specific things occur right away. Number one is we can't reach our highest cognitive functioning and thinking abilities. We literally cannot make our best decisions. Secondly, our immune system drops down significantly, allocating that energy to the sympathetic response, the real threat or "perceived" in the environment. Thirdly, we can't learn any new information. No new information can come into the system if we are in a fight or flight state because it has been taken over by our sympathetic nervous system. It is not concerned with how you can live a happier, healthier life when it perceives the threat of a hungry bear chasing it. Lastly, it causes a massive amount of disease within the body, wreaking havoc over time.

Consider this scenario: if, upon waking, the first thing we do is immerse ourselves in the news or social media, and get sucked in emotionally, we inadvertently trigger a mild fight-or-flight response. The emotional impact of negative news permeates our being, influencing our emotional state, which in turn governs our autonomic nervous system's response. By subjecting ourselves to a continuous stream of negativity, comparison to others, criticism and judgement, mixed with separation from God, we unwittingly undergo a process of disempowerment, pessimism of the heart and indoctrination of the mind. This spotlights the critical importance of exercising discernment in curating both our external environment and internal mindset.

Especially in the early morning upon waking up and later in the evening when we are going to sleep, as we are in a more open and vulnerable state. Moving into and coming out of a theta state, not beta brainwave activity, which is the guardian and gatekeeper to our subconscious. Ever wonder why the news is first thing in the morning waking up and right when going to bed? Besides the weather, its vastly negative and seeps directly into the subconscious. The perfect "program."

This occurrence stems from a deliberate lack of education regarding these inner workings. The reason for this omission is clear: if we comprehended our own mechanisms and recognized the pervasive influence of media manipulation on society and the toxic culture's parasitic grasp on us, we would emerge as empowered individuals. Armed with this understanding, we would refuse to passively accept the manipulation imposed upon us, thereby reclaiming control over our own destinies.

Indeed, embracing gratitude enables us to transcend the confines of separation and lower frequencies. If we were to visualize a scale of emotions and frequencies, we would observe that feelings such as guilt, shame, anger, greed, and jealousy resonate at extremely low frequencies. Conversely, emotions like hope, joy, and inspiration vibrate at higher frequencies. By ascending this emotional scale, we can witness the profound impact on our bodies, minds, and overall well-being as higher frequencies imbue us with vitality and resilience.

Individuals who maintain a state of gratitude, love, optimism and joy navigate life distinctly different from those mired in anger, hate, jealousy, greed, or negativity. These two groups operate within different frequencies or realities, profoundly influencing their mindset, health and worlds. Those consumed by lower emotions often contend with more health issues as their bodies resonate at lower frequencies. In contrast, individuals embracing gratitude and positivity experience enhanced well-being, reflecting the higher vibrational frequency of their existence and their body responds accordingly.

Masaru Emoto conducted groundbreaking experiments demonstrating how intentions and words can profoundly influence water molecules and their structural formation. In his renowned work, 'The Hidden Messages in Water,' Emoto placed droplets of water in individual Petri dishes, inscribed with a single word wrapped around each dish. After rapidly freezing these Petri dishes, he captured the process on camera, revealing astonishing results. Water exposed to words of joy, inspiration, love, and compassion formed mesmerizing structures characterized by symmetry, beauty, and a golden white hue. These findings illuminate the profound impact of positive intentions and affirmations on the molecular structure of water, highlighting the interconnectedness of consciousness and the natural world.

In contrast, the Petri dishes adorned with words of hate, separation, evil, greed, and anger yielded starkly different results. The water within these dishes froze into snowflakes with grotesque and misaligned structures, devoid of the harmonious symmetry observed in their counterparts. These dissonant formations bore a dark hue, reflecting the negative influence of such intentions on the molecular composition of water. Emoto's experiments highlight the profound impact of human consciousness and intentions on the structural formation of water, providing compelling insights into the interconnectedness of thought, emotion, and the natural world.

In reality, the implications of Masaru Emoto's experiments are staggering. The mere influence of a word inscribed on a piece of paper and placed near water can orchestrate profound changes in the molecular structure of this essential element. When we consider that our bodies and the Earth itself are predominantly composed of water, the significance magnifies exponentially. Every thought we harbor, every emotion we cultivate, reverberates through the vast network of water molecules within us and throughout the planet. It accentuates the intricate dance of frequency modulation that permeates existence, further highlighting the interconnectedness of mind, body, and the natural world in a symphony of cosmic resonance.

Undoubtedly, delving into the intricacies of stress reduction and understanding the dynamics of our neurochemical's allows us to glimpse into the realm of quantum healing. It's a realm where the spotlight of attention directs the flow of energy, where our thoughts weave a tapestry of feelings that resonate through our bodies on a molecular level. Moreover, we're not solitary travelers in this quantum landscape; our experiences are intertwined with those of the collective. Thus, as we navigate the corridors of our own healing journey, we simultaneously contribute to the collective tapestry of human experience, shaping and reshaping the fabric of reality with every thought, feeling, and intention. An ever-changing landscape upon the cosmic dance of eternity.

When immersed in negative environments or surrounded by negative individuals, our well-being can be significantly impacted. Therefore, it's crucial to exercise mindfulness and attentiveness regarding the spaces we inhabit and the company we keep. By consciously limiting our exposure to such negativity, we safeguard ourselves against its adverse effects and cultivate environments conducive to our growth and well-being. Do not fall prey to those who attempt to bring you down to their level through guilt-tripping or shaming.

Maharishi Mahesh Yogi was a pioneer in recognizing the transformative power of coherence and positivity cultivated through meditation. He observed that when just the square root of one percent (1%) of a population practiced a singular focused meditation, it significantly enhanced the quality of life within that society. This increased coherence fostered greater national harmony and well-being. Moreover, this internal harmony radiated outward, positively impacting international relations and diminishing global conflicts as well.

Through practices like meditation and prayer, the collective power of even a small group focusing on love, gratitude, peace, and blessings has been profoundly recognized. This concerted effort has tangible effects on our communities, homes, and nations. Crime rates decrease, health outcomes improve, and individuals experience numerous personal health benefits. Moreover, stress, depression, and anxiety are reduced, contributing to a more harmonious individual and thriving society.

In the practice of body-mind medicine, it's essential to reconnect the mind with the body through deep breath and presence, allowing us to release stored distress and reclaim our sovereignty. This process enables us to confront and process the emotions and sensations within us, leading to transformative healing. By honoring what arises and listening to our body's wisdom, we can follow its guidance toward resolution. Whether it's through movement, expression, or cathartic release, we must heed the body's cues for discharge and resolution. Avoiding, suppressing, or distracting ourselves from these experiences only perpetuates disconnection and prevents true inner peace. To find solace within, we must embrace this journey of integration and allow ourselves to come home to ourselves fully.

This is why many people resort to various distractions to escape their inner turmoil. They become fragmented and disconnected, distancing themselves from their true selves and others around them. To counteract this, we must re-establish the connection between the mind and body, engaging in slow, deliberate breathing and allowing ourselves to fully experience our emotions. Coupling this with EFT, fasting and cold therapy yields profound results. By acknowledging and confronting what needs to be addressed, we can begin the process of releasing stored disturbances. It's crucial to understand that healing and empowerment requires us to confront our pain and discomfort head-on; avoiding it only allows it to gain more power over us. As a wise college teacher once told me, *"Secrets keep us sick."*

The nervous system, in its essence, is straightforward. Western medicine often suggests lengthy psychotherapy sessions, costing substantial amounts of money, under various modalities like CBT and DBT. While these approaches may offer temporary relief and aid in cognitive understanding, they fall short in discharging the deep-seated trauma stored within the limbic system. This is because our nervous system doesn't communicate through words; it communicates through sensations and feelings. It's through feeling that true healing occurs, not through mere cognitive analysis or verbal expression.

Approaches like EMDR or EFT prove to be significantly more effective, as many, including myself, have personally experienced. Following intense childhood trauma, my psyche employed a self-preservation mechanism, causing a disconnection from my body. However, it wasn't until I engaged in EMDR therapy in Hawaii that I could reunite with my complete self. The experience was profound; for the first time, I felt fully embodied, experiencing sensations like feeling my facial hair—a sensation that had eluded me for years.

Reconnecting with my body felt like emerging from a dense, unfamiliar forest into the clarity of sunlight. It was a revelation, offering newfound sight to things I had never before perceived. I vividly recall my therapist's gentle guidance after the profound reconnection: *"It's okay. Tell little Kye where you are. Show him how you got to Hawaii."* As I traced my journey on a map, recounting each step from my birth in Utah to growing up in Wyoming, then my travels across the country fighting fires, then from living in Mexico to traversing various corners of America for work. The realization struck me like a bolt of lightning: *"I'm in Hawaii? Holy crap! How did I get here?!"*

My therapist chuckled as he witnessed the process of unification unfolding before his eyes. *"Pretty cool, huh?"* he remarked. *"You did a pretty good job! Look at your body and how strong you are."* In that moment, I truly felt my body and saw myself as I hadn't in nearly two decades. A chuckle bubbled up from within me, and I laughed like a little kid, exclaiming, *"Damn, I'm like a Greek God. You did good, buddy."* Smiling ear to ear.

Whatever arises within us, no matter how uncomfortable, we must allow ourselves to feel it in order to reveal it and heal it. If we suppress it or deny it, it will persist, causing disease, disorder, and disconnection because we are not acknowledging and honoring that aspect of ourselves. Instead of pushing it away or avoiding it, we must face it head-on and say, *"Yes, I need to feel this. Yes, I need to go through this process."* Only then can we truly move forward and find healing and resolution through empowerment.

It can be uncomfortable, but the real question is, where is your mindset in all of this? How strong is your willpower?

Are you truly committed, within your faith and mindset, to heal and shift into a new perspective and reality that honors yourself and your journey? You have the power to choose your path. It's challenging to remain in a state of pain and suffering indefinitely, just as it is challenging to embark on the journey of healing and growth. However, on the other side of that journey lies hope, joy, and a renewed sense of purpose.

Many individuals seek distractions, but often become ensnared in this repetitive cycle of consumption, rather than addressing their pain and actively participating as generators, creators, and producers of life.

As we embrace the principles of holistic healing and delve into the realm of body-mind medicine, we begin by granting ourselves permission to acknowledge and honor whatever emotions arise within us, regardless of how insignificant or trivial they may seem. We never berate ourselves or gaslight our own experience. Even i f something appears inconsequential on the surface, if it stirs up an emotional reaction within us, it demands our attention. We must courageously venture into the depths of our emotional wounds, illuminating them with the light of consciousness. By doing so, we disarm their power to control our lives, freeing ourselves from their grip.

Some of you might be thinking, *"Im' different, it won't work for me.'* And for that I call BS. Yes it works, yes it is possible, because I've done it, and many people have done it because they believe it. When doctors or therapists say, *"You're not going to heal, you'll always be this way or you're never going to walk again."*

Consider if you want to fight for your limitations because if you do you'll keep them. I have seen people who are like, *"Nope, I don't believe that. I rebuke that."* And they are the very ones turning the impossible into possible, creating change and miracles in their lives.

Refuse to allow anyone else to impose a version of reality upon you that doesn't resonate with your truth. Embrace empowerment by embracing radical honesty, radical accountability, and radical truth about where you currently stand. It's crucial to acknowledge our present circumstances with compassion, recognizing that hatred breeds more hatred, greed fuels more greed, and suffering begets more suffering.

Resistance only intensifies polarity. Instead, let us approach ourselves and others with compassion, understanding that those who have caused us pain were themselves operating from a place of disconnection.

When we cultivate compassion within ourselves and extend it to others, we begin to understand that everyone is doing the best they can with the resources they have, even if those resources seem very lacking at times. It's an acknowledgment that everyone is carrying their own burdens, facing their own struggles, and navigating their own internal battles. Even those who exhibit rudeness, cruelty, or mistreat others are often projecting their own inner turmoil onto the world around them. In a reflective universe, their external actions mirror their internal state – they're treating others as they treat themselves. Recognizing this dynamic allows us to respond with empathy rather than react with anger or resentment. As we begin to realize *"Oh they're sick, they're literally spiritually sick."*

It can be ordinary for people to interpret others' behaviors as personal attacks, but in reality, it's often a reflection of the other person's inner state rather than a true reflection of ourselves if we are in our truth and noble character. As Don Miguel Ruiz teaches in his book *"The Four Agreements,"* one of these agreements is to not take things personally. When we internalize this wisdom, we understand that the way others treat us is a reflection of their own perceptions, beliefs, and emotional state, not an accurate assessment of our worth or character. We're each operating within our own worldview, and what others project onto us is merely a reflection of their own inner landscape.

Cultivating a mindset rooted in compassion, forgiveness, and gratitude shifts our perspective to embrace a higher reality guided by divine empowerment. Belief in a higher existence, the divine orchestrated by God, offers us a profound anchor amidst life's tumultuous seas. To believe that we are solitary beings adrift in the universe is a fallacy, leaving us disconnected and adrift in a sea of chaos. In the realm of resilience, faith, belief, and gratitude to our Creator become indispensable pillars, guiding us toward healing and wholeness.

When I healed from my motorcycle accident rapidly and was working out three months later, every doctor said, *"How are you doing this? This is impossible!"*

I experienced rapid healing because I made a conscious choice to embrace these very principles that I had learned from my mentors and the wisdom contained in the books I had read. Instead of succumbing to blame or self-pity, I took ownership of my situation. Yes, I was the one with alcohol in my system. Yes, I was the one involved in the motorcycle accident. And yes, I could have lost my life. However, I know that I was spared for a purpose greater than myself. I see my survival as a divine intervention, a second chance granted to me for a significant reason. My mission now is to share my testimony, to illuminate the transformative power of choosing growth over despair. Rather than dwelling in anger or self-rejection, I chose to approach my circumstances with gratitude and compassion. I embraced my reality and resolved to seize control of my life, recognizing this experience as my most profound learning opportunity yet.

A mentor of mine always said, *"We always find what we are seeking."* My response at first was, *"How do I know what I am seeking? How do I know what it is I truly believe?"* I feel many of us are unconscious of what our mind is seeking and unaware of the programs that have been silently running below the surface. We've become over taken and have had so many programs running unconsciously in our lives.

As we observe the ramifications of our flawed societal programming, it becomes evident that these issues permeate every aspect of our collective existence. Taking a moment to step back, question established norms, and cultivating an open mind unveils a reality that is both jarring and disconcerting. Once we begin to glimpse the truth and comprehend its implications, there is no turning back. Opening Pandora's box irreversibly alters our perception, forever shattering the illusion of blissful ignorance. Yet, despite the unsettling nature of this revelation, it ultimately grants us a profound sense of liberation, for true freedom can only be attained through awareness and understanding.

In this book, I offer my testimony, my truth, and the profound experiences I've undergone. I recognize that countless individuals are grappling with pain and suffering, unsure of where to seek solace or find answers. Despite their efforts, many feel trapped in a cycle of despair, with hope seemingly out of reach. Through my words, I aim to extend a beacon of hope to those who are struggling, offering guidance and inspiration gleaned from my own journey of healing and transformation.

I am driven to convey a powerful message of hope and possibility to those who may feel lost or trapped in despair. I want them to understand that beyond their current struggles lies a realm of hope, truth, and unimaginable blessings. By embracing faith and surrendering to the divine guidance of God, the architect of the universe and the source of our souls, we can embark on a transformative journey toward a life beyond our wildest dreams. It requires stepping into the unknown, allowing ourselves to be reshaped into something entirely new—something we have never envisioned—guided by the principles of compassion, forgiveness and moving forward boldly.

It ultimately leads us to tap into our ultimate power and connection within ourselves. By not allowing external influences to sway us, whether it be the world's chaos or the actions of others, we open ourselves up to receive divine guidance and connect with our inner voice. This state of receptivity allows us to align with our true essence and purpose, empowering us to navigate life with clarity and resilience.

As we embark on this inner journey and remain committed to doing the necessary work, we pave the way to manifest an existence that resonates with our highest ideals. Through unwavering honesty, raw vulnerability, and authentic truthfulness about our current state and aspirations, we open ourselves to divine guidance. By surrendering to God's wisdom and allowing it to illuminate our path, we co-create a reality that aligns harmoniously with our soul's purpose and highest aspirations.

As I gaze upon the vast landscape of not just my own nation but nations around the world, I am struck by the prevalence of suffering. I am left pondering the root causes behind the plight of countless homeless veterans and the pervasive challenges to our mental and emotional well-being. Why is it that we prioritize material possessions over genuine human connections? And how can we justify treating our fellow brothers and sisters across the globe with such disregard and indifference? These questions weigh heavily on my heart as I seek to understand the complexities of our shared human experience.

As my awareness deepened, I found myself grappling with anger as I confronted the perceived injustices and flaws in our world. Yet, I soon realized that our perception of reality is deeply personal and shaped by our individual conditioning and experiences. While we share this world with others, each of us inhabits a unique universe of thoughts, beliefs, and emotions, co-creating our reality alongside others.

What resonates as truth for us may not align with someone else's reality or framework of understanding. Our individual backgrounds, culture, upbringing, experiences, personalities, and traumas shape how we perceive ourselves and the world around us. Thus, we do not perceive the world as it is but rather through the lens of our own unique perspective and beliefs.

For instance, if we hold the belief that people are inherently bad, our perception of the world will align with this belief, shaping our experiences accordingly. This belief acts as a lens through which we interpret events and interactions. Therefore, if our focus is on seeing people as bad, it tends to manifest as a self-fulfilling prophecy.

Our minds have a remarkable ability to seek out evidence that validates our beliefs and perspectives, regardless of their accuracy due to our RAS (reticular activating system.) What we perceive as true for ourselves is often what we notice and encounter in our reality. While delving deeper into quantum mechanics is beyond the scope of this discussion, it's crucial to highlight its implications for us.

As our understanding of the universe deepens, we realize how much we have yet to uncover. At the forefront of both science and spirituality, a profound revelation emerges: everything is energy vibrating at various frequencies. This realization leads us to the paradoxical conclusion that we are simultaneously comprised of nothingness and everything.

Challenging circumstances often reveal two distinct responses: those who rise and those who fall. The outcome hinges on the orientation of our heart, mind, and focus. Closed and burdened hearts lead to sinking, while hearts anchored in faith, hope, and the divine within us propel us through turbulent seas to the shores of safety and tranquility.

While I understand the challenges inherent in this journey, I can attest that prayers, mantras, and maintaining focus on our divine connection greatly facilitates connections with supportive individuals. Our vibe attracts our tribe. If negativity pervades our environment, it's crucial to sever ties with those fostering such toxicity. Negativity spreads like wildfire if given the chance. Infecting all those it comes in contact with. All things are transient, including our troubles and, ultimately, our physical existence. Embrace the present, nurture your faith, persevere, and relinquish fear, for it corrodes the soul. Our souls endure eternally; only our earthly vessel bids farewell.

Our souls are beyond anything we've witnessed here on the physical plane. I had the privilege of participating in a ceremony for the summer solstice led by a revered Hawaiian Kahuna named atop Mauna Kea. Known as the tallest mountain on Earth from its base on the ocean floor to its summit. Mauna Kea holds profound spiritual significance and is regarded as sacred Aina or land.

As the ceremony commenced in Hilo at dawn, the golden hues of the sun illuminated the horizon, signaling the beginning of our sacred journey. We gathered to offer prayers and lay offerings at the revered Naha stone, a monumental symbol of strength and resilience, believed to have been lifted by King Kamehameha himself, showcasing his legendary power and fortitude.

As we listened to Uncle's prayers in the ancient Hawaiian language, we tenderly placed our offerings, adorned in tea leaves, upon the stone, bowing in solemn respect to Akua (God) and the sacredness of the moment. While immersed in prayer, I felt a tingling sensation, like tiny sparks of electricity coursing through my hands, igniting a profound sense of awe and anticipation. In that instant, I sensed the extraordinary significance of the day ahead, brimming with sacredness and magic.

Ascending gradually up the slopes of Mauna Kea, we ascended beyond the veil of clouds, entering a realm that felt otherworldly. The mana, or spiritual energy, of the sacred mountain, permeated the thin, pure air, electrifying each breath with its presence. Our group converged at the summit, where a stone altar, known as the Heiau, stood. With reverence, we trod the final steps to this hallowed ground, feeling the ancient whispers of the land beneath our feet.

Gathered around the stone altar, we joined our Hawaiian elder in prayer, our hearts and minds united in a collective plea to the divine. With offerings laid upon the sacred ground, we sought peace, protection, and healing for our world, our communities, and all nations.

In the midst of our prayers, a profound stillness enveloped us as if time itself had paused. Standing atop the world, bathed in the golden light of the sun, it felt as though a celestial portal had opened, enfolding us in a divine embrace of love and grace.

Following the prayers, a brother invited me to partake in a sacred ritual known as the administration of hape´. This ritual involves gently blowing ceremonial tobacco into the nasal passage to ground the individual and facilitate the emergence of inner experiences. Although non-psychedelic, it carries profound significance and has been practiced by tribes worldwide for generations. Tuning into my intuition, I received affirmation to participate and proceeded with a sense of safety and readiness.

Seated cross-legged on the ground, my heart overflowed with a sincere prayer to connect with my soul in a profound way. It may seem unconventional, but I harbored a deep desire to witness my soul beyond the confines of my physical body, to glimpse the essence of our intelligence and spirit. And in that moment, I sensed that this sacred space was the perfect setting for such an endeavor.

Moments before the administration, I gazed up at the sky and felt an overwhelming wave of love cascading down upon me. It was as if God Himself was peering down, whispering, *"Continue onward. I am proud of your resilience despite all you have endured."* Then, in an instant, the ceremonial tobacco was blown into my nasal passage, filling me with warmth and a profound sensation. While not my first experience with hape, it was the first time I encountered my soul. It defied description, unlike anything I had ever known. In that moment, it became clear: we are beings of light confined within these mortal vessels. Reclining on the sacred Mauna, I surrendered to its embrace, drifting away from my physical form.

Propelled beyond my physical confines, I soared into a realm of radiant light, beholding my soul in its full glory. Overflowing with boundless joy and love, my soul appeared expansive, a luminous presence enveloped in gold. In this transcendent state, I perceived myself as a Titan, akin to an action figure perched upon a grapefruit representing Earth. Surrounding me were the majesty of galaxies and stars, a testament to the divine creation crafted by God.

In a flash of realization, I recognized myself as pure light, pure joy, and pure love, wholly dedicated to glorifying God. Yet, amidst this divine revelation, towering demonic entities materialized, armed with savage weapons and malevolent intent. Their colossal forms swung mighty blows at my luminous being, each strike resonating with the force of a supernova's explosion. Despite their onslaught, a revelation emerged from their infernal whispers: *"We can't touch him... he's directly connected to God!"* In response, I erupted into laughter, unleashing a defiant proclamation: *"You cannot lay a hand on me! I am directly linked to God, blessed by the creator of heavens and cosmos, Alpha and the Omega, Lord of the skies!"* With a surge of golden radiance akin to a nuclear blast, I returned swiftly to my earthly vessel atop the sacred mountain.

Following my profound encounter on the sacred Mauna, I came to a pivotal realization. For so long, I had sought a soulmate externally, yearning for a profound connection and partnership. Yet, in that transformative moment, I understood that true completeness lies within myself, in my connection with the divine. No external individual could ever fill that role. Thus, I recognized that my foremost relationship is with the divine and myself—a foundation for genuine empowerment and soul-level healing.

In the wake of this profound revelation, I gained a deep understanding of our inherent magnificence and power as individual souls intricately connected to God, our creator. It became clear to me that God has endowed us with everything we need and bestowed upon us immense powers to navigate our earthly existence. Yet, there exists a concerted effort to conceal the truth of our profound connection and inherent power.

In truth, this realization strikes fear into those who oppose it, for when we awaken to our ultimate truths and unite with God within us, we become unstoppable. We embrace our rightful roles as heirs to His Kingdom and wield His authority through Christ on Earth.

Wherever you find yourself on your journey—striving for better health, seeking healing from challenges, or grappling with trauma—remember: Anything is possible! Miracles have unfolded in my life repeatedly, defying limitations. Never confine God or your circumstances to predetermined boundaries or put cosmic and infinite intelligence into a box. Don't accept limitations imposed by others; as Jim Quick says, *'If you fight for your limitations, you get to keep them.''* With even the tiniest bit of faith, like a mustard seed, coupled with the right mindset, prayers, mantras, and positive affirmations—declaring with all your heart, mind, and soul—anything becomes possible. Stay positive, remain grateful, keep your spirits high, and forge ahead with boldness!

"Setting boundaries is an act of self-love, not selfishness." - Unknown

Chapter 10: Boundaries and Self Value

Tragically, many of us navigate through life without mastering the art of establishing and maintaining healthy boundaries, articulating our core values, and respecting our own worth. This seemingly straightforward yet profoundly impactful skill often eludes us, leading to a cascade of chaos, scarcity, and disconnection in our lives. The very root of self-sabotage, toxic relationships, and detrimental coping mechanisms can often be traced back to our inability to effectively communicate our needs and hold firm boundaries. Whether due to a lack of understanding, societal conditioning, or past experiences, we find ourselves mired in patterns of behavior that perpetuate pain and suffering. Both with ourselves and others.

Perhaps we were never taught how to assert ourselves confidently and assertively, or maybe our upbringing stifled our ability to recognize and honor our intrinsic needs and values. Regardless of the cause, the consequences are stark:

fractured relationships, unfulfilling partnerships, and a pervasive sense of discontentment.

Yet, within this realization lies a glimmer of hope—a recognition that true transformation begins with acknowledging our limitations and committing to cultivating healthier patterns of interaction. By embracing the power of assertive communication and self-advocacy, we can rewrite the script of our lives, forging connections based on mutual respect and understanding.

As we embark on this journey of self-discovery and empowerment, let us remember that our worth is non-negotiable, and our boundaries are sacred. By honoring ourselves with compassion and authenticity, we pave the way for a future defined by harmony, abundance, and genuine connection.

In my experience, the core issue lies in a lack of self-love and self-worth. We often seek external validation at the cost of neglecting our own intrinsic value, leading to unnecessary suffering. Recognizing this pattern enabled me to understand one origin of my hardships.

First off, we need to understand what a boundary is, how it functions, and how we can effectively utilize this to maintain healthy relationships with ourselves and others in our lives.

As we establish healthy boundaries, we unlock a newfound sense of personal power, value, and self-esteem. Through this process of boundary-setting with ourselves, society, and the world, we cultivate greater confidence and connection. By valuing, affirming, and esteeming ourselves in a healthy manner, we can fully express our authenticity and sovereignty, leading to a more fulfilling life. We choose to disengage from anything that does not align with our values or contribute to our sense of meaning and importance.

In essence, personal boundaries are the internal limits and guidelines we establish within relationships, reflecting our core beliefs. Those with healthy boundaries have the ability to assertively say "no" when necessary while also welcoming intimacy in compatible relationships aligned with their values. Individuals with high levels of self-love and self-esteem maintain healthy boundaries that filter out anything incongruent with their personal values and worth.

Crucially, it's essential to understand how to protect ourselves and preserve our energy when our boundaries are consistently violated, as well as what actions to undertake.

Consider this example: We've all encountered individuals who seem to have perpetual conflicts with others, constantly attributing blame to external factors. They often feel unappreciated, undervalued, and misunderstood, projecting negativity. Typically, these individuals struggle to establish and maintain healthy boundaries, both with others and themselves. They habitually say *"yes"* without considering their own values or needs, making them susceptible to being taken advantage of by others who exploit this vulnerability, whether consciously or not.

Often overlooked is the fact that our internal boundaries, rules, and agreements shape our belief systems, and conversely, our beliefs influence how we establish boundaries. This internal framework serves as a guide for how we permit self-treatment and allow others to treat us. What's crucial to recognize is that we are consistently the common denominator in our experiences, yet we may fail to acknowledge this. Projection onto others often stems from a deficiency in understanding how to value ourselves, uphold self-esteem, and establish healthy boundaries—a shortfall rooted in a lack of self-love and self-worth.

Many times, people are not taught the skills in a healthy family or cultural environment while they are younger, creating a vicious cycle of victimhood, unaccountability, and toxicity within the environment.

Until we grasp the importance of setting boundaries, we will likely encounter ongoing issues, feeling undervalued, misunderstood, and neglected, particularly by ourselves. If you find yourself in this situation, know that it's alright—I empathize. I've faced similar struggles countless times, permitting both others and myself to disregard my boundaries repeatedly. This pattern only led to unnecessary resentment, hardships, and pain.

At times, we may have lacked the chance to assert, *"This is not for me. I won't allow this in my life. I refuse to be treated this way. These are not my values."* Particularly in familial, educational, or religious contexts where choices were limited during our formative years.

Many of us have not had the opportunity to learn how to navigate ourselves and the world due to past or ongoing chaos. It has become our accepted reality, though it is far from normal. It's not normal to exist in a state of anxiety and depression, unable to articulate our needs or establish boundaries. It's not normal to feel fearful of expressing ourselves or advocating for our values and needs.

It's challenging to acknowledge that sometimes we inadvertently contribute to or permit problems by failing to maintain healthy boundaries. We endure hurt, wounds, and trauma simply because we weren't aware of what we didn't know. We subject ourselves to these hardships because we weren't taught otherwise. That's why I'm sharing this insight— to help us learn and grow from our experiences.

Clear communication is paramount, and many interpersonal conflicts stem from a lack of defined boundaries and miscommunication. When individuals encounter issues with others, it often traces back to unclear or unestablished boundaries from the outset of the communication process.

An exemplary illustration of a healthy boundary within the family might sound like this: *"Dad, I want to let you know about a boundary I'm setting. I prefer not to discuss political, religious, or spiritual topics with you as they tend to cause conflict between us. I love you and value our relationship, which is why I'm establishing this boundary. If it's crossed repeatedly, we may need to take a break from communicating for a period of time."*

When individuals disregard the boundaries you've set, it indicates a lack of respect for your values and boundaries.

Consequences for boundary violations are necessary. Holding boundaries within the family unit can be challenging because it's what we're accustomed to—it's where we grew up, and these are our blood relatives. Until we gain awareness, we often perceive unhealthy family dynamics as normal. Some may not realize they're born into toxic environments, mistaking dysfunction for love. However, recognizing this reality is essential for breaking free from harmful patterns.

It's a harsh reality to accept that we were born into imperfect families and societies where, despite their best efforts, we may have been left wounded and broken. However, it's crucial to remember that they did the best they could with what they had. Remembering involves recollecting the parts of ourselves that have been overlooked or suppressed, integrating them to achieve wholeness once more.

While life-altering experiences and traumatic events can lead to complex trauma, entwining us in unconscious patterns and coping mechanisms. Unraveling these patterns takes time and effort. The key, learned from personal experience, is to be patient and compassionate with yourself throughout the journey. It's uncomfortable initially, but with practice, we learn to regulate our emotions, connect with ourselves, and find calmness. Over time, we adapt, becoming more resilient and grounded in the process.

Reconnecting with parts of ourselves that we've closed off due to trauma involves deeply honoring our bodily sensations. It's a process of learning to regulate by focusing on the breath and the body. By anchoring ourselves in the present moment through grounding and focused breathing, we discharge the bound-up energy, which can manifest as inflammation and disease in the body left unchecked and unacknowledged.

So, get ready for a wild ride because this journey is yours and yours alone. No one else can walk this path with you —it's uniquely yours. If you've felt the stirring of something greater, something that fills you with both fear and excitement, then the time to answer the call is now. It may seem daunting, even impossible, but deep down, you know it's your destiny, your passion, your mission, your gift. Embrace the intrigue and allure of what lies ahead.

All because a question slips into our mind. What if? What if I let go, what if I trusted, what if I stop fighting and blaming and running? What if I just surrendered? What if I healed and I was able to achieve this and follow my dreams? A few of the most powerful words, *"What if?"*

As we embark on the journey toward our highest destiny and follow our hearts, the universe will test us to gauge our commitment. It challenges us to let go of hurt, forgive, surrender to the unknown path and move forward. What are we willing to sacrifice for what we truly believe in? If we cling to our limitations, we perpetuate them. So, ask yourself honestly: *What are you fighting for?*

When I left the mainland of the US, I was willing to fight for a new life. I left everyone and everything I'd ever known. Coming to an entirely new place without ever being here once. Upon arriving on the Island, I didn't have a vehicle for quite sometime and was in a very remote part. For nearly two years I was hitch hiking, riding my bike, taking the bus and friends loaning me their cars when it was an option as I couldn't even buy a vehicle because of my credit from bankruptcy and losing everything.

It was so uncomfortable but God was teaching me a valuable lesson to learn how to completely and entirely trust him and the plan. I told him, *"Dude this sucks! Ive always done what I wanted and gone where I wanted! I feel like a little kid."*

His response was, *"Goooood, you are learning how to trust me and my plans, not your plans."*

It forced me to be with myself in the jungle and made me feel like I was going insane. After running for years I was forced to sit and be still and it was the most uncomfortable thing as I hadn't ever really done it. I'd spent afternoons crying and yelling re-establishing this connection with myself that had been severed from years intense fire operations, drinking, drugs and abuse.

Years as a fire fighter and experiencing such a tumultuous upbringing warped my system. Much like individuals in high-stress roles, such as emergency services personnel, firefighters, police officers, EMS, and military members, that face significant challenges. Their bodies endure a constant barrage of stress hormones and chemicals, leading to damage not only to their mental and emotional well-being but also to their physical health over time. Operating in a perpetual fight/flight/freeze response mode, their autonomic nervous system (ANS) undergoes adaptations, altering the brain's neurochemical thresholds to cope with internal and external stressors. This results in a heightened sensitivity, requiring a more intense stimulus to evoke a response compared to before or numbing out because of the intense nervous system arousal.

Once this cycle begins, the brain-body connection seeks to replicate the same level of chemical response it initially experienced. Consequently, we may turn to various substances or behaviors to numb ourselves from the extreme discomfort or seek dopamine and adrenaline rushes. This can manifest as turning to alcohol, drugs, food, pornography, sex, gambling, or shopping—anything to distract or numb ourselves and bridge the gap caused by the altered baseline. Addiction often precedes trauma stemming from the disconnect within our system. To heal, we must learn to reconnect with ourselves.

The cycle of addiction is progressive and insidious. Over time, we find ourselves needing more and more to cope as our body becomes increasingly dependent on chemicals and habits. This dependence leads to a deeper disconnection from our true selves, dimming the vibrant essence of life that we are meant to embody and operate from. Extinguishing the brilliant sparks of life that we once were.

As trauma expert Dr. Gabor Maté emphasizes, the significance of an event is determined solely by the individual who experiences it. What one person perceives as traumatic may not resonate as such for another. Our perceptions, thoughts, and ways of operating vary greatly, making the experience entirely subjective. Thus, our journey of reintegration is uniquely ours, requiring acceptance of all aspects of ourselves and the cultivation of a relationship with our nervous system.

Once we tap into the present moment, it's essential to honor exactly where we are, as we cannot exist anywhere else but in the now. This encompasses all aspects of our experiences, habits, attitudes, and behaviors accumulated throughout our lives—the good, the bad, and the ugly. The transformative shift occurs when we embrace complete and radical acceptance coupled with radical responsibility. While challenging, this choice is far preferable to remaining trapped in limiting patterns, perpetuating unresolved trauma, and living disconnected from life and ourselves—a truly detrimental state. So, ultimately, we must choose our path, recognizing that both options present their own challenges.

To live a more authentic, enriched, and empowered life, we must examine our reactions, responses, and behaviors across all levels. This mindset fosters growth, expansion, and forgiveness. We release the tethers to our past and anxieties about the future, embracing the present moment fully. By embodying the now and basking in the golden rays of gratitude, we illuminate a path toward a bright and empowered future.

Experiencing challenging events like mental, emotional, physical, or sexual trauma, particularly during our formative years, can inflict profound damage and alter our brain, behavior, and self-perception. Healing from such trauma involves a process of unlearning and reprogramming ourselves, striving to return to a state of wholeness. By holding space within our hearts, minds, and bodies, we create an opportunity to acknowledge and feel our emotions fully, thereby fostering coherence among all aspects of ourselves.

As humans, we often resort to various distractions to avoid confronting our inner thoughts, memories, feelings, and emotions. But consider this: WHAT IF... you dared to sit with those emotions, allowing them to surface and be acknowledged? WHAT IF... you chose not to numb yourself with substances or escapism but instead sat with yourself and focused on slow, deep breathing, perhaps incorporating techniques like Emotional Freedom Technique (EFT)? The result could be revolutionary—a breakthrough beyond the thresholds we've been avoiding through distraction.

We are the sum of our collective experiences up to this point, and every experience—both negative and positive—has shaped us into who we are today. Remarkably, you are your own hero in this journey! You are uniquely equipped to handle and navigate through everything you've encountered because it's all a part of you. You're the sole caretaker of your own journey. Are you beginning to grasp the magnitude of this realization?

Many of us lack the coping mechanisms and skills needed to effectively navigate trauma and stress, especially when we are younger. During our formative years, we are particularly susceptible to the influences of our environment. But now is the moment to embrace healing, empowerment, and illumination! Our world is in need, and so are we. It's time to rise up and shine brightly!

If you've endured such experiences, whether in your youth, like myself, or at any point in life, I want you to know this, you are not broken. Although it may feel that way, we must accept that nothing is inherently wrong with us.

I understand it may be difficult to comprehend, but truly, nothing is wrong with you. What you're experiencing is a natural response to the events you've endured—a result of the aftermath of those experiences. Such reactions are common in response to trauma; it's not personal. It's directly related to the events themselves. So, here's the good news: You are not broken. You're simply misaligned and in need of recalibration.

So, find a mirror, gaze deeply into your own eyes, and affirm, "*I'm not broken. It's a normal response, and my body knows how to heal. I can and will make it through this! I love you, you sexy mother trucker!*" Seriously though, breathe that in! It's normal. The things we do to regulate and cope, even though they seem "counter-intuitive or bad," are normal responses. So be easy on yourself. You are learning how to navigate this complex world of internal existence while operating in the 3D material world.

When I first grasped this concept, everything fell into place. I thought, *"Oh, I understand now. It's normal. I'm not broken, nor do I need fixing. I simply need to allow my biology to run its course."* Trauma occurs when we're unable to release the energy from it in a healthy manner. The energy becomes trapped in the limbic system, the part of the brain responsible for our behavioral and emotional responses, particularly those crucial for survival.

So, when the energy within our physiological biology cannot complete its natural cycle, we become ensnared in a continuous cycle of sympathetic nervous system arousal. This perpetual state prevents the completion of the cycle, leading to lasting damage from the ongoing effects.

It's when our biology transitions into pathology. We become trapped within the limbic system, where the fight-or-flight response remains perpetually activated, leading to significant breakdowns over time. Our bodies fail to distinguish between events that occurred recently and those from decades ago. When trauma remains unprocessed, our bodies perceive ongoing threats stored in memory and emotional centers like the hippocampus and amygdala of the limbic system, prompting a constant state of protection.

We can draw valuable insights from our animal counterparts, as explored in Peter Levine's book "Waking the Tiger." Consider the example of a bird: after crashing into a window and possibly being knocked unconscious, its brain shuts down temporarily. When it regains consciousness, it shakes itself off and often flies away unscathed. This shaking is crucial; it allows the bird's biology to complete the cycle and reset to a healthy baseline. Unlike humans, the bird's experience doesn't become pathological because it lacks the neocortex's tendency to overthink and become stuck. Instead, it flies off to live another day.

Experiencing guilt and shame following a painful event or trauma is a common reaction and can manifest in various behaviors. I understand this firsthand—I spent years feeling worthless, inadequate, and burdened by the weight of the world. These feelings stemmed from unresolved trauma, compounded by a lack of awareness of its presence and how to address it. Consequently, I struggled to value myself, set healthy boundaries, and communicate effectively in my life.

Time and again, I found myself entangled in relationships—with people, substances, lovers, or businesses—that weren't conducive to my well-being. If only I had possessed the ability to say no, to value myself, and to establish healthy boundaries at that time, the journey would have been much smoother and gentler. Yet, in retrospect, without those struggles, I wouldn't be The Miracle Man writing this book today. So, it all balances out. You're welcome—I've done the heavy lifting to share these insights now. The key not only lies in you taking action, but in maintaining faith and hope, keeping the spark alive within our hearts. We must embrace the notion that God has a brilliant plan if we trust and allow it to unfold, courageously stepping into the unknown, one foot in front of the other.

How can we blame ourselves for what we didn't know at the time? We were simply doing the best we could with the tools and knowledge available to us, even if that meant enduring some tough experiences. But growth requires awareness, and we can't grow if we don't acknowledge what we don't know. That's why it's crucial to cultivate a relationship with ourselves, expanding our consciousness into our bodies and reconnecting with the present moment through the breath. By returning home within ourselves, we can witness and hold space for whatever unfolds, as I've emphasized numerous times before.

As mentioned previously, our world operates on a cognitive reward system from the moment we enter it. It's a performance-based society where rewards are granted for performance and withheld otherwise. However, this system contradicts the workings of our nervous system, which are both advanced and straightforward. Fundamentally, our nervous systems crave acknowledgment, validation, connection, love, and respect.

If our emotions stem from the seat of our fight/flight/ freeze response, it stands to reason that embracing what is alive within us is the most logical approach. This entails seeing, feeling, and holding whatever needs to be witnessed, allowing it to process naturally. Without judgments or criticisms, we simply hold space for what needs to be held—no fixing or fault-finding, just honoring the visceral experiences we've encountered.

This is how people, events, or situations can exert control over us—when we become entangled in emotional reactions to external or internal stimuli. For example, if someone directs negativity or rudeness toward us, they seek to emotionally hook us, enabling them to feed us their negativity. If they can provoke an emotional response or investment from us, they feel victorious. That's why it's crucial not to take anything personally.

We often believe we can rationalize our way out of pain or trauma, using our cognitive minds to strategize, conceptualize, theorize, or analyze philosophically in search of a solution. However, this approach doesn't align with the workings of the nervous system, which is rooted in feelings and sensations. Therefore, to effectively address our nervous system, we must engage in a relationship grounded in feeling and reconnect with it on that level.

One of my cherished soul sisters, Sandra, who has been an immense source of support beyond measure, shared words with me that will forever resonate. She's a wise medicine woman with a radiant soul, and I'm honored to pass on her wisdom to you. During a moment of deep emotional processing regarding my past experiences with my ex-wife and my time in Mexico, Sandra held space for me with profound insight. She said, *"We have to feel it to heal it. We can't heal what we don't feel."* Those words struck me like lightning. Suddenly, I realized I had been avoiding feeling my emotions for far too long. Accepting this truth, I committed to sitting with my discomfort, embracing the growth that awaited me, no matter how uncomfortable it might be.

When we endure trauma, it fractures parts of our being. Our mind latches onto a distorted version of ourselves, shaped by the trauma we've experienced. This creates a separation from our true essence, our highest self, the purest manifestation of our existence. It's an unconscious attachment to a skewed perception rooted in false information. To undo this distortion, we initiate the process of healing by releasing stored trauma through somatic experiencing, reconnecting with our felt senses and bodily sensations and challenging the false paradigm.

The remarkable truth is that I firmly believe in our capacity to change, heal, and evolve, even in the face of adversity—an experience I've undergone personally. With the right tools and techniques, alongside lifestyle adjustments and protocols outlined in my coursework, our bodies demonstrate an astounding ability to regenerate and rejuvenate. Just like a miraculous spaceship, our bodies possess innate healing capabilities; while sometimes they require assistance, the healing process unfolds naturally. By reconnecting with our natural roots, we empower ourselves and align more deeply within.

At a certain juncture in our journey, we must acknowledge our sovereignty and reclaim authority over our lives. It's about embracing the power of our own free will, choices, and beliefs, aligning them with our inner truth. Instead of seeking validation or affirmation externally, we must look within ourselves. This empowers us to live authentically and purposefully, not just for our own fulfillment but also in service to others.

We've imposed limitations on ourselves for far too long. We've been inundated with falsehoods, distorted narratives, and divisive ideologies. These lies perpetuate notions of separation and division, driven by manipulated cultural narratives, cultural Marxism, and hedonistic materialism. Consequently, we've allowed false beliefs, societal conditioning, labels, and judgments to dictate our lives.

Attaining wholeness and connecting with the divine is the ultimate treasure, the purest gold. When we achieve this level of sovereignty and inner autonomy, we no longer rely on external sources for validation or fulfillment. We are whole and complete within ourselves, fully engaged and grateful for life. Our acts of giving stem from an overflow of gratitude, love, and joy within us, not from a place of seeking validation or completion from others.

Relying on others' approval or love rather than affirming ourselves and our own needs traps us in a cycle of dependency on external validation. When we live for praise, we die to criticism. While it's undoubtedly beneficial to have supportive people in our lives, it's essential to esteem our own identity, establish healthy boundaries and engage in conscious communication. Valuing ourselves and the divine above all else ensures that our relationships are built on a foundation of self-respect and authenticity.

Craving validation from family, friends, associates, or romantic partners can lead to eventual pain. When we rely on others to fulfill our needs, we become vulnerable to manipulation and control. Dependency on external validation stems from a sense of lack rather than wholeness, making us susceptible to being controlled by our desires.

Embracing an empowered life on our own terms is infinitely more fulfilling. It invites adventure, romance, success, joy, and peace to flourish. This journey begins when we empower ourselves, becoming deeply present, aware, and conscious of our values and boundaries. Through this heightened awareness, we navigate life authentically, crafting experiences that align with our true selves and manifesting the best outcomes for ourselves.

It's a profound shift when you transition from pain, sorrow, depression, and anxiety to a state of gratitude and happiness. After enduring suffering for so long, waking up one day to feelings of appreciation, love, and care is truly transformative. It marks the beginning of healing—a beautiful journey that I deeply cherish. Having experienced my own struggles, I'm committed to supporting others to prevent them from enduring similar hardships if I can help them.

As we begin to honor ourselves and embrace our authenticity, we naturally cultivate a deeper sense of self-worth and confidence. This process strengthens our values and belief systems, enriching our lives and enhancing our overall sense of value and empowerment.

As we recognize and embrace our own value and worth, aligning it with our skills, training, and offerings, we naturally elevate our value. This newfound self-awareness leads us to become more discerning in our interactions and choices. Deepening our understanding of our true essence, we tap into the profound uniqueness of our spirit and soul, recognizing its rarity and significance. A soul with a unique blueprint and energy.

Empowered connection is the right direction a mentor would say to me. It's about how we connect and engage and learn and feel. Just ensure you are connecting to that which is empowering, uplifting, and not draining and life-sucking.

For the longest time, I couldn't grasp why someone would endure a toxic relationship. In college, I'd hear stories of girls staying with abusive partners, and I'd think, *"Just leave him, dump his ass."* It seemed so straightforward until I found myself in an intensely toxic relationship. Amid the chaos of 2020, I crossed paths with a woman in the Miss America Pageant circuit, connected to influential business figures. Ignoring numerous red flags, I fell into the trap, buoyed by my ego. In reality, it turned into a tumultuous ordeal; she struggled with significant mental and emotional issues hidden beneath a composed exterior. On the outside, she appeared fine and composed, but behind closed doors, she was very wounded.

In the simplest terms, it was a complete shit show. Despite knowing it was extremely unhealthy and wrong, I found myself still entrenched in the relationship. All because I didn't hold healthy boundaries and was sucked into sexual pleasure. Reflecting on those events, I recognized it mirrored the trauma cycle from my youth, with my mother's yelling, screaming, and gaslighting. Eventually, I came to understand she was a narcissist, a realization not made lightly or as a trend. Those who've truly experienced it can empathize. Recovery took time and intensive therapy due to the profound damage inflicted.

People even noticed how off I was and affected by it, my fire chief even said, *"What's wrong with Kye? What happened to him?"*

After years of learning and spiritual growth, I came to understand that being an empath often draws narcissists, and that's precisely what occurred. Unresolved childhood dynamics with my mother left parts of me disempowered, making me susceptible to repeating the pattern. While it's uncomfortable to acknowledge, it's a dynamic that plays out frequently.

We will find ourselves in similar situations until we grasp the lessons they offer and transform accordingly. It's crucial not to let these experiences dictate or manipulate us; instead, we must opt for a higher path. Acknowledging our role in these situations and taking responsibility is part of the journey. Though challenging, it's also incredibly empowering. Following such an experience, I embarked on a profound journey of self-discovery and gained a deeper understanding of myself.

Indeed, the narcissist and empath represent two contrasting aspects of the same spectrum. While narcissists seek to fulfill their needs by manipulating their external surroundings through domination and control, empaths tend to manipulate the internal state of others, often at their own expense. Empaths often immerse themselves in the emotions and interactions of others, striving to save or fix them. This dynamic often results in the empath assuming the role of the victim while the narcissist adopts that of the aggressor.

Always remember, appearances can be deceiving. While someone may seem well put together externally, it's crucial to look beyond surface impressions and observe their actions and behavior. True insight into someone's internal landscape comes from understanding their actions and how they treat others rather than relying solely on their appearance or words.

As you embark on the journey of implementing these principles into your life, prepare yourself for transformative shifts. Begin today by honoring your worth, respecting your time, and embracing the uniqueness of your soul. Have the courage to release anything that no longer serves your highest good. While this path may present challenges, the liberation and tranquility awaiting you on the other side transcend your current comprehension. Embrace this profound journey with an open heart, knowing that the rewards are nothing short of miraculous.

"Miracles happen every day, change your perception of what a miracle is and you'll see them all around you." - Jon Bon Jovi

Chapter 11: Miracle Flow

Gaze upon the world with a renewed perspective, and you'll witness the intricate dance of nature unfolding effortlessly. From the ebb and flow of the tides to the rhythm of the changing seasons, every aspect of the natural world follows a divine blueprint. In every blade of grass, every towering tree, and every creature that roams the earth, there lies an innate wisdom guiding their existence. Take a closer look, and you'll realize that everything in the universe pulsates with life, both around us and within us. We are intricately intertwined with the cosmos, each of us a vital thread in the fabric of existence.

Often, we overlook life's magic as we hustle through our days, consumed by tasks and obligations. We become human doings rather than human beings, disconnected from the divine flow of the universe. God seeks to work through us, yet we find ourselves disconnected, distracted and entangled in struggles, both external and internal. We force and grind our way through life, missing the truth of our divine origin. Instead, we cling to artificiality and superficiality, surrounded by fake food, news, culture, and relationships. In moments of calm reflection, we sense that something vital is missing amidst the facade—a yearning for a deeper, more authentic connection beyond the superficialities of our environment.

It begs the question, *"Why do we as humans love to be in and amongst nature? How is it that a golden sunset and bright morning sunrise evoke such peace and serenity within us as we pause and admire the vastness of the world?"*

Because it's our origin. Our lineage traces back to tribal ancestors who thrived in harmony with nature. Today's sprawling metropolises, with their concrete jungles and artificial surroundings, are a departure from our natural heritage. We've paved over paradise, replacing it with soulless structures and artificial light. In doing so, we've severed our connection to the natural world, isolating ourselves in oversized homes and cubicles. Despite our apparent *"connectivity,"* we've become deeply disconnected from ourselves, our hearts, and our global community. We've unwittingly woven ourselves into an artificial matrix, straying far from the flow of the natural universe.

Hence, to forge a brighter future for generations to come—one marked by safety, freedom, and peace—we must acknowledge the unnatural aspects of our current world. The agents of chaos that are thriving from our division and dismay. Many of our societal norms and materialistic pursuits are profoundly abnormal. We've allowed ourselves to be ensnared in a culture of separation, greed, and the prioritization of possessions over human connections. Unaware of the spiritual conflict unfolding around us, we've been led astray by diversion and demoralization. Completely unplugged from our ancestors and the magnificent feats from the ages past that were accomplished and laid down for us to move forward.

Many are unaware that Earth serves as the ultimate training ground for our souls and spirits to evolve. As the universe expands, so does our consciousness and the evolution of our souls. Life embodies both growth and decay, symbolized by the eternal battle between yin and yang, light and dark. If we seek true freedom, peace, and prosperity for ourselves and others, it's imperative to reconnect with the flow of our lives within our own hearts and allow our souls wisdom to come forth bravely.

Having experienced it firsthand, I understand how we become entangled in the false belief that external possessions will bring happiness. Society reinforces this notion, as it conveniently aligns with its agenda. However, true joy and happiness are never found in external acquisitions. Why though? Because they originate from outside of ourselves and it's always an inside job.

Similarly, our thoughts, feelings, and emotions serve as signals that interact with the external universe. Within our bodies lies an internal universe containing the intelligence of the world as our bodies are born from the earth. We are interconnected with everything because we are a part of everything. Our universe operates based on our belief system, which encompasses our thoughts, feelings, and emotions, shaping our experience of the world.

Likewise, those who are experiencing disconnection, separation, and pain are the ones who need love the most. As humans, we are inherently designed for genuine and authentic connection. The crucial step is to reconnect with our own internal universe, allowing ourselves to become whole and empowered from within.

Likewise, we have the capacity to evolve and thrive through the challenges we face, should we decide to do so. We can transform our struggles and pain into victories if we make the choice. It's about embracing an attitude that declares, *"Despite the hardships I've endured, I opt for a better life. I commit to investing more energy into growth. I believe in a supportive God that aligns the universe with my highest aspirations and self-realization."*

Similarly, this understanding offers us an endless array of parallel realities, boundless options, and limitless opportunities for transformation. It hinges on our perception of life and our proactive engagement with the universe, shaping our reality through the choices we make.

Similarly, I've discovered it profoundly rewarding to approach life as if we're surfing its waves. Attempting to battle the ocean inevitably leads to defeat, as the ocean always prevails. Conversely, passively waiting for the tide to change only results in being overwhelmed. However, when we master the art of surfing life's waves and move harmoniously with its rhythms, we can enter a state of profound harmony, joy, and fulfillment. Life isn't working against us; it's working for us. We've simply forgotten how to engage in the dance.

In the aftermath of riding a wave, we often reflect, feeling a sense of exhilaration and accomplishment. Yet, as any surfer can attest, there are times when we're wiped out by the waves. It's part of the experience. However, some individuals choose to retreat from surfing altogether after a painful wipeout. They opt to sit on the sidelines, watching life pass them by, filling their days with material possessions and distractions, falsely believing they're truly living. In reality, they're being consumed by life, mere spectators rather than active participants in their own journey.

So, the pivotal question remains: Will you rise again to ride the wave? Will you mount the horse once more? Will you dare to believe and hope again? Will you step boldly into your greatest potential? Can you muster hope and faith once more? Are you willing to declare, *"Not today! Today, I choose a different path! I'm done with this garbage mindset. I deserve better, I can achieve better, and I will be better!"*

If we fail to make a decisive choice, others will make it for us—our family, friends, lovers, institutions, religion, or even, God forbid, the government. Thus, life slips through our fingers as we grow older, bitter, and filled with regret. The greatest betrayal is to squander the gift of life unopened.

Imagine for a moment returning to where we come from, and God, creator, All-father, says, *"Wow...you were given this divine gift of life, A life designed just for you, and you return the gift completely wrapped! You didn't even open it! You left your dreams, hopes, and everything on the sideline!*

You disconnected from the kid within your heart and became bitter, cold and scared! What a waste!"

Truthfully, I believe we are all children within our hearts, solely pretending to be adults in big costumes. Reconnecting with our inner child teaches us how to play, enjoy life, laugh, and not take everything so personally or seriously. In order to achieve this state, though, we have to step into the unknown, surrender to the flow of the divine, and let go of all that we have been conditioned with. As it says in (Matthew 18:1-3) *"Truly, I say to you, unless you turn and become like children, you will never enter the kingdom of heaven."*

If we yearn for a brighter life and a transformed world, we must venture into uncharted waters where we've never ventured before. It might feel daunting, but you know what's even scarier? Remaining stagnant, rooted in the same place throughout your life—never exploring, never experiencing, never loving, and never creating. Just existing as a mere consumer is draining rather than contributing. That's the true terror. To live out an entire existence without truly living it. Indeed, the richest repository in the world is the cemetery, brimming with unrealized dreams, untold stories, and unshared gifts—buried out of fear and hesitation.

As emphasized earlier, our individual missions, talents, and perspectives are uniquely ours. It is incumbent upon us to uncover how we can best serve others by sharing our authentic selves and enhancing our own value, thereby enriching the lives of those around us and the world at large. Cultivating inner fulfillment necessitates delving into the unknown—the void we've explored in depth in preceding chapters. Undoubtedly, growth, expansion, and learning demand effort. It's a challenging journey, yet the rewards far surpass anything we could have imagined otherwise.

If you find yourself going through hell, keep moving forward until you reach heaven. During my recovery from the motorcycle accident, I was determined: *'This is not where I'll remain. I refuse to let this dictate my destiny. This too shall pass.'*

Yes, I made a mistake. I messed up. But I didn't let it define me. Instead, I turned it into my greatest learning opportunity. That's why I'm sharing the lessons I've learned with others. If we could just trust, even for a moment, that despite all the chaos, God and the universe are benevolent and guiding us toward individual and collective growth, we might find the healing medicine we need.

While effort is undoubtedly necessary, it must be directed intelligently to yield benefits. Otherwise, we risk expending energy in futile endeavors, remaining stuck where we shouldn't be. It's essential to take a step back, assess the situation, and ask ourselves: *'How can I implement just a 1% change to improve? How can I show more compassion to myself and others? How can I open myself to love, courage, bravery, and gratitude?'* Gratitude, in particular, holds immense power, leaving no room for anger, fear, judgment, criticism, or unrealistic expectations – the very prisons that confine us within our minds and relationships.

The solution lies in letting go and embracing a more elevated perspective, recognizing the interconnectedness of all existence. Every action ripples out, influencing the whole and shaping a world unlike any before. Despite our differences, we all share this planet. It's about navigating life with the knowledge we've acquired and striving to do better.

At times, life can be deeply heartbreaking and soul-wrenching. Yet, when we lean in, trust, and combine faith and hope with action, transformations occur. What if you meet the love of your life? What if you start that business? What if you write that book? What if you fully show up? It's when we tap into our creative potential and exert effort that we begin to encounter truly magical and indescribable experiences.

Recently, I've been practicing a meditation prayer inspired by the notion that God loves to bless us abundantly. I put this belief to the test by expressing gratitude daily for everything I have and creating a gratitude list. Then, I say, *'Grant me the eyes to see, the ears to hear, and the heart to feel your presence. Show me how loved, blessed, and anointed my life is so that I may freely share what I receive!'* Remarkably, things started to shift as I consistently transmitted these words, feelings, and emotions to the universe and to God in my prayer and meditation. It's a powerful reminder that He listens, and the universe listens, just as our cells listen.

Every aspect of existence carries a spirit and energy. By aligning with the positive energy within ourselves, connecting with God, and fostering an empowered, grounded, and grateful state, we start to witness the outcomes of these states. Some term it magic; others label it miracles or manifestation. Regardless, it's the result of allowing ourselves to perceive, hear, see, and experience something beyond our present reality, thereby paving the way for its manifestation in our lives.

Imagine how liberating it would be to fully embrace self-love and forgive yourself completely for any perceived shortcomings or past mistakes. Extending that forgiveness to others as well and making a sincere commitment today to embark on a new journey forward. Letting go of the burdens of the past – the criticisms, unmet expectations, and pain – and invite God wholeheartedly into your heart, mind, and soul.

It's within reach, and the path is surprisingly simple. While it may not be easy, it's straightforward if you open yourself up completely. Place your hand over your heart and speak from your soul, saying, *'God, I ask for forgiveness. I love you, I thank you and I'm sorry. I acknowledge my shortcomings, my moments of anger and bitterness. Today, I choose to turn the tide in my life.'* Do this for 21 days and watch what happens. Because if not now, then when? If not you, then who? Today holds the potential for miracles, but only if you're willing to embrace them. Today marks the opportunity for profound change if you simply allow it. Let go of the burdens you've carried for so long.

Why persist in the same cycle of suffering year after year? Enduring the same pain, the same sorrow, and the same stagnant situations—how can that be called living? It's not life;

it's suffering. You were meant for more than mere survival; you were born to thrive.

Imagine waking up and realizing that today is your last day on Earth. Just 24 hours, and then it's all over. How would you spend that time? How would you act? You'd live each moment to the fullest, wouldn't you? We need to approach every day as if it were our last. I call it *'The Last Day Living'* mindset.

Imagine living each day not in panic or fear but in deep presence and gratitude for everything we have. If today were our last, what would truly matter? Would we fret over trivialities or cherish moments with loved ones? None of us know when our last day will come. Embracing this perspective cultivates gratitude and reverence for what's truly important.

So, the question lingers: amidst adversity, how do we evolve? How do we shape a brighter outcome? How do we cultivate stoicism, shielding ourselves from negative external influences? And most importantly, how do we nurture gratitude and empowerment while traversing through hardship?

I understand it's challenging, but it's immensely rewarding. Embracing this path is far superior to resisting life's flow, obstructing our growth, and stifling our dreams.

Numbing, running, and resisting demand enormous energy that could be directed toward more constructive endeavors.

In essence, are we aligning ourselves with the flow of life through gratitude, creativity, and authentic self-expression, embracing elevated emotions and feelings? Or are we disconnecting from life, resisting its currents? To manifest the life we envision, the one destined by God, we must transcend our current limiting beliefs. We need a clear, heartfelt vision, a North Star, a unique direction solely ours.

To truly shape the life we desire, we must first assess our current position in every aspect. Conducting a life audit involves examining our belief systems, self & worldview, predominant emotions, and habitual states of being. Through a series of reflective questions, we gain insight into our feelings and beliefs. Armed with this awareness, we can embark on a transformative journey, challenging and replacing outdated beliefs. This process accelerates our growth, bridging the gap between where we are and where we aspire to be, compressing time and avoiding the futile cycle of aimless striving.

Merely contemplating change is not enough; we must equip ourselves with strategies, tools, and tactics to take decisive action. Recognizing the profound influence of our emotional states on every facet of our lives, we must delve into the core of our beliefs about ourselves and the world. Gratitude serves as a transformative force, regardless of our circumstances. By adopting an attitude of gratitude and seeking opportunities to serve others, we shift from self-absorption to meaningful engagement with the world. My own journey reflects this shift: for too long, I focused solely on myself, unaware of the disconnection from my heart and from God.

When we're connected to our heart and God in an empowered way, we automatically want to share the beauty of life and what we're experiencing with others.

As someone who has traversed a tumultuous path riddled with mistakes and needless suffering, I implore you to confront the difficult questions. Embrace what surfaces with unwavering faith, hope, and gratitude, propelling yourself toward a brighter future through decisive action. Perhaps your circumstances aren't ideal—be it in finances, relationships, health, or spirit. We all harbor aspirations for more, sensing the potential for growth and fulfillment within us. It requires a courageous surrender to the inner stirrings as we boldly navigate the journey, refusing to be swayed by distractions along the way.

The realization that life isn't fair is a crucial milestone on our journey. Instead of expecting ease, we strive to grow stronger with each challenge. It's our responsibility to embrace action and power, shaping the life we desire, for our dreams are also seeking us. The pivotal question remains: Are we willing to transcend negative emotions and take decisive steps toward our goals, be it in health, wealth, or fulfillment? Embracing success and empowerment opens the door to a realm of endless possibilities.

We have boundless opportunities to cultivate our skills, unlocking our potential for growth and expansion. Unlike trees rooted in one place, we're free to move away from toxic relationships, unfulfilling careers, and limiting beliefs. Today, we must make a non-negotiable decision: I MUST have a better life. I MUST achieve wealth. I MUST prioritize my health. I MUST be healthy. I MUST be empowered. These are not mere wants but essential mandates for our well-being.

In my journey, when I felt unfulfilled and sensed I wasn't on my highest path, I summoned the courage to explore new territories. Though daunting, I'm profoundly grateful for these leaps. They led me to embrace expanded versions of myself, guided by God's illuminating presence on unfamiliar paths. Remember this: God's love for us surpasses understanding. He desires blessings and abundance for each of us, nurturing us as heirs to His Kingdom.

When we wholeheartedly surrender to our highest self, aligning with our ideals, values, and God's presence, miracles unfold. This isn't mere sleight of hand but the manifestation of divine blessings due to our unwavering hope and faith in something greater. It's the tangible expression of God's energy and spirit enriching our lives.

I earnestly yearn for everyone to experience enduring joy and profound peace. However, to safeguard these precious treasures, we must remain vigilant, for there exist malicious forces in our world. These forces are sinister, parasitic, demonic and intent on sowing chaos and destruction. I believe they are not of this Earth and harbor disdain for humanity, perpetuating lies, deceit, and discord to cloud our minds and hearts.

We must shield our minds, hearts, and spiritual energy to fortify ourselves, our families, our communities, and our world Ohana against these insidious influences. By standing up to evil and embodying virtue, bravery and courage with positivity, we can serve as beacons of light, inspiring positive change in the lives of ourselves, others and the world.

When you send out a heartfelt message to the universe, being honest and authentic, you never know how it might return to you. The universe operates in mysterious, synchronistic ways. I've experienced this miraculous flow countless times, and looking back, it's truly divine and awe-inspiring.

This is how I found myself living in Hawaii. Back in 2021, I was residing in Salt Lake City, UT, fresh from a divorce in 2020 and bankruptcy. During this period, I was employed by the Federal Government as a Public Information Officer, serving on command teams for National Wildfire Incidents. My journey in the fire service had taken me from hands-on fieldwork to more elevated positions over the years.

The fire season had just commenced, and I was anticipating being dispatched to a wildfire. One morning in early April, I found myself at a coffee shop adorned with my cherished Rudraksha mala beads. These beads held profound significance for me, having been gifted by a friend. They symbolized my survival of my NDE, affirming my vitality, health, and resilience even after such a harrowing ordeal.

The coffee shop, nestled on Highland Drive, buzzed with eager patrons awaiting their morning caffeine fix. Amidst the crowd, I couldn't help but notice a woman behind me sporting striking, spiked hair.

"I like your hair," I remarked. She graciously replied, *"Thanks, it's my signature look. I'm from Honolulu, Hawaii. I like your beads. They resemble Kukui nuts, but they're different."* As she mentioned the islands, a hush seemed to fall over the surrounding chatter, and I could sense her unmistakable Hawaiian heritage.

"That's fascinating. I've never been," I replied. *"I'm Kye, although it's not the Hawaiian 'Kai.' It originates from my 16th-century Germanic tribes, meaning 'keeper of the key' or 'bringer of light.'"*

Drawing closer, she met my gaze with sincerity and declared, *"It doesn't matter. Your name sounds like 'Kai,' and the islands will call you."*

As I chuckled in disbelief, she leaned in closer, fixing her gaze directly on my soul. *"You have a drum, don't you?"*

Her question hung in the air, though she already knew the answer. Suddenly, the bustling coffee shop fell silent, leaving only her and me enveloped in a charged energy. Stunned by her insight, I had to ask, *"How the hell do you know about my drum?"* It was a drum I had acquired in 2020, a special buffalo hide drum obtained after becoming certified in Reiki in Mt. Shasta.

Her response was calm and measured as she smiled lightly, *"You must learn to play the drum to sound the call, so others can hear the call. We need to bring 'Kai' back to the islands and back to the people."* Her words carried a weight of seriousness, and I could feel the depth of her sincerity piercing through. It was as if she was delivering a message directly from the divine, tailored specifically for me in this sacred encounter. Stunned into silence, I stood there, grappling with the profoundness of the moment.

"Coffee for Kye' The barista yelled out. I popped out of my trance and said to the Hawaiian Lady, *"Alright... I believe what you are saying. I'm open."* I grabbed my coffee, said goodbye and thank you for the conversation, and went on my way, smiling and thinking, *"Oh man, that was intense."*

A week later, I received the call to head to a fire in Arizona, just outside of Phoenix. As I made my way down the tarmac at the Salt Lake City airport, a man brushed past me, sporting a Hawaiian shirt adorned with a tribal turtle (Honu) emblazoned across the chest. It was as if the image leaped off his shirt and struck me right in my third eye. *BAM!* I was shaken to the core, and without hesitation, I whipped out my phone and snapped a picture of it. The man was startled, muttering, *"Umm... okay. I got this shirt in Hawaii,"* as I briskly walked away, lost in the moment.

Arriving in Arizona and heading to the Incident Command Post (ICP), it was on the third day when a local farmer showed up and handed us three bags of cherries, expressing his gratitude for our firefighting efforts. As he presented the cherries, I noticed the same Tribal Honu symbol on his right wrist. Once more, it seemed to hold immense significance, captivating my attention instantly.

Inquiring about his turtle tattoo, I could sense it held a profound story. With a smile, he shared, *"My granddaughter planned a trip to Hawaii, but her friend couldn't go at the last minute. So, she invited me instead. We swam with sea turtles, a truly magical experience. I got this tattoo to commemorate it."* He revealed that he had stage four cancer at the time, and after the trip, his cancer miraculously vanished in less than two months.

Stunned, I exclaimed, *"That's incredible!"*

He nodded, *"Yes, those turtles saved my life.*

A few days later, while driving to a different section of the fire, we passed a sign for Turtle Coffee Co. I couldn't help but chuckle to myself at the coincidence. The sightings of Honu symbols seemed to multiply from there, becoming even more frequent.

Upon my return to Salt Lake from the fire in Arizona, I took a stroll around Liberty Park. As I wandered, a couple approached me and asked, *"Hey, how long have you lived in Hawaii?"* Perplexed, I responded, *"I've never even been to the islands."* They seemed surprised and said, *"Oh, we thought you lived in Hawaii."* Puzzled by the odd encounter, I walked away, wondering about the strange connection they perceived.

Believe it or not, people from Facebook, whom I hadn't spoken to in many, many years or ever, started messaging me out of the blue. They said things like, *"Enjoy your life in Hawaii! When are you moving to Hawaii? Have an epic life in Hawaii!"* It was all so "random," as I hadn't mentioned anything about moving or Hawaii or ever contemplated it to anyone. What made it even more unusual was that none of them could explain why they said it; they just felt compelled to. It felt strangely right to them as if it were simply meant to be.

During this period, I was called to join a Prevention and Education Team tasked with educating the public about fire safety and implementing fire bans in designated forest areas. Our duties involved traveling around the forest, distributing fire safety materials, and ensuring that people were taking necessary precautions, especially during severe weather conditions, to prevent wildfires.

One morning before our shift, we stopped at a convenience store to grab gas and some water. As I picked up two bottles of water and a snack. I noticed the water was from Hawaii, which seemed odd as I've never once in my life seen water from Hawaii.

The cashier, with long hair and a hippie vibe, rang up my items and exclaimed, *"Wow, Bruh, That's super weird!"*

Glancing at the checkout terminal, I saw the total was $8.08. Confused, I asked him, *"Why?"*

He dramatically replied, *"It's 808, man!"*

Still puzzled, I asked, *"What does that mean?"*

He chuckled and explained, *"Bruh, this is water from Hawaii, and its price with tax is $8.08. That's the area code in Hawaii!"*

Surprised, I said, *"Damn... That's crazy!"*

He then looked at me seriously and said, *"It's a sign, man, the islands are calling."* As I left for our operational period.

Halfway through the day, we reached one of the most remote parts of the forest, where we encountered a lone camper at a campground. After giving him the fire safety spiel and some Smokey swag, as we were leaving, I happened to glance to my right and saw the largest beach towel I'd ever seen. And what was proudly displayed on it, soaking up the sun's rays? A majestic Honu.

In disbelief, I exclaimed, *"Holy Shit!"* startling everyone. *"What's wrong?"* they asked.

"Oh, nothing," I replied, *"just having a moment with myself."* Chuckling to myself, I couldn't shake the feeling that things were getting weirder by the minute.

Later that evening, after a day filled with all these bizarre encounters, we went out for dinner and parked the rental car. As we exited the restaurant and approached our vehicle, I couldn't help but notice a car parked next to ours with a bumper sticker featuring the shaka sign, three Honu, and the words *"Hang loose in Hawaii."* It felt like the universe was playing a cosmic joke, and I couldn't help but laugh at the synchronicity of it all.

The frequency at which signs and synchronicities were manifesting seemed almost unbelievable. Upon returning to Salt Lake City after the fire assignment, I received an invitation to join a sweat ceremony with tribal elders from the Lakota tradition. Despite some initial hesitation, I felt a compelling inner urge to attend.

Upon arriving at the venue, located an hour away from Salt Lake City in the countryside, I encountered an elder—a figure akin to an uncle in Hawaiian culture. He shared his profound experience on the Big Island of Hawaii, describing it as one of the most spiritually transformative encounters of his life.

As the sun dipped behind the mountains and the evening air grew cooler, we engaged in conversation by the flickering fire. Amidst the crackling embers, he revealed a tattoo acquired during his time on the island, sharing how it facilitated a profound connection with his heart and soul. He spoke of a profound gift bestowed upon him by the island.

As the sweat ceremony commenced, we solemnly entered the lodge, following the traditions of the Lakota people. With reverence for our ancestors and all living beings, we bore our prayers and offerings, seeking connection and guidance.

For those who have yet to experience a traditional sweat lodge led by knowledgeable and respectful guides, I highly recommend it. Countless individuals, myself included, have undergone profound transformations and healings within its sacred confines. After an indescribable journey that defies words, the ceremony concluded, and we convened for a communal meal and shared our stories.

The uncle came up to me and handed me a gift from Hawaii and a card for an eco-retreat center.

He said, *"I feel this is for you."*

I replied, *"I don't plan on going to Hawaii anytime soon. I am engaged in Federal Wildland Fire operations and travel around the county in the summer."*

He looked at me, smiled, and said, *"That's cool, but I know this is for you. Just keep it with you."*

A little over a week later, my fire chief gave me a call and told me bluntly, *"Kye, we are canceling the fire program,* and you're going to have to find another agency and fire station to sponsor you."

Baffled, I replied, *"It's the middle of the fire season. California and everywhere else is burning up. What the hell are you talking about?"*

He replied in a short manner, *"Sorry, and best of luck."* And hung up.

At this point, I was really pissed off and disappointed, very angry at all the things that had unfolded. It was the middle of the fire season, and I couldn't continue to fight fire because I didn't have a fire station.

After a week of self-reflection, aka being pissed off and angry, I went out with some friends to go and drink to escape the anger. That night something very remarkable happened.

A girl from Facebook reached out to me and said, *"I feel you are from the islands and belong near the water."*

Telling her, *"I'd never been to any islands. I love the water though."*

She was adamant and told me the same thing the aunty from the coffee shop told me, *"The islands are calling you. The water wants you near her."*

Right after her response, I passed out as I was already pretty smashed from the night of drinking.

Waking up in the morning, I reviewed my messages to see what I had said. And what unfolded was something beyond.

In my last response to her, a voice replied from deep within my soul, a voice I had never heard in my entire life and it came out in my drunken stupor, *"I need to go home, I need to go to Hawaaiiiiiiii....."* With the word Hawaii lingering on as I passed out, not remembering what I had said until reviewing it in the morning. Upon reviewing it, chills went down my spine as I knew my destiny was calling, .

After the soul expression, I mustered the courage to dial the number on the card I had received. To my surprise, the voice on the other end revealed they were an eco-retreat center seeking a Marketing Director with my skill set. Excitedly, I shared my experience working with numerous national and international companies. They offered me the position on the spot, complete with room and board, two farm-to-table meals daily, and the opportunity to run the marketing department, all while receiving a modest stipend.

Even after all the signs, the synchronicities, and the opportunity that was presented before me, I still wasn't 100%

convinced about moving to Hawaii. It wasn't until I was eating dinner with my aunt and she laughed at me after I told her the entire story.

She said, *"How many signs does God and the universe have to give you? Don't you think you should listen to him and move to Hawaii? Are you really that thick-headed?"*

After our conversation and many prayers, I knew it was the right thing to do. So I bought a one-way ticket to the Big Island of Hawaii in September of 2021 and left everything and everyone I'd ever known, to move to Hawaii. A place I'd never set foot on, moving to one of the most remote parts of the island with only a backpack, a small suitcase, my drum and a modest savings to my name. It was like Mexico all over again besides the fact that I literally knew no one and had no connections.

I arrived late at night in the middle of September when the plandemic was still going on. I had to overcome one of my greatest fears at the time and that was crossing over the ocean at night. Because If the plane goes down you are in the middle of the ocean far away from everything and everyone with some really big stuff swimming around.

When I arrived, I stayed the night in Kona and woke up, realizing that I needed to get to the other side of the island. At that time, the buses were few and far between. And an Uber to the other side would have been $250 bucks, and a cab much more.

With my customary composure and optimism, I embraced the morning and headed for breakfast. Seated at the counter, I watched the sunrise paint the mountain and bathe the bay in golden light. Suddenly, I spotted a gentleman who bore a striking resemblance to a friend I'd met in La Paz, Mexico— a real estate colleague from England.

Walking over to him and his wife, I said, *"Sorry to bother you guys, but you have a doppelgänger and this is his picture!"* I presented the picture to him and his wife.

His wife started chuckling and said, *"Oh my gosh, it's you, babe!"* He was less than convinced and didn't see a resemblance at all.

He then said to me, *"Hey, we are going to the other side of the island? Do you want a ride?"* I smiled and replied, *"I would love a ride. I'm so glad you asked!"*

Accompanied by him and his wife, I enjoyed a delightful two-and-a-half-hour car ride to the other side of the island, celebrating his birthday and their anniversary along the way. They kindly dropped me off in a charming town called Keaau, just a short 20-minute drive from my destination.

As soon as they left, nearly 20 seconds later, another vehicle pulled into the same EXACT parking spot of the coffee shop they dropped me off at, rolled down its window, and the gentleman said, *"Hey, do you need a ride?"*

Responding eagerly, I said, *"That would be divine, yes, please."*

He let me know that he was an Uber driver and was picking up a girl in the coffee shop, and he would ask her if it was OK with her. She got into the Uber, and he talked with her for a moment. Then, he rolled down the window again and said, *"She said it's fine. Put your bags in the trunk and hop in."*

This is not an exaggeration at all. I put my bags in the trunk, looked up to the sky, thanked God as I chuckled, and got into the vehicle.

After a short ride, and she was getting off at her stop, she said, *"Take him wherever he needs and just change the location, and I'll pay for his ride."*

The driver looked at me in the rearview mirror and said, *"It must be your lucky day."*

I replied to him, smiling ear to ear, *"I just arrived last night, and I've never been to Hawaii before. Honestly, right before you picked me up, a couple I met at breakfast in Kona dropped me off at the same spot you parked in. Giving me a ride from the other side of the island. What a trip."*

The uncle chuckled and said, *'Wow, looks like the red carpet was rolled out for you. The island must have invited you for a real reason."*

And so, as if orchestrated by some divine hand, I found myself standing at the entrance of my destination. No prior arrangements had been made for rides or travel plans, for I had unwavering faith that everything would fall into place, guided by the hand of God. Remember, never resist the flow; instead, seek out the signs, and keep your eyes and heart open to the messages the universe and God are sending your way. Surrendering to the divine flow and taking each step with trust can lead to a life far more magical than we ever dared to imagine.

"God's power is made perfect in weakness." - Unknown

Chapter 12: GodPower or Willpower?

Willpower is the cornerstone of living an extraordinary life and unlocking our highest potential. Yet, many struggle with inaction and an inability to control impulses, lacking the essential tool of willpower. It is a divine gift bestowed upon us to harness and wield in our journey toward greatness. By mastering the art of restraining immediate gratification and resisting impulses, we cultivate resilience and pave the path to achieving more. Willpower empowers us to transcend the allure of instant dopamine hits and stay focused on our long-term goals. Only when we harness the strength of our willpower can we conquer obstacles, attain success, and manifest our deepest desires.

Willpower serves as a potent tonic across various facets of our lives—be it mental, spiritual, or physical. From committing to daily exercise routines to maintaining financial stability, from fostering consistency to enhancing overall well-being, willpower is indispensable. When either internal or external influences begin to derail us from our path, it often signifies a deficiency in willpower, accompanied by weakened boundaries, low self-esteem, and diminished self-worth.

To cultivate resilience and fortify our willpower, we must venture into challenging territories beyond our comfort zone. These experiences catalyze growth by compelling us to take action and demonstrate unwavering dedication. As we aspire to evolve into a stronger, wiser, and more self-directed individual, we must equip ourselves with every available tool to navigate toward brighter horizons.

A powerful technique I gleaned from one of my mentors is the use of power-phrased mantras. These phrases serve as focal points for our minds and attention, igniting energy toward a specific goal or aim. One particularly impactful mantra that has guided me through life's various journeys is: "I will my will to be: (_____)", allowing me to fill in the blank with aspirations such as success, happiness, gratitude, love, health, or outgoingness.

Whatever challenge you're facing, use the power phrase mantra to counteract limiting beliefs or disempowered thoughts. For example, if you're feeling insecure or shy, your counter-power phrase mantra could be, *"I will my will to be confident. I will my will to be outgoing. I will my will to be gregarious."* Implementing this simple practice can yield profound changes in just a few moments. With consistent use, you'll forge new neural pathways through neural plasticity, shifting toward a more empowered version of yourself.

I vividly recall reciting variations of this mantra while running for miles: *"I run effortlessly for miles. I possess boundless energy."* Whether it's in this exact form or not, the concept remains the same. I refer to it as PMP (Positive Mental Programming) – the practice of directing our minds toward uplifting and empowering thoughts coupled with physiological changes. This leads to powerful emotions and feelings, which, in turn, drive diligent actions.

Combining power phrases with changes in physiology, such as adopting power stances and postures, enhances the transformation process. Our physiology follows our psychology, so when you're feeling low or disconnected, try jumping up and down while shooting your hands in the air like a champion, all while reciting a few power phrases. You'll be amazed at how quickly the switch flips to a more impactful state. Learning to manipulate ourselves in this way is key to achieving specific and desired states of being.

Once you begin to understand the direct correlation between our physiology and psychology you can see it manifest in every facet of our life and others as well. Take for instance the individual who's head is drooped with shoulders slumped over as he's walking. What do you think their internal dialogue and state is? Are they brimming with confidence and empowerment? Indeed not, they are more than likely feeling down and depressed. Begin to look at others body postures, mannerisms and how they carry themselves and speak and you'll begin to dissect their internal states and psychology from that. This will help you to better understand your own self more deeply as well.

Once we start gaining momentum, we become like an object in motion that stays in motion. For those who have been at a standstill for years, it requires more energy and effort to get moving again. This is why having our mantras, rituals, and routines is crucial – they provide the structure for consistency, strength and resilience needed to shape the person we aspire to be. It's essential to complement our actions with positive thoughts, affirmations, meditation, prayer, and, most importantly, taking MASSIVE action.

While we are bound to make mistakes as humans, dwelling in guilt, shame, or despair isn't productive. Instead, we should embrace the concept of failing forward and failing fast. We must inspire and motivate ourselves to reach our highest potential, especially when we feel unhappy and disconnected because ultimately, it's up to us to bring about positive change in our lives.

Having our North Star guides us as we invest considerable time and energy in becoming the best versions of ourselves. We disregard naysayers, doubters, and haters, staying focused on our path, mission, goals, and dreams. Seeking validation, security, or materialism from others only leads to disappointment, as true fulfillment is an inside job. By aligning our will with the divine will, we unlock the path to genuine happiness and fulfillment.

Consider this: why seek guidance from those who aren't headed where we aim to go? Placing undue importance on others' wisdom, advice, or direction when they're lost themselves is akin to the blind leading the blind. Many are confined by societal molds, living within limited versions of reality and resigning themselves to playing small. Refuse to shrink yourself down. It's in this smallness that dreams wither, hopes fade, and life becomes mediocre. Don't settle for growing old with bitterness and resentment because you lacked the courage to go all in.

Many, including my former self, felt adrift in life because of not being in alignment with God's will. Instead, they follow the dictates of parents, family, society, and culture, forsaking their true essence and divine potential. This disconnect stems from scarcity, inauthentic programming, wavering faith, and the allure of superficial consumerism and material pleasures. Yet, these distractions offer fleeting satisfaction, leaving one questioning their persistent emptiness. The cheap thrills of entertainment, food, friends, and culture are mere placeholders for genuine fulfillment. I've chosen a different path—one guided by God, leading to my highest destiny. And I extend an invitation to fellow seekers of spiritual truth to join me on this journey.

We must align ourselves with the divine and our highest selves because God and the universe are ever-present guides. Life serves as a training ground, offering opportunities for learning, growth, and self-development. If everything were effortlessly handed to us without endeavor or challenge, we'd lack the character and depth that adversity fosters. In today's society, where instant gratification reigns supreme, many resort to fleeting pleasures to numb the existential void. However, our spirits yearn for challenges that foster growth. It's essential to remember that God never presents us with challenges beyond our capacity to overcome.

In overcoming my addictions, recovering from a life-threatening motorcycle accident, and rebuilding myself after heartbreak, divorce, and bankruptcy, I realized that my journey was not solitary. It was a collaborative effort between myself and the divine forces of God and the universe. Reconstructing, rebuilding and empowering myself in the jungle literally from NOTHING, with God and Me, in one of the most remote places on the island in the middle of the pacific ocean is where my legend was birthed.

The path to greatness is not paved with ease. As we become more dedicated, focused, and selective in our pursuits, we generate greater energy and momentum. This transformation often sets us apart from those around us— family, friends, and lovers. We undergo profound changes, morphing into versions of ourselves that our environment has never witnessed before. It's natural for others to feel left behind or to express their doubts and criticisms. Yet, we must recognize that their reactions are not personal. Our mission is paramount, driven by the truth in our hearts and our calling. As the adage goes, *"It's none of my business what others think or say about me."* Our focus laser like on our path, steadfastly moving forward with unwavering conviction.

Abandoning ourselves is the surest path to eternal suffering and regret. We know deep down that we're capable of achieving more, yet we allow ourselves to drift away from our true essence. In doing so, we cast blame on others, convincing ourselves that the world is conspiring against us. But in truth, the betrayal lies within us. It's our own actions that drive us further from our hearts and aspirations. This self-betrayal is the ultimate treason. Look closely, and you'll see the telltale signs of self-loathing in those who have forsaken their connection to God and their dreams. They wear bitterness, anger, and negativity like a cloak, easily spotted by those who know where to look.

Each of us is endowed with a unique mission, intricately intertwined with our talents, abilities, and life experiences. God and the universe have crafted a divine plan for us, conceived long before our names were ever spoken. Yet, to discern this plan, we must quiet our minds, steady our hearts, and listen intently in the silence. Too often, we find ourselves consumed by the rush of the future or the weight of the past, neglecting the profound presence of the eternal now. Our lives become a frenetic race, mistaken for a sprint when it is, in truth, a journey—a singular pilgrimage that belongs to each of us alone. Yet, we allow ourselves to be ensnared by the trappings of materialism, the lure of social media, and the ceaseless clamor of social interactions, friendships, and relationships. We are caught in a relentless cycle of distraction, overlooking the quiet wisdom that awaits us in the stillness of our souls.

Too often, we allow ourselves to be drawn away from our own essence, a path I've personally traversed countless times. Invariably, we forsake ourselves long before anyone else has the chance to do so. Yet, the crux of the matter lies in returning to our core, reclaiming the essence of our true selves before life's myriad experiences obscure our vision. It's about turning to God with an open heart and asking, *"What is your will for me? How can I lead a more fulfilling life? How can I unlock my fullest potential and capacity?"* It's a stance of receptivity, a willingness to learn, and an openness to divine guidance.

You could say the true challenge lies not in the pursuit of our dreams but in refusing to accept a life of discontent and bitterness, severed from our true selves and the divine of our world. All because we've neglected to honor our own aspirations, failing to carve out the space and time needed to pursue our deepest desires. Throughout history, great men and women of all ages have achieved remarkable feats by heeding the call of their hearts, undeterred by the chorus of doubters and critics. They understood that God's hand guided them and that the universe would furnish all they required as they bolstered their faith and hope through action, believing they could move mountains. Our past struggles and setbacks matter little in comparison to the choices we make today. What truly counts is our gratitude in this moment, our commitment to taking small steps forward, and our unwavering resolve to follow the path that calls to our soul.

Change is not an overnight phenomenon; it unfolds gradually, much like the shifting of seasons. We're striving for incremental progress, a mere 1% improvement each day, which, over time, can dramatically alter the course of our lives. This is the power of taking baby steps. Just as we approach eating an elephant one bite at a time, we must honestly assess our current position in various aspects of our lives. Where do our finances stand? What about our relationships, spirituality, and overall health—mentally, emotionally, physically, and communally? Are we contributing positively to ourselves and our community? By confronting these challenging questions head-on, we unlock the real insights needed to propel us forward.

To truly progress, we must summon the courage to confront our reality with unfiltered honesty—a task that demands bravery and authenticity. An unexamined life, as the saying goes, is not worth living, yet many choose to numb themselves rather than face their inner truth. It's a daunting prospect, delving into the depths of our hearts for fear of what we might discover.

For the longest time, I sought fulfillment in external sources—a partner, a career, financial success. I believed that these would complete me and make my life perfect. Yet, I failed to acknowledge my own needs and neglected the treasure buried deep within. Caught in the web of societal and religious conditioning, I looked outward for answers when, all along, the guidance I sought resided within—in my heart, in my connection with God.

Among the saddest souls are those who have forsaken themselves, losing sight of their beliefs and drowning in despair and self-pity. Without hope or faith, they languish in the depths of desolation. Yet, with unwavering belief and divine guidance, we possess the power to shape our reality. By fixing our gaze on our north star and visualizing our destination, we can chart our course one step at a time, one day at a time, one task at a time.

So, what's your next move, your next small step forward? In truth, we hold an abundance of tools, resources, and technology to not only enrich our own lives but also uplift others. How can we contribute our unique gifts to the world, fostering prosperity, inclusion, and deeper connections among all humanity? It's time to shift the paradigm from one of conflict and greed to one of shared abundance and unity across the globe. Honoring our unique and individual creed, color and community. Preserving and protecting that which is virtuous, moral and upright. Unifying together to push back the tides of injustices and evil we are seeing executed by the global elite who seek to destroy and diminish our culture, heritage, and history.

Nurturing robust families and steadfast communities rooted in a profound sense of empowerment and reverence for their people, culture, heritage, and traditions. It's not about superiority or inferiority; it's about embracing our identity with pride and extending that same respect to others. If everyone gets to love their folk, I sure as hell get to love mine and my ancestors as well. Together, let's celebrate our uniqueness while embracing the rich diversity of our shared humanity.

Recognizing that imperfection is inherent in every culture, every individual, and every society, we can cultivate forgiveness and compassion toward humanity. While we must not condone wicked behavior or wrongdoing, we have the power to choose light over darkness. Our mission is to restore our own wholeness and release what does not serve us - the pain, the hurt, the anger, the sorrow, the lies. Rather than clinging to them like burning coal, we can simply observe and let them go.

The miracle lies in your uniqueness. There has never been anyone like you, nor will there ever be. Your perspectives and experiences shape a one-of-a-kind view of the world. I believe that if more people embraced their uniqueness, it could profoundly alter the fabric of our existence and how we interact with one another. Together, we could usher in a transformative change, not only for our present lives but for the generations yet to come. Our empowered actions today can contribute to a legacy that fosters stability and harmony for future generations of our people and our planet.

How can we unite people toward a common goal of improving our world? I believe the answer lies in embracing the love of God within ourselves and recognizing the divine essence of human life. By leveraging our unique talents and abilities, we can strive toward our highest truths and resist forces that seek to undermine our collective well-being. It's crucial to acknowledge the existence of pervasive evils and systems that perpetuate enslavement, regardless of our geographical origins. Across continents, power structures manipulate nations and humanity through debt, usury, and fractional reserve banking. They saturate us with propaganda fueled by hate, conflict, fear, and scarcity, sustaining their war machines while sacrificing our loved ones for profit. They taint our food and water and impose restrictions on our freedom of expression.

In my studies with various mentors, I learned that we are each a note in the symphony of the universe. Every one of us vibrates at a unique frequency, expressing ourselves in our own distinct melody. So, what music do we emit into the world? Is it a tune of anger, hate, and despair or one of gratitude, joy, and inclusion? Our lives compose a grand symphony, blending together the pieces of our past, present, and future into a harmonious masterpiece.

Therefore, if we're dissatisfied with our current situation, we must confront our own self-deception and be authentically vulnerable with ourselves. Only we truly understand our inner landscape, and we're often adept at deceiving ourselves. I've certainly been guilty of this in the past, putting on a facade of happiness while feeling dead inside. It wasn't until I faced myself in the mirror, acknowledging all aspects of myself—the good, the bad, and the ugly—that I recognized my reality. *"This is where I am."* Realizing there's nowhere to escape, for wherever I go, there I am.

I've made decisions in my life that were solely mine, and some of them didn't turn out as planned. They weren't ideal, but in the moment, I did what I thought was best with the resources available to me. I firmly believe that when we have faith in a higher power and trust that the universe is supportive, we can transform our experiences into valuable lessons. These lessons become medicine for our growth, allowing us to evolve and positively impact the lives of others. However, without belief in something greater, we risk stagnation, resigned to a bleak existence devoid of hope for brighter days.

Having weathered numerous challenges and triumphs at a young age, I now find purpose in sharing my journey—its highs, lows, and the invaluable lessons learned. My selfish aim is to extend a hand to those navigating similar struggles, offering them the hope and resilience I've cultivated along the way. Through my own experiences, I've discovered the path to fulfillment, joy, and empowerment. Every twist and turn in our lives, every moment of pain or triumph, contributes to the rich tapestry of who we are. Nothing is wasted; everything is woven into the fabric of our existence.

Life offers us but one chance, one fleeting opportunity to make our mark. Some moments pass us by, never to return. This truth became vividly clear to me during my time in Mexico.

In La Paz, I once found myself in an unexpected situation with a well-to-do couple I had collaborated with on media production. They generously invited me to join them for a day of water skiing on their fancy boat. However, as luck would have it, I woke up late that morning with a pounding hangover. Frantically, I rushed to the marina, but by the time I arrived, their boat was already pulling away.

My initial reaction was one of frustration and regret. *"Damn it, I'm late,"* I muttered to myself. Nevertheless, I swiftly parked my car among the others and dashed to the edge of the marina's rock wall. With the couple only a stone's throw away, I pondered how to catch their attention. Without a second thought, I began shouting and waving my arms frantically, hoping to signal them amidst the bustle of preparations.

Equipped with my snorkeling gear, I made a spontaneous decision to plunge into the water and swim toward their boat. Although apprehensive about venturing into the vast ocean alone, I forged ahead, shouting, *"Hey, I'm here! Wait for me!"* as I stroked toward them. Despite my efforts, they failed to hear my calls and sped off, leaving me behind.

It was a missed opportunity, one I regretted deeply. My tardiness, stemming from a night of indulgence, had cost me dearly. Hesitation further compounded the situation, delaying my dive into the water. In the end, my reluctance proved fatal to my chances. It's a sobering reminder that showing up promptly, staying sober, and seizing opportunities without hesitation are paramount. After all, some opportunities are fleeting, never to return again.

The unexpected passing of my cousin's husband, leaving behind his young family, shook me to my core and thrust death to the forefront of my thoughts once again. Tears flowed freely as I grappled with the stark reality that none of us are exempt from mortality. Deeply connecting me again to the reminder that life, fragile and fleeting, can be extinguished in an instant. Contemplating our mortality, I realized that death is the ultimate equalizer—we all meet our end eventually. Yet, beyond the physical realm, our spirits endure eternally. And the place we come from is beyond anything in comparison or comprehension to this realm. Embracing this truth imbued my life with newfound purpose and urgency. Each day becomes a precious opportunity to strive for growth, to honor our journey, and to pursue our true calling with unwavering determination.

If connecting with the concept of mortality feels daunting, focus instead on what you genuinely desire in life and what you have the power to influence. Take small, deliberate steps forward, fueled by faith and hope, knowing that progress is inevitable with faith and action. Even when the journey feels like navigating through hell, keep moving forward.

When we surrender to the divine will of God and the universe, uncertainty may arise, and fear may creep in. Yet, with unwavering faith in ourselves and the greater plan, remarkable things unfold. The path ahead may be uncertain and fraught with obstacles and detours but trust that it ultimately leads to a place of fulfillment. Despite the twists and turns, the journey always ends in redemption, IF WE CHOOSE IT! That, I can assure you.

I stand here today with profound gratitude for every trial endured. These challenges, while formidable, have sculpted me into the resilient, connected, divine man of God I am now today. I view them not as burdens but as invaluable lessons that have shaped me into the person I am. With each trial, I gather strength, wisdom, and resilience, empowered by the realization that this is my story—no one can diminish its significance.

This is what I have to bring to you. I have to share this with you, as it's a story of hope, resiliency, and courage. So, be courageous, hopeful, and faithful because there is evil in this world, and if we're not connected to God, the holy spirit, and our highest selves, life can get scary and depressing. We have to focus on the good things in our lives and decide, "*No, I demand that I do more and be more. I must have this divine connection to God and myself. I must have a healthy family and relationships. I must be wealthy and share the goodness of my life.*" If God is for us, who can be against us?

The more we have, the more we can give. But look around; we've got too many people in the world flaunting their million-dollar watches and fancy cars, which do absolutely nothing to give back. Congrats, you've reached a level that not many can! But here's the burning question: *Are you giving back? Are you helping others become better versions of themselves? Or are you just being a selfish little B?*

Let's face it, a majority of celebrities and influencers swim in wealth and influence, yet it seems they're only out for numero uno. That's disappointing, isn't it? Because if you've made it to a certain level and have the status, wealth, and influence, but you're not using it to uplift others, or impact the world in a positive way, well, that's the biggest slap in the face of humanity. You've been blessed with more, so more is expected of you. Now, I'm not saying you should give away everything you own, but for damn, DO SOME GOOD!

Congratulations to those with the means, connections, and wealth. But let's cut the crap. I'm calling you out. It's time to step up and join the cause, to lend a hand to our communities, nations, and families. The best way to help? Use your platform and influence to stand against evil and spread a message of hope and unity, empowerment and virtue. Because here's the harsh truth: evil thrives when good men and women sit idly by and do nothing. Scared to act, scared to stand up, scared to have fingers pointed at them.

Our youth are under siege, hyper sexualized and bombarded with twisted ideologies and vile propaganda. They're targeted because, let's face it, you control the youth, and you control the future. Our morals, norms, and culture are under relentless attack from every angle. Society is crumbling before our eyes despite having the money, tech, and means to build a better world. It's cultural Marxism and Neo-liberalism at its finest, corroding our nations and distorting truth and decency. So, are you going to sit and watch, or are you going to stand up and be part of the solution and stop being a coward?

I'm urging people to take a stand for what they know is right. It's time to deepen our connection with God and ask ourselves, *"How can I do better? How can I give back? How can I contribute more? How can I be a channel for God and the divine?"* Because every one of us has the power to make a difference in this world, even if it's just a small one. Together, we can transform this world into something truly beautiful. Our planet provides us with everything we need - clean air, fresh water, nourishing food. So, how can we unite to bring about meaningful change that benefits everyone?

We are all part of humanity, and we all deserve access to fresh, healthy food without harmful chemicals, clean water free from toxins, safe housing, supportive communities, and the right to be proud of who we are, what color our skin is and have caring individuals who uplift us. Not perpetuate indoctrination and madness. It's time to come together and make these rights a reality for every person on this planet.

As I conclude this chapter, my prayer and hope resonate deeply within these words. It's my fervent wish that through sharing my experiences in this book, we can all be drawn together in divine purpose with God. May our collective journey inspire us to strive for better to create a tapestry of life woven with bravery, compassion, and unity. Let us compose a majestic symphony of existence, each note harmonizing to create a world where all souls flourish and thrive.

"Believe you can, and you're halfway there." - Theodore Roosevelt

Chapter 13: Belief Systems

From the moment we enter this world, we find ourselves enveloped within a system that shapes us through established cultures and structures. Whether it's the religion we're born into, our national heritage, societal norms, government, or educational institutions, these elements weave a framework of belief systems around us from the very beginning of our existence. It's as if we're handed a script before we even have the chance to discover our own voice.

Yet, there commonly comes a point in our lives when something stirs within us, urging us to seek beyond the confines of our upbringing and conditioning. We begin to question the narratives we've been fed and the roles we've been assigned. It's a moment of awakening, where we realize that we do have the power to shape our own experiences and beliefs.

To embark on this journey of self-discovery, we must peel back the layers of conditioning and examine the core of our belief systems. We must dare to question the very fabric of our reality and how we perceive ourselves and the world around us. Only by challenging our preconceptions and embracing a mindset of curiosity and exploration can we truly uncover our authentic selves and forge our own path forward.

The conditioning imposed on the vast majority of people often serves to disempower and disconnect them from their true selves and the Divine. Rather than nurturing the human spirit and fostering empowerment and creativity, our societal programming is geared toward a cognitive performance-based reward model from day one. We're taught to constantly strive for achievement and success in order to feel worthy of love and acceptance, perpetuating the belief that human value is contingent upon external action and validation of such.

This systemic approach creates a relentless cycle of chaos and suffering, pushing individuals into an endless pursuit of material gain. It's as if we're trapped in a never-ending rat race, chasing after the next material cheese as dictated by societal norms.

Coming to terms with how deeply ingrained this programming is can be disheartening. Our systems of governance and institutions are designed to uphold this cognitive performance paradigm, reinforcing the notion that adherence to this system is the sole measure of our worth. It's infuriating to realize that our programming is rooted in hedonistic materialism and cutthroat corporatism, perpetuating a cycle of exploitation under unregulated capitalism that disproportionately benefits the few at the expense of the many.

Recognizing the extent of corporate greed and the complicity of governments in perpetuating it necessitates a keen sense of critical thinking. Corporate entities wield immense influence over politicians through unethical lobbying practices and financial incentives, manipulating legislation to maintain control and pacify the population.

In understanding the nature of the human spirit, we grasp its supernatural and eternal essence within the confines of our temporal physical bodies in this finite 3D realm. Despite inhabiting this world, we must realize that our true essence transcends it. Our consciousness and soul are eternal, existing beyond the constraints of time and space, while our physical bodies are transient vessels. In this temporal realm, everything is fleeting and impermanent.

For many, coming to terms with this reality proves challenging. The comfort of conformity often outweighs the discomfort of questioning deeply ingrained beliefs. Yet, it takes immense courage to challenge the status quo, especially when it's clear that the norm doesn't always align with truth or correctness and often seems amiss. The elephant hiding in the corner of the room.

The pervasive conditioning that saturates our society keeps the populace ensnared, controlled, and manipulated through media, propaganda, and marketing tactics. Rather than nurturing vibrant, resilient, and content individuals, our societal structure often feels like a soul-crushing machine. From every angle, we're bombarded with messages dictating that we're not enough unless we perform to certain standards, possess specific possessions, or meet societal benchmarks. This creates a distressing dichotomy between the 'haves' and the 'have-nots,' perpetuating a cycle of discontent and inadequacy.

In our educational system, which ideally could foster creativity and innovation, standardized testing reigns supreme. This system prioritizes conformity, producing obedient workers rather than encouraging critical thinking and challenging authority. It molds individuals into predetermined roles, stifling creativity and individuality. Consequently, not everyone thrives within this rigid structure, leading to a system that categorizes individuals as either winners or losers based on their ability to conform rather than their unique talents and potential.

Living a fulfilling life and realizing our true potential necessitates awareness. Choosing to be unconventional involves breaking free from societal conditioning and reclaiming autonomy over our own beliefs and actions. Otherwise, we risk being passively molded by a system that thrives on greed, division, and hatred. Many individuals are ensnared in a web of delusion and cultural indoctrination, making it difficult to discern truth from falsehood. By freeing ourselves from this programming, we create space to connect authentically with our inner selves and challenge prevailing narratives.

Once we grasp how the system operates, we can navigate it to our advantage rather than feeling ensnared by its constraints. Too often, people accept the status quo unquestioningly, clinging to the notion that *"this is just how things are done."* However, upon closer examination, this blind adherence to tradition reveals itself to be irrational and nonsensical.

Consider the paradox of our society: We dwell in what appears to be the wealthiest nation globally, yet a significant proportion of the populace (80-90%) teeters on the edge of financial instability, living paycheck to paycheck. Without constant labor, most Americans would face financial peril within a mere month, unable to meet even basic expenses. Furthermore, despite residing in a highly developed and "educated" society, a majority grapple with profound mental and emotional distress. This phenomenon epitomizes modern-day consumerist enslavement, with individuals experiencing profound anguish and despondency. Astonishingly, our nation grapples with record-high rates of suicide, substance abuse, depression, obesity and anxiety, casting doubt on the notion of progress in a seemingly advanced and affluent society. Clearly, we're not being '*educated*' we are being brainwashed. Where is the education in financial literacy? Where is the education in entrepreneurship? Where is the education in critical thinking and leadership? Where is the true nutritional education? Oh, that's right......

It's because the authorities do not care about us. This is a system created to keep people being slaves and indoctrinated. We have more than enough money and technology to be able to ensure the prosperity of all people across the planet, not just our nation. Once you awaken to what is happening, you can't really put it back in the box.

Consider the influence of our belief systems, sculpted by the relentless barrage of news, media, radio, TV, magazines, and what some may call "CULT-ure." It's a toxic brew, poisoning our minds and perceptions. Shockingly, a staggering 99% of our food wouldn't even pass European import standards due to its chemical contamination. Yet, we're practically coerced into consuming this poison within our own borders. Neurotoxins lurk in our water, while chemtrails manipulate weather patterns and pollute the very air we breathe. Our foundational beliefs, shaped by such influences, have strayed far from their origins and the wisdom of our ancestors. It's high time we acknowledge that much of what we've been taught is nothing but utter bullshit.

The puppeteers behind the central banking system, in bed with the WHO, WEF, and UN, often hailed as supreme elitists, perpetuate this madness worldwide to keep the masses sick, enslaved, and indoctrinated. Rooted in their corrupt fractional reserve banking and usury running rampant, so evident in enslaving the nations and pillaging the wealth of it. Resulting in deliberate inflation of goods and services and the loss of the value of the currency.

In the eyes of our sick care system, our well-being holds little value; in fact, America, the supposed beacon of progress, struggles as one of the world's unhealthiest nations. Why? Because a sick populace means billions in profits for the medical industry, a cured patient translates into lost revenue.

As we undergo the process of deconditioning, it's crucial to extend compassion to ourselves. After all, we had no hand in the creation of this dysfunctional system—be it government, society, religion, politics, or culture. It's imperative that we discern the good from the bad, focusing our energies on what's effective and positive, what we can change, and what we can improve upon, uniting together and doing our part to bring more love and awareness.

We've been thrust into a pre-existing system, one riddled with inefficiencies and dysfunctionality, designed to exploit and ensnare individuals. It's imperative to recognize that this system thrives on division; unity among the populace would spell its demise. Consequently, the ruling class maintains its hold while the masses remain divided, too preoccupied with the struggles of daily life to discern the larger picture. They love to stoke the fires of racial conflict while we're losing the class war.

It's abundantly clear that a vast majority of our politicians have little regard for the welfare of our people or our nation. Our hard-earned taxpayer dollars are being funneled away while our own citizens suffer. Veterans who bravely served our nation now find themselves homeless and battling PTSD on the streets. They're being neglected and forgotten. Meanwhile, dare I say, Bolshevism aka Marxism-Leninism with neoliberalism spreading like wildfire, indoctrinating our governmental and educational institutions through cultural Marxism, communism, leftism and wokeism. This blatant disregard for our children's future and national heritage is a direct assault on our culture and family values, sowing seeds of chaos and discord. In the absence of a strong family structure, our youth are exposed to relentless sexualization and moral decay, further alienating them from their true selves and their connection to God.

Manipulating and controlling a nation becomes all too easy when you sow confusion, dominate the younger generations, and feed them lies. After all, they represent the future. Corrupting the minds of children is akin to sabotaging the very foundation of our future. It's disheartening to acknowledge, but we must confront the reality that our belief systems are being systematically infiltrated with deceptive and subversive ideologies, philosophies, and theories. These insidious influences are corroding the fabric of our society, culture, and families, evident in the widespread illness, division, and polarization plaguing our nation and many others. From coast to coast, the symptoms of this malaise are glaringly apparent, fueled by a relentless barrage of misinformation from the media and societal institutions. Merely take a look around within our cities. The rising homeless population, the escalating drug problem, crime running rampant, the atmosphere of despondency, distress and indifference toward it all. The national border crisis and slew of forced and mass illegal immigration. The unsafe undertone for our women to walk safely in the very communities of their ancestors. To me, this is absolute bastardization of the very fabric of our society.

From my perspective, it's abundantly clear that bipartisanship is a thing of the past. The political landscape is now dominated by a Uni-party, manipulated by a technocratic oligarchy and beholden to corrupt corporatism purely supporting their own interests and unscrupulous lobbyists. It's imperative that people wake up to the reality that the infrastructure and very safety of our once great nations and communities are being dismantled. Our hard-earned tax dollars are being squandered through unregulated spending, manufactured wars, dishonest foreign endeavors, backwater corporate bailouts, and frivolous spending, all the while neglecting the welfare and safety of our very own citizens. It's systemic, calculated and coordinated. Assuredly not by mere "chance or coincidence."

Corrupt politicians and leaders in bed with monopolized corporatism, lining their pockets with our hard-earned tax dollars. Profiting from warmongering, corporate greed, and the destruction of our planet. While pharmaceutical drug lords deceive the public and manipulate the honest and hardworking folk, who want nothing more than to provide a good life for their families. Placing these orchestrated bailouts all on the backs of our American citizens who labor tirelessly to simply provide a life for their families.

The belief systems propagated by these entities are leading individuals to commit heinous crimes against one another, all while the American populace suffers the consequences. The mantra seems to be: *"Pay your taxes, consume toxic food, absorb our propaganda, stay divided, remain ignorant and unhealthy. Don't speak up, while we plunder your nation and allocate billions for warfare, immoral gender studies, demonic propaganda and line our pockets."*

At the heart of it all lies the desire for more control, the pursuit of wealth and the destruction of that which is virtuous. Morality takes a backseat when profit is the ultimate goal. In this system, people are mere pawns, easily swayed and manipulated by the allure of money and status and the talking heads on the media. The insidious spread of harmful ideologies engineered by those in power extends far beyond our borders, affecting the global populace. The pace of tyranny and oppression is accelerating, leaving us struggling to keep pace with the onslaught of manipulation and deceit. People have been fighting a race war when we are all together losing the class war.

At the core of every human being lies a deep yearning for love, acceptance, and purposeful engagement. Yet, our society instills the belief that possessions equate to love and acceptance, in tandem with perpetuated madness of the hearts and minds of our people and planet. As a result, individuals relentlessly pursue material success, hoping to be perceived as worthy and enough. Don't misunderstand what I am speaking about; wealth, money, and material means are very, very useful tools, but they are terrible masters.

God owns all the gold and silver; we are solely stewards of it while we traverse these realms. The problem has become that we've made it our God, everything over everyone and not giving back to those who need our help and assistance.

However, this pursuit often leads to exhaustion, despair, and a deterioration of mental and emotional well-being. The events of 2020 have only exacerbated this crisis, with alarming rates of depression, anxiety, and suicide among young teens and men yet society remains largely indifferent to their suffering.

There is an ongoing and intentional academic, intellectual and spiritual effort to subvert our Western society and what we're witnessing is the deliberate orchestration of cultural Marxism, and is certainly a calculated effort to subvert our society. Those behind it will stop at nothing to discredit dissenting voices, labeling them as "conspiracy theorists" or purveyors of hate speech. But my very journey from the depths of death, addiction, and despair to my profound encounter with God, leading to overwhelming joy, fulfillment, and purpose, I've been gifted the key of truth and connected the dots. I understand that my perspectives may be deemed unorthodox, earning me labels such as heretic by some, hero by many, radical by opponents, genius by a select few, and madman by disbelievers. Yet, the truth remains undeniable. Just look at the decay of our societal fabric, including our morals, virtues, values and our entire culture.

Who controls the levers of influence in Hollywood, the music industry, and the government? Who inundates our airwaves with messages glorifying violence, sex, and substance abuse? It's time to question these narratives and confront the forces working against us as citizens.

We must observe with clarity the manipulation and promotion of false societal constructs. To reclaim our autonomy, we must dismantle these fabricated cultural norms and establish alternative structures. Our freedom and control are under siege, and it's vital to recognize the deceit, coercion, and manipulation we face. Embracing our divinity and spiritual essence is key to this empowerment. Our freedom and purpose are not bestowed upon us by governments, institutions, or individuals but by the hand of the almighty God, Creator of the universe, the divine, great spirit, the all-encompassing and all-pervading omnipresent fabric of the divine truth. Therefore, we must cultivate belief systems rooted in gratitude, appreciation, and love, fearlessly confronting the world's injustices through bravery and courage.

Stepping beyond our comfort zones is where we find true fulfillment and empowerment. Sharing the truth of the light and joy within us, pushing back the darkness that would love nothing more than to extinguish our torches of hope.

Illuminating a beacon for those who have the valor to brave the arena; despite the sweat, bruises, critics and setbacks, they are the ones propelling change forward. Yet, the majority remain cowardly, fearing criticism and ridicule due to their limited beliefs: the fear of failure and the dread of judgment from others, placing other powers above the very power of GOD whom has gifted them the very life they live.

The true winners recognize that failure is merely a stepping stone on the path to success. They've fallen a thousand times but rise again with unwavering determination. They possess a clear understanding of their goals and refuse to be swayed by external influences. They steadfastly reject anyone or anything that attempts to dictate their capabilities and God's plan in their lives.

It's imperative that we scrutinize our belief systems in light of this. We must remain cognizant of the beliefs we hold not only about ourselves but also about the world around us. How do these beliefs shape our actions and perceptions? What are our aspirations and dreams? How do we engage with our inner dialogue? Evaluating and adjusting our belief systems is crucial as they significantly impact every aspect of our lives, for better or for worse.

I refuse to accept that everything happening around us is all love and light, as new agers say because it is not. We must aspire to envision a brighter future for ourselves and our planet. My mission is to challenge the status quo and inspire the creation of something superior. It's painfully evident that our current system and society are sick, and this is unacceptable to me. That's why I urge people to challenge the prevailing narrative and engage their intellect and critical thinking skills. Instead of being swept away by emotions, we must objectively evaluate and assess our circumstances to foster positive change.

It's baffling how easily the general populace can be swayed and controlled, even by sensationalist reports or rumors, leading to destructive riots instead of rational responses. Fighting against their own tribe rather than the ones whacking the beehive. We must grasp the extent to which our beliefs shape our actions and how they've been manipulated against us. When individuals in positions of power lack integrity and moral strength, they exploit others for personal gain, leaving us to question the state of our collective values and direction. If we continue down this path, it's clear we're not headed in a positive direction. It's imperative that we reassess our beliefs and reclaim our moral compass to steer society toward a better future.

Let us grasp the weight of our collective responsibility. The future of our nations, cultures, planet, and world hangs in the balance, awaiting the united strength of men and women who dare to alter the course of history like never before. I implore you, for the sake of future generations, to stand tall, stand strong, and embrace hope with unwavering faith. Remember, God has a plan, but it requires our active participation. Let us courageously step forward and allow ourselves to be instruments of divine purpose, shaping a tomorrow that surpasses our wildest dreams.

"Magic exists within us; it's the spark that ignites our deepest passions and guides us toward our true purpose." - Unknown

Chapter 14: Your Magic

Our individuality is a masterpiece crafted by the divine hand, each of us a unique thread in the tapestry of existence. From our soul's blueprint to our life experiences, every aspect of our being contributes to the intricate design of who we are. This intrinsic uniqueness, shaped by divine personality and perspective, holds immeasurable value not only for ourselves but also for others and future generations. Embracing our individuality unlocks the door to profound self-realization and enriches the world with the beauty of our authentic selves.

Those who have left a permanent mark on the world understood their inherent worth and the unique contributions they had to offer. They recognized a deeper purpose in life, a distinctive design meant specifically for them. These visionaries understood that conventional beliefs only scratch the surface of what life truly offers. By embracing their authenticity and refusing to succumb to fear or conformity, they reclaimed their power and allowed their innate magic to shine through. They honored the divine spark within themselves, connecting to the vast intelligence that birthed the cosmos and, in doing so, became the best versions of themselves.

As we embrace our uniqueness and strive toward our highest potential, we tap into the divine essence within us. Through this connection, we gain clarity on how our past experiences have shaped us and how they can be leveraged for our growth and expansion. What was once painful becomes a source of wisdom, propelling us forward on our journey.

Undoubtedly, life presents us with its share of challenges, serving as the crucible for our transformation. Yet, it is through these trials that we discover our resilience and emerge as our best selves. To evolve, we must lean into the process, trusting in its ability to refine us like a whetstone, sharpening our character by stripping away what no longer serves us. Challenges provide the contrast necessary for growth, much like the sun relies on the stars of the night or the warmth of summer is defined by the cold of winter. Embracing these contrasts allows us to fully appreciate the richness of our experiences and the depth of our growth.

Our uniqueness empowers us to co-create with the divine. In the vast expanse of existence, everything originates from the etheric realm through focused thought and intention. This preexisting potential, accessible to all, exists within the mind of God. However, it is our individuality that brings forth tangible creations from this realm of possibility. Consider the marvels of our modern world—telephones, lights, cars, airplanes, the internet—all born from the fertile ground of someone's imagination, effort, and unwavering faith. Each innovation, a testament to the power of focused intention and inspired action guided by our unique perspectives, creativity and the will of the Divine.

Within each of us resides a creative spirit yearning for expression, transcending the boundaries of our physical, mental, and emotional selves. Our unique spirituality and intelligence possess the power to shape realities previously unseen. It is our individual journey, our personal goals and aspirations, that drive us forward on the path of creation.

To shape the formless into reality, we must embrace our current circumstances and capabilities as our starting point. While some may seem to start with more advantages in life, material success or societal status doesn't dictate our ultimate destination. Adversity and challenges are not barriers to greatness; rather, they are the crucibles that forge individuals of extraordinary resilience and strength.

THE MIRACLE MAN

Those who persevere through difficulties, maintaining hope and faith in the face of adversity, often emerge as beacons of inspiration. The truth is that we hold the power to manifest miracles in our own lives and the lives of others. When we align our beliefs with the divine forces of the universe, miracles become not only possible but inevitable. History is replete with examples of such miraculous transformations, reminding us of the boundless potential within each of us.

We must cultivate faith and unleash the boundless potential of our imagination, reaching beyond the confines of our past experiences. It is imperative that we question the paradigms that govern both individuals and society, envisioning a future that is more equitable and prosperous for all. By challenging the status quo and dismantling archaic systems of corruption, we pave the way to a brighter future for our coming generations.

What would life's purpose be if it revolved solely around the individual? How shallow and unfulfilling it would be, consumed by the pursuit of self-interest. Yet, when we shift our focus to serving others and leveraging our unique perspectives and imaginations to contribute something meaningful to the world, life gains profound significance. By embracing this ethos of service and creativity, we transcend the limitations of the self and forge connections that enrich our lives and the lives of others.

Realizing that you are destined for greater things, meant to achieve more, become more, and explore beyond your current limitations, propels you toward a path of expansion and growth. Embracing life's challenges as opportunities for learning and development, you ultimately discover profound joy, empowerment, and purpose aligned with your passions. We wouldn't value anything if everything came to us easily and we didn't have to work for it. We wouldn't be able to know the strength of our character if there was no resistance.

The greatest figures in history emerged from the crucible of pain, hardship, and relentless struggle. Driven by resilience, they refused to be defined by their circumstances, recognizing the boundless potential within. They understood that their trials were catalysts for growth, igniting the eternal flame of greatness within. Conversely, those who falter in the face of adversity often lack the inner strength, character, and spiritual connection to endure. Blinded by the illusions of their minds, they fail to recognize the brilliance of their souls.

The strongest souls are forged not by avoiding difficulty but by embracing it and emerging stronger. Drawing from past experiences of resilience and perseverance, we navigate current challenges with confidence and determination. Reminding ourselves of the trials we have overcome reinforces our inner strength, allowing us to face adversity head-on with the unwavering belief that we will prevail once again.

When we recognize that our experiences have sculpted our character and contributed to our growth, we unlock the transformative power within. Our journey becomes a tapestry woven from both joy and adversity, each thread contributing to the vibrant mosaic of our lives. Embracing the dynamic nature of existence, we adapt, evolve, and glean wisdom from every encounter. Suffering persists only when we resist growth, clinging to outdated patterns that no longer serve our highest good.

The magic that surrounds us and emanates from within blossoms through self-love, acceptance, and a connection with the divine. In this wondrous world, every moment offers boundless opportunities for growth and adventure, a stage upon which miracles unfold. Yet, without belief and action, the seeds of possibility remain dormant. To manifest miracles, one must become an active participant in their own destiny, seizing the reins of agency and embracing the transformative power of action.

My life has been enriched by a myriad experiences, each serving as a catalyst for soul growth. Contrary to popular belief, our existence extends beyond the confines of the material world; we inhabit a vast, multidimensional cosmos teeming with life and energy. Within this quantum reality, the universe orchestrates synchronicities and delivers divine messages, guiding us along our journey. Whether we perceive them as intuition, psychic insights, or profound observations, these manifestations of guidance connect us with our ancestors, angels, God and spiritual guides. By embracing this expansive perspective, we open ourselves to a wealth of wisdom and experiences beyond our wildest imagination.

There exists a realm beyond the limits of our physical senses, one that beckons us to explore its mysteries. As we venture into this divine realm, even just a crack, we unlock the potential to shape our own reality and catalyze transformation in both our lives and the lives of others. Central to this process is the recognition that where focus goes our energy flows and what we give attention to grows. By cultivating gratitude and directing our thoughts toward higher planes, we align ourselves with the guidance of the divine, allowing miracles to manifest in our midst.

As we embark on our journey of personal and spiritual growth, we may encounter resistance from those who do not resonate with our path. This contrast highlights the evolution of our reality and may result in a natural distancing from relationships lacking in mutual dedication. While it can be challenging for loved ones to not fully support our transformation, this shift underscores the importance of prioritizing our own growth and well-being. As our focus shifts toward personal development, learning, and wellness, some relationships may naturally fade away. It's essential to honor each individual's unique journey and embrace the changes that accompany our quest for personal evolution.

We often become reflections of the company we keep, shaped by the influences of those closest to us. It's essential to reflect on the individuals with whom we surround ourselves and consider how they contribute to our growth and well-being. Are they champions of our uniqueness, encouraging us to embrace our gifts and imagination? Or do they diminish our spirit and hinder our progress? Let us gravitate toward environments where we are celebrated, not just tolerated.

Creating a nurturing environment that supports our growth and expansion is paramount. We must distance ourselves from those who hinder our progress and seek out like-minded individuals who foster critical thinking and challenge conventional wisdom. By questioning the status quo and delving deeper into our understanding, we liberate ourselves from the constraints of media and societal norms.

People may label you as crazy, disconnected, or weird because you challenge cultural norms and societal programming. However, it's important to recognize that you are a unique soul with a distinct mission and purpose. Embracing this truth will lead you out of your comfort zone and prompt you to question your beliefs, but ultimately, it propels you toward a more meaningful and authentic life path.

When I first began writing this book, I had long hair that was braided into Viking braids. After the events that were orchestrated on Maui in the Lahaina fires and the death and destruction that took place, I was devastated and extremely heartbroken. Grieving for the islands and Ohana that I now called home, which had saved me. The very day it happened, I was in Montana on a fire assignment, laid up in the hotel with an extremely high fever and thought I was going to die being boiled alive, nearly going to the hospital not knowing what was going on, as I never get sick. A friend then messaged me asking me if I knew what happened, as I had no idea.

A few days later, in a prayer to God, I expressed to him that I was raging mad and full of sorrow, knowing the whole situation was wrong and that foul play was at hand. Especially being involved in the highest level of fire operations nationally for over a decade. I told him I wanted to help in any way I could, not with just this situation, but that I was serious about being used as a divine conduit for service to our planet and our people in a grand and magnificent way. In a sincere prayer, I pleaded with him that I would do whatever he asked me to do, only that he showed me exactly what to do, no matter the cost.

His response was, "*Give me something that you love and hold sacred and dear and prove to me how serious you are.*" At that very moment, I knew what I had to do, even though I was 100% against it. Deep within, I knew that I had to cut my hair, all of it and shave it off in a ceremony of sacrifice and mourning. I didn't want to do it at all, as I had built up my mana and connection with having it. A few days later, after praying and thanking this connection, I had formed spiritually, literally crying as I was cutting off a part of me that was sacred.

After having it cut off, I was going to donate it to Locks of Love, but I knew I had to bring it back to the island. Keeping the ponytail in my bag wrapped up in a cloth as I traveled across America for work and then made my way back to the islands in December, 4 months later.

While I was Christmas shopping for my family with my friend Shekinah, we stopped at a little store right outside of Kailua-Kona. I noticed a very large white conch shell on a shelf behind the store as I was parking.

Coming around the corner I talked with the uncle there and asked him, *"Whose truck is that that has the big sticker that says TEAM JESUS."*

He replied confidently, smiling, *"That is mine."*

I laughed and said, *"Team Jeeesusss! Yeah, buddy, that's what's up. What about that conch shell? Who is that? I feel it calling to me and believe it's wanting to come home with me."*

He raised his eyebrows in response and said, *"That's mine. It washed up on the shore just right down the road as I was walking on the beach in the morning 3 days ago. I haven't seen one that big since I was a little kid; it's a very rare thing."*

I nodded, acknowledging what he had just said and the significance of it, and replied, *"How much do you want for it? I'll take great care of it. I feel it wants to be used in ceremony."*

He paused for a moment, looked me in the eyes, and scanning me up and down looming at my soul and said with approval, *"For you... $10."*

Shocked and in awe as something like that could go for hundreds of dollars, I respond, *"Whaaaat? Are you serious? No way..."*

He smiled at me with a big hearty smile and said, *"Take good care of it. It's yours now."* As my eyes were tearing up, I gave him $10, a big hug, said mahalo, and went our way.

After researching how to clean, polish and drill out the conch to make a horn, I ever so carefully completed the task a few days before the winter solstice in 2023 and waited for guidance after testing the conch out by the sea. It was remarkable being on the lava rocks barefoot as the sun was going down with golden colors spanning across the sky and me blowing the conch as it echoed across the waves.

As we are being guided and allowing ourselves to be directed, we listen to a small, intuitive feeling and thought. In my case, it hasn't been a loud booming voice but a still soft voice on what to do. That's exactly what happened as I was directed to go to the Volcano the next night for the winter solstice and gift my hair in prayer to God, with Tutu Pele as my witness and the Aina holding space. Taking only the conch, my drum, sage, and some tea leaves, I knew exactly where to go, as I had been there many times prior with close friends and local spiritual elders for ceremonies.

This time was different, though. I'd be going alone at night with no one around. When I arrived in the parking lot, just after 10pm, there wasn't but a single car that was just getting ready to leave.

They told me, *"There is nothing to see; the volcano isn't active. It's cloudy, cold and sprinkling rain."*

And then they were gone. While I was in the parking lot, I texted my friend Shekinah, *"There is no one here. I am all alone. It is very different with no one around and kinda trippy being surrounded by the jungle."*

She responded, *"Guess it's time to be brave."*

I knew I had to go all the way to the crater rim, which was miles and miles down an old trail, and there was no way around it.

At that moment, I said to myself, *"If I die, I die brave, and I come with deep respect, aloha and a pure heart."*

Once I began walking down the path, I was guided to not use a light unless it was absolutely necessary for the parts that were dangerous. There was barely light enough to see as I made my way down the trail in the darkness. After 20 minutes, I emerged out of the jungle forest and was in the open, where more light shone through the clouds. While I was walking down the path, I could see columns of steam rising up from the crater, which formed into what appeared to be very large human forms. Walking with me as I walked, dozens of them, not more than a few hundred yards away. It was extremely unnerving as I could feel them watching my every step, marching in the night as guardians.

I communicated with them, saying, "*I am here on God's errand for a divine purpose, carrying a pure heart of aloha. I acknowledge you and mahalo for being here.*" After speaking that, I felt it cleared the air and that I could proceed onwards toward my destination.

After hiking for what seemed like hours and, overcoming the fear of the darkness, and being alone on a volcano in the middle of the Pacific Ocean with no one around for miles in the late hours of the night, I made it to the rim of the crater. Once I arrived, I took out my drum, placed the conch on the ground, gifted the sage and its leaves and began praying, allowing myself to be a channel. Tears of sadness started streaming down my face as I picked up the conch shell and began blasting the horns song out into the night and the blackness of the caldron, turning in each direction for a full circle.

The air shifted directions and a sense of peace fell over me as I placed the conch back on the ground and grabbed my hair in my right hand. Standing at the edge, I raised the hair clasped in my hand high into the sky, yelling, "YOU WANTED TO KNOW HOW SERIOUS I WAS! HERE I AM! I GIVE YOU EVERYTHING GOD! MY HEART, MY SOUL, EVERYTHING I AM!" And with all my might and the prayer in my heart to be used as a divine channel for God, I tossed my hair, that was braided in a ponytail, off into the darkness that was before me.

Dropping to my knees, I wept like a small child yearning to be loved. Moments later, I grabbed my hand drum (Arjuna) and started channeling all the anger, masking the sorrow into the drum as I pounded the mallet against the buffalo hide. Each thunderous echo reverberating around the crater like the waves of a crashing storm. Releasing primordial howls from deep with my soul out into the night.

Then something very, very strange happened. The caldron had been black as the night, inactive, but as I was drumming, the interior of the volcano began glowing, brighter and brighter, magma from below rising closer to the surface. And what began to form beneath was mind-blowing. A glowing red heart right below the surface formed and began beating and pulsing with me as I was drumming. It was something beyond the realm of explanation and ordinary and an honor to experience and witness. Right then, I knew my prayers had been heard. I kneeled in gratitude, said, *"mahalo nui loa Akua,"* grabbed all my things and began the journey back to my car, mesmerized by the experience that had just unfolded.

Many may not understand your perspective or be able to witness the miracle, but a few will. Despite the challenges, it's crucial to stay true to the course set by your heart and soul's blueprint. This is your divine purpose, bestowed upon you by God. My survival and supernatural experiences are a testament to this truth. Sharing my journey to testify that our past struggles do not define us and are not who we are in the slightest.

These experiences, just like any others, can be viewed as valuable lessons. They've shaped our values and provided insights not being gained otherwise. This is where the magic lies—turning adversity into growth. Utilizing the trials and trauma as rocket fuel for our expansion. It's about forming an internal ecosystem where external factors hold less sway. Embracing a stoic philosophy allows us to focus on personal development and sharing our unique gifts with the world. Our business is not what others think of us; it's about cultivating positivity, gratitude, compassion, and joy within ourselves.

How we perceive others reflects our internal view of ourselves and the world. While it's crucial to stand firm in our values and beliefs, deep joy and fulfillment cannot be solely found in material possessions alone. Gratitude for the present moment in all we are experiencing is paramount, as it invites more blessings into our lives. By embracing gratitude for what we have, we open ourselves to receiving even more from the divine.

Comparison truly steals our joy. When we measure ourselves against others, we diminish our own uniqueness and value. Our journey is not theirs, and our worth cannot be defined by external standards. Embracing our individuality is where our true magic lies. Spending every moment with ourselves is vital to being kind to ourselves and cherishing our own company. Without self-compassion and self-worth, external achievements will never bring lasting contentment.

We are divine beings inhabiting remarkable physical vessels. Our bodies are truly marvels of nature, each uniquely crafted by the hand of God. Depression and anxiety often arise when we compare ourselves to others rather than embracing our own inherent uniqueness and expressing gratitude for our individuality.

Some friends or family may resist our journey because it challenges their own perspective. We must not allow others to confine us or diminish our power, as every individual possesses their own unique magic and creative potential. Just as each person has their own fingerprints, they also have a distinctive personality, preferences, and talents. Embracing this diversity enriches our world with vibrant colors and a multitude of experiences.

Consider a world where everyone is identical. Without contrast, we wouldn't even perceive color. It's the uniqueness of each individual that brings magic to our world. By harnessing the power of our thoughts and imagination, we tap into the realm of manifestation and unleash our true magic.

Focusing our perceptions, thoughts, and self-image to shape the reality we experience for something beneficial and highly useful. Recognizing this power within ourselves unveils the true magic that lies within.

Aligning with God's will and the universe's flow of unfolding occurs when we allow our soul's expression to flourish unimpeded by fears or external judgments. Though not effortless, having faith in a greater purpose initiates positive change. Through dedication and effort, we can manifest greater achievements and transformations.

Anything worth having is never easy to attain. It requires effort, dedication, and the willingness to weather storms. So, as we journey forward, let us pause and reflect: What are we striving for? What foundations have we laid? What masterpiece are we crafting with each step we take?

In life's unpredictable seas, we cannot control the wind that blows, but we possess the power of self-control. Like skilled sailors navigating vast oceans, we learn to adjust our sails, adapting to the winds of change. Despite the tempests that may rage around us, our self-mastery guides us safely through the roughest waters, steering our ships toward our chosen destination.

As we continue our voyage, let us embrace the challenges that lie ahead with courage and determination. For it is through these challenges that we refine our character, forge our destiny, and ultimately chart the course of our own epic journey.

"Healing is not just about recovery; it's a journey of self-discovery and transformation, leading us to wholeness and inner peace." - Unknown

Chapter 15: Heal the Hurt

It's crucial to acknowledge that life presents challenges to everyone, irrespective of outward appearance or social status. Regardless of wealth, fame, or cultural background, we all share in the human experience of joys and sorrows. Despite our differences in religion, beliefs, or upbringing, we are all part of the same global community and encounter similar struggles. While life can be difficult and unjust, we strive to make the best of our circumstances. As we gain understanding and grow in maturity, it's a natural cycle toward endeavoring to improve ourselves and our world.

The most direct route to understanding this truth and unraveling the complexities of our existence is through cultivating compassion and forgiveness. This entails extending compassion not only to ourselves for our own mistakes and missteps but also to others and the events of history. By learning from past experiences and drawing parallels to present circumstances, we empower ourselves to navigate life with greater wisdom and resilience.

In the wake of challenging experiences, the last thing we desire is to remain imprisoned. I've personally navigated this struggle, witnessing loved ones succumb to the weight of their unresolved pain, allowing it to consume their being entirely. Clinging to criticism, resentment, and judgment is akin to poisoning oneself, confining us to a suffocating existence. This self-imposed confinement not only breeds suffering but also inhibits growth and liberation. Just as love knows no bounds, neither does suffering. Our chosen path shapes our reality, dictating whether we dwell in the depths of despair or rise to embrace the expansiveness of love and possibility.

Even amidst profound adversity, some individuals maintain remarkable positivity, kindness, and compassion. Conversely, others, despite possessing material wealth and status, endure inner turmoil and suffering due to a disconnection from their authentic selves and from the love of God. Remaining in such dissonant states prolongs suffering and veers us off course from our authentic paths and divine purpose. Embracing greed or selfishness only amplifies this suffering. Hence, it's imperative that we consciously choose forgiveness and reconciliation each day, embodying the

Hawaiian principle of "Ho'oponopono" — forgiving the past, ourselves, and others — to realign with our hearts and souls.

Following everything I endured, there was a time when resentment and anger consumed me. It wasn't until later that I realized the preciousness of the present moment — a gift that shaped me into the person I am today, fostering growth within my character. Imperfection is inherent in our journey, for life itself is a continuous learning experience.

Our existence is inherently dualistic, encompassing both Yin and Yang, light and dark. Without contrast, our experiences would lose their meaning. Just as the seasons change, so do our emotions and circumstances. In honoring the full spectrum of human experiences — from joy to sorrow — we acknowledge the transient nature of life. Everything, whether happiness or pain, is fleeting, and to remember this too shall pass.

Most of the time, we want to create what we think is right based on our programming, so we try to compel, demand, and shape things the way we think they should end up. However, it's not the wisest course of action or God's purpose for us.

Spirituality entails allowing God and our higher selves to illuminate our path from a vantage point beyond our limited perspective. Like a benevolent observer, God watches over us, cognizant of every detail. Even when our intentions seem pure, it's crucial to question them and seek guidance from our intuition, as unseen pitfalls may lie ahead. Surrendering, though not easy, proves to be the most fruitful path. Delving deep into our hearts and souls, we forge a profound connection with the divine, relinquishing control to a higher power that orchestrates the universe. In surrendering, we open ourselves to compassion, love, and forgiveness, inviting miracles to manifest in our lives according to divine timing.

Moreover, we are intricately shaped by our environment, our inherent traits, and the legacy of our ancestors — that is our origin story. These are the attributes we inherit and embody. Yet, everything within our surroundings and thoughts is remarkably adaptable; through the marvel of neuroplasticity, we possess the capacity for profound transformation, birthing new neural pathways, fostering healing, and experiencing expansive growth.

Similarly, our identity is not bound by who we were yesterday; we hold the power to redefine ourselves at any moment. Yet, we often cling to justifications for our actions, hesitant to release control. Instead, we can choose surrender, acknowledging our vulnerability amidst life's storms, whether of our own making or not. Trusting in a higher power, we seek guidance and embrace the potential for transformation.

When we open ourselves to guidance, it often reveals itself in extraordinary and serendipitous ways, facilitated by prayer and meditation. Each of us possesses the capacity for personal revelation, which may manifest through chance encounters, meaningful signs, encounters with animals, or divine interventions. These occurrences underscore the profound interconnectedness of all things. Embracing this connection allows its magic to flow through us more abundantly, enriching our lives in unimaginable ways.

Is it nature or nurture that shapes us? Or perhaps it's a combination of both. Through the lens of epigenetics, we understand that we hold the power to alter our circumstances to a certain degree. By embracing emotions of joy, gratitude, and embodying our highest selves, we can initiate profound transformations. We need not perpetuate suffering; it is a choice we make.

I urge every reader of this book to embrace their inner superhero. Love yourself fiercely, not in a narcissistic manner, but with genuine affection and confidence, recognizing your divine essence as a son or daughter of the universal divine light. You are a unique creation, your fingerprint and eyes unlike any other in the cosmos. Embrace your individuality and recognize your inherent worth.

I'm granting you permission to love your life, to forgive yourself, and to release the pain, the past, the struggle, and the hurt. You have to choose all this. I cannot choose for you. Take this opportunity to make a firm and resolute decision so that when you wake up tomorrow morning, you can declare, "*I don't care what happened in the past. I'm choosing to be a better person. I'm choosing to change this. I'm choosing to be 1% better today. I'm choosing forgiveness, I'm choosing to be my own superhero.*"

Our hearts beat ceaselessly within us, silent yet steadfast, guiding us through the tapestry of life's journey, unseen yet omnipresent. It is evident that an invisible force animates our existence, sustaining us in its boundless embrace. As we honor this life force, its vibrancy and magnitude amplify, permeating every facet of our being. In reverence, we acknowledge the luminosity of our spirit and soul, cherishing the precious gift of life bestowed upon us.

With this understanding, I grant you permission to embrace your brilliance, to radiate with pride in who you are and the love that resides within your heart. Let your light shine boldly, even if society deems it unconventional. Why would we heed criticism, judgment, or shade from those who don't even cherish themselves? Let us rise above the opinions of others and embrace our authenticity unapologetically.

This is why you must embody your inner superhero. Embrace your inherent greatness and pursue your dreams and passions, for within you lies a unique creation waiting to be born from the depths of your heart and mind. Understand that without consistent effort and faith in your capacity to evolve, your aspirations will remain unfulfilled. With God, all things are possible. Throughout history, human beings have achieved remarkable feats through the divine power within them. Nothing occurs by chance; every event is a thread woven into the fabric of a divine plan. Solely awaiting the individual to open up and be utilized as a paintbrush in the hands of the divine.

When we redirect our attention to something beyond our current circumstances, our energy follows suit. This shift enables us to reclaim a childlike state of being — carefree, joyful, and fully present in the wonder of the world. To honor and embrace our emotions fully, we must first acknowledge and experience them without distraction. Just as children immerse themselves in the moment, we, too, can find contentment by surrendering to the depth of our feelings and releasing them without inhibition.

To alleviate our pain, we must prioritize avoiding distractions. Often, we resort to various diversions instead of confronting our emotions head-on. By staying present with our inner experiences and reassuring ourselves that our feelings are valid, we pave the way for genuine growth.

I firmly believe that mystical and extraordinary experiences are within reach for everyone, as I've encountered them firsthand throughout my life. These inexplicable phenomena, often dismissed as "woo-woo" or paranormal, become tangible when we open ourselves to them. Whether they're perceived as extraterrestrial or beyond conventional understanding, embracing these experiences allows us to connect with the universal force that animates all existence, propelling us forward in the cosmic dance of life.

I'm deeply grateful for the opportunity to pen these words, to share my journey, and perhaps offer solace or inspiration to even a single individual. It's a profound miracle to be able to extend a helping hand through the pages of this book. To impart my experiences and insights in the hopes of offering assistance to those who may find resonance in my story. Having witnessed considerable suffering in our world, I'm compelled to take action. Fearlessly and unapologetically, I lay bare my truth, guided by a steadfast belief in the message I'm called to share — a message I believe is aligned with the divine will.

For many years, I allowed fear to dictate my authenticity. Repeatedly told I was *"too much," "too positive,"* or questioned for simply being myself, I grappled with self-doubt. But those voices no longer hold sway. We must honor our souls and the depth of our experiences. It is individuals like us who have catalyzed the greatest transformations in history. They dared to believe in their vision, even sacrificing their lives to leave behind a lasting legacy. This is my aspiration: to leave a legacy that inspires and empowers future generations. Through sharing my journey and the wisdom gleaned from it, I aim to equip others with the tools and insights needed to navigate their own paths with courage and purpose, igniting a perpetual spark of life for generations to come.

It only takes one spark to ignite a million flames. The question remains: *Will you be that spark? Will you kindle within yourself the flames of passion, hope, and faith and venture into the unknown, guided by a calling that resonates deep within your soul?*

In life, everyone faces hardships. No soul emerges unscathed from the journey, for we all endure trials that test our strength and resilience. It's said that the most brilliant souls often encounter the fiercest battles, for before arriving here, they, in a way, choose to undergo specific experiences. Our consciousness, intelligence, and spirits transcend time, seeking new adventures with each manifestation on Earth or elsewhere. Some souls, perhaps more seasoned than others, are drawn to profound experiences, equipped with the innate ability to navigate challenges with confidence, as they had foreseen their capacity to do so before their arrival.

A dear friend once reminded me that it is our duty to honor ourselves and heed the calling within us. No one else can fulfill this responsibility for us. We must remain steadfast on the path that resonates with our truth despite the challenges and distractions that may arise. It's a daunting task, but one that is essential for our growth and fulfillment.

There have been stretches of time where I woke up day after day, engulfed in despair, feeling as though life had lost its meaning. Despite my efforts, I remained trapped in a cycle of despair. It wasn't until I surrendered control and earnestly called upon a higher power, saying, *"God, I need your help. I can't bear this existence any longer,"* that I found a glimmer of hope. Today, I owe my survival to the grace of God. Each time I surrendered and asked for help over the years more was revealed as I grew in my understanding and connection.

As I penned this book, an unshakable sliver of sadness lingered within me, defying all efforts to erase it. It persisted, a silent specter of sadness. Then, a chance encounter with a kindred spirit led me to a deliverance service in Kona. Despite my reservations, an inexplicable pull urged me to attend.

On a Thursday night, I found myself at the service, drawn in by the uplifting music. It felt like any other church gathering until the pastor stood and called for prayer and confession. Skeptical, I watched, expecting the usual religious routine. Then, almost against my will, I found myself stepping forward in front of the small stage.

Upon arrival, members of the prayer team greeted me warmly, assuring me of the power of confession and the potential for miracles in my life. With a heart unexpectedly open, I found myself uttering words I never thought I'd speak:

"I am a sinner, an adulterer, a former drunkard, and a lustful man. Please help me, Jesus. I give you my life" They then anointed my head with holy oil, and started praying for me and then rebuking demons and casting them out in Jesus' name. In an unexpected turn, they even rebuked the spirit of religion, and suddenly, a door swung open.

Dropping to my hands and knees, I found myself coughing uncontrollably, wailing, and screaming. My body began to convulse and shake uncontrollably as they brought over a trash can as I coughed fiercely from deep within me. Coughing so hard and so long that I spat up a small amount of blood.

Feeling this darkness latched onto my heart and soul, almost nearly gone, I spoke the words in my mind, *"Jesus I've heard about you my entire life but I DON'T KNOW YOU. You must be real, you have to be real. Please help me, Jesus!"* And then *POOF* it was gone. In that instance, the darkness that was surrounding me was gone and these ethereal lightning-blue electric eyes appeared in my mind saying, *"It is finished.'*

Witnessing and experiencing something utterly unfamiliar, I sensed a profound shift within me. It was as if something had been expelled from my being, and I keenly felt its departure—a weight lifted, darkness dispelled, and an anguish that had long plagued my soul now banished. As the process concluded, my vision sharpened, my hearing became acute, and my heart felt unburdened. I knew I had been set free, released from the grip of vampiric, demonic energies that had haunted me for an unknown duration. Over the course of four weeks, I diligently attended the healing services, delving deeper each time and witnessing remarkable transformations unfold within me.

After traversing myriad spiritual paths—from psychedelic journeys to men's groups, from workshops to rehab —I reached a pivotal moment where all these experiences paled in comparison to the profound liberation I obtained. Through my confession and deliverance, I unearthed a depth of freedom that transcended any earthly pursuit. It was a revelation that surpassed mere healing; it was a soul-level transformation. Witnessing the immense power of this release, I found myself yearning for others to encounter this same level of peace and serenity—a peace that surpasses understanding and a serenity that anchors the soul amidst life's storms.

Through my journey, a profound realization dawned upon me: while many may claim to "know" Jesus and be acquainted with his teachings, few have truly encountered him and experienced the transformative power of deliverance. This encounter unveils the deepest wells of grace, mercy, and compassion—an experience that transcends mere knowledge or belief. It's an encounter that illuminates the heart with a profound understanding of divine love and redemption, leaving an indelible imprint on the soul.

Once we commit to a decision, we surrender control over its consequences. Sometimes, our choices unwittingly invite negative energies into our lives, resulting in pain or harm inflicted upon loved ones or ourselves, leaving wounds that seem indelible. While we cannot rewrite the past, we can embark on a path of healing and inner peace through the boundless mercy of God and the transformative power of restoration found in Christ.

Breaking free from the chains of sin, guilt, shame, and societal conditioning while reclaiming our divine essence is a daunting task. Yet, it's a noble pursuit that brings forth profound rewards. Amid life's storms, it's crucial to acknowledge your intrinsic value and the impermanent nature of your current challenges. You are not defined by your circumstances or past choices; you are an infinite being with limitless potential. Instead of tethering your identity to fleeting situations, ground it in the divine essence from which you originate—God. Remember, each of us is a reflection of the divine, entrusted with the precious gift of life to navigate and transcend earthly trials.

I firmly believe that by unwaveringly pressing forward with faith as our guiding light and having a clear north star, we can cultivate lives of profound fulfillment and purpose. I am resolute in my belief that I will manifest my aspirations of nurturing a loving family and joining forces with an exceptional Germanic Goddess. Together, we will embark on extraordinary adventures around the world, savoring luxurious experiences and sharing our God-given gifts and talents. Our journey will be marked by unforgettable moments as we touch lives and contribute to the betterment of our planet and humanity. Through workshops, seminars, conferences, and packed stadiums pulsating with the energy of divine love, we will inspire others to join us on this transformative journey. This vision embodies my highest calling, and I am actively working to manifest it into reality.

One of my mentors once told me, *"Kye, always keep your fork with you."*

When I first heard it, I said, *"What the heck do you mean by 'always keep the fork with me?'"*

He replied, *"We always keep the fork with us because dessert comes last. The sweetest things come after the darkest of nights. The lowest of the lows are preceded by something in the glory of the sun, basking in its brilliance once again."*

Life resembles a roller coaster, an exhilarating odyssey brimming with unexpected twists and turns. Despite society's portrayal of it as a relentless race, what exactly are we racing toward? Ultimately, we are born, we live, and we die—everything in between merely embellishes our journey. Along this path, there exist no fixed rules dictating our trajectory. While societal norms may attempt to impose a predetermined path, they lack inherent truth. We are not obligated to conform to societal expectations; rather, we possess the autonomy to forge our own unique path. Often, these societal constructs serve to disempower and divert us from our true essence. It is crucial to realize that genuine liberation stems from breaking free from these confines and embracing the authenticity of our existence.

At some juncture in history, every one of us—each ancestor—belonged to a tribe, gathering in circles, intimately tied to the earth, and safeguarding our legacy through the art of storytelling. This ancestral heritage resonates within us, intricately woven into the fabric of our DNA from time immemorial. Through rekindling our connection to our roots, embracing our authenticity, and paying homage to our forebears, we stride purposefully toward forging a luminous future for our children and the countless generations that will follow.

I firmly believe that at the core of every individual lies a yearning for love and fulfillment in life. However, conflicts, materialism, greed, alienation, and illness often plague our existence, propagated by agents of chaos seeking to sever our connection to the divine. While we are not God entirely ourselves, we are mini g's, not the OG's, but we possess the power to co-create with the divine in our universe through our decisions, actions, and creations. In embracing our capacity to speak, write, craft, engage, and create, we unlock the potential to shape our lives in beautiful and meaningful ways.

As we emerge from the transformative journey of healing, empowerment, and awakening, we find ourselves standing on the precipice of destiny, poised to embark upon a quest of epic proportions. Armed with the brush of co-creation, we unlock the symphony of harmony and invoke the alchemy of love through our communion with God and the divine realm.

May every endeavor reverberate with the resounding echoes of love, echoing throughout the cosmos. Let our actions carve pathways through the very fabric of existence, painting the vast expanse of the universe with the vibrant hues of passion and purpose. In this magnificent odyssey called life, we are not mere bystanders, but rather protagonists in a cosmic saga, destined to etch our own tales of valor and transcendence upon the annals of eternity. Therefore, let us seize each moment with the fiery zeal of warriors, for in the crucible of time, it is here that legends are forged and immortality is claimed.

So, heed the call of your dreams, the whispers of your passion, and let greatness be your mantle. Embrace the superhero within, for it is you who holds the power to shape destinies and sculpt realities. With unwavering determination and boundless courage, traverse the realms of possibility and ascend to the zenith of your potential. Know that in every step, every leap, and every triumph, the universe conspires in your favor. For I believe in you, in your capacity to defy limits, and in your ability to illuminate the world with the brilliance of your spirit. So go forth, fearless and resolute, for the cosmos awaits the awakening of your legend!!!

As we draw the curtains on this epic odyssey, I am deeply grateful for your presence and companionship on this remarkable journey. Together, we have ventured through the realms of healing, empowerment, and awakening, navigating the twists and turns of life's grand tapestry with courage and resilience. Your unwavering support and shared moments of reflection have enriched this adventure beyond measure. From the depths of my heart, I extend my sincerest gratitude for joining me, the Miracle Man, on this profound exploration of the human spirit. May our paths continue to intertwine, and may the echoes of our shared journey resonate throughout eternity. I wholeheartedly believe in the greatness that resides within your soul. Embrace it, and witness the miracles that unfold. Thank you for being a cherished part of this extraordinary experience.

With deep honor and profound sincerity, your brother in arms, the lighting lion,

Royal Kye Aurelius Funk

PS - If you found this book helpful, insightful and adventurous, please leave a review on Amazon and share it with friends and those whom you'd feel would benefit from it.

www.ingramcontent.com/pod-product-compliance
Lightning Source LLC
Chambersburg PA
CBHW021027130626
46552CB00005B/1711

9 798990 443341